D1528216

Interpersonal Relations

Interpersonal Relations

A THEORY OF INTERDEPENDENCE

HAROLD H. KELLEY
University of California, Los Angeles

JOHN W. THIBAUT
University of North Carolina

LIBRARY
FLAGLER COLLEGE

A WILEY-INTERSCIENCE PUBLICATION

JOHN WILEY & SONS, New York · Chichester · Brisbane · Toronto

Copyright © 1978 by John Wiley & Sons, Inc.

All rights reserved. Published simultaneously in Canada.

Reproduction or translation of any part of this work
beyond that permitted by Sections 107 or 108 of the
1976 United States Copyright Act without the permission
of the copyright owner is unlawful. Requests for
permission or further information should be addressed to
the Permissions Department, John Wiley & Sons, Inc.

Library of Congress Cataloging in Publication Data

Kelley, Harold H.
  Interpersonal relations.

  "A Wiley-Interscience publication."
  Bibliography: p. 329
  Includes indexes.
  1. Interpersonal relations. I. Thibaut,
John W., joint author. II. Title.
HM132.K43   301.11   78-164
ISBN 0-471-03473-8

Printed in the United States of America

10 9 8 7 6 5 4 3 2

Preface

Nearly two decades ago we published a book (Thibaut & Kelley, 1959) on the social psychology of groups. That book, along with rather similar ones by Homans and by Blau, has been incorporated into a tradition that has come to be called social exchange theory. Although we are pleased to be identified with such distinguished company, we cannot let the terminology pass without demurrer on two counts. First, our book did not pretend to develop a theory and, second, we were concerned with much more than social exchange. What the book did intend to present was a conceptual framework for the analysis of problems of interdependence in small groups—questions of attraction to the group, power and control, status evaluations, social norms, coalition formation, and the like. In a subsequent smaller work (Kelley and Thibaut, 1969) we extended the analysis to deal with informational interdependence, specifically as it applies to group problem solving.

The present book represents our joint work over the last decade. When we began it our aim was to revise our earlier book by reviews of empirical studies since 1959 that would illustrate, elaborate, justify, or perhaps prove troublesome for our conceptual framework. Relevant research was abundant and for a while we proceeded with the revision. But in that process new ideas occurred to us and as they gradually developed they captured our interest. We set aside the plan for revision and decided to write a new theoretical book. In this book, beginning with some key ideas in the earlier work, a further and more systematic analysis of inter-dependence in two- and three-person groups is developed. It constitutes, then, not a revision of *The Social Psychology of Groups* but a companion volume.

This book presents a taxonomy of patterns of interdependence, a set of indices for evaluating their properties, and an analysis of their psychological antecedents and of the ways in which they become transformed by personal values and policies. Processes of attribution and self-presentation are analyzed in the context of interdependent actions in the group. Finally, a fresh conceptualization is proposed for the process of negotiation and coalition formation. We believe the treatment of our ideas to be sufficiently cumulative and systematic to warrant describing it as a *theory*; hence we have subtitled the book "A theory of interdependence."

As has been true for our past coauthored works, this book reflects a truly joint effort. The mutual moral support and intellectual stimulation on which our collaboration is based have been necessary conditions for carrying this project through to completion. It would certainly not have been possible for us to work together for the required amount of time without the understanding support of those persons on whom we each are most dependent—our wives and children. They have assumed without question that what we were doing was important enough to warrant the inconveniences created by the many trips and visits between Chapel Hill and Malibu. When aware of the substance of our work, they have been helpful with comments and examples, as illustrated by Constance Thibaut's calling attention to the letter from Plato used in Chapter 8. Both our joint work and preparation of the book have been greatly facilitated by National Science Foundation Grants, GS-33069X to Kelley and GS-40601 to Thibaut.

Although we take full responsibility for the content, we have had the benefit of careful and thoughtful critiques from many students and colleagues. Graduate students in seminars at both Los Angeles and Chapel Hill have highlighted errors and points of unclarity. Special acknowledgement is due Charles G. McClintock and his colleagues at the University of California, Santa Barbara, who gave us a very helpful group commentary on a near-final draft. Phillip Bonacich and Dean Pruitt are to be thanked for their careful and expert readings of a last draft. Finally, we are indebted to Toney Dixon at UCLA who, with great patience and care, saw the entire draft through its final preparation and typing.

The quotations from Tolstoy's "Family Happiness" translated by J.D. Duff are reprinted from *The Kreutzer Sonata and Other Tales* by Leo Tolstoy (World's Classics, 1940) by permission of Oxford University Press.

HAROLD H. KELLEY
JOHN W. THIBAUT

Malibu, California
Chapel Hill, North Carolina
January 1978

Contents

Interpersonal Relations

1

Introduction and Overview

The interdependence matrix for a dyad describes the way in which the two persons control each other's outcomes in the course of their interaction. It is constituted by specifying the behaviors important to the relationship that each of them may enact and by assessing the consequences for both persons of all possible combinations of their respective behaviors. Thus each cell in the matrix defines a possible interpersonal event. The flow of their relationship can be described in terms of the sequence of particular cells through which it moves.

The interdependence matrix plays a pivotal role in the analysis and understanding of the dyad. On the one hand, it reflects the various ways in which psychological and situational factors impinge on the pair. The pattern of interdependence summarizes the consequences for the pair of the abilities, needs, and evaluative criteria each person brings to the dyad as well as the manner in which these two sets of personal dispositions engage with each other. The pattern is similarly indicative of the external resources at their disposal and of the task and environmental constraints within which they operate. On the other hand, the interdependence matrix describes the joint and individual problems the two persons face in their relationship and certain of the means available to them for solving these problems. Thus the matrix portrays the kinds and degrees of power they have over each other by means of outcome control and the bases they have for influence through threats, appeals to social norms, and other communications. These aspects of the pattern have implications for whatever interaction process, norms, and roles will develop if the two persons achieve a stable and satisfactory relationship or, if they fail to do so, the nature of the conflict that will characterize its dissolution. In short, the interdependence matrix is an exceedingly useful conceptual device for moving *from* the psychological and situational bases of interpersonal relations *to* the processes and structures characteristic of successful relationships and the conflict and disruption in the unsuccessful.

The nature of the interdependent relationship is not always fully or accurately understood by the participants. Furthermore, even when it is fully and accurately assessed, the outcome matrix does not always indicate unequivocally the course of action to be taken. However, although we must keep these caveats in mind, this simple and obvious point is to be emphasized:

If a person knows (or thinks he knows) the contingent relations between his own and his partner's actions, on the one hand, and his own outcomes, on the other, he has a basis for deciding what to do himself and/or what to attempt to induce the partner to do in order to affect his own outcomes beneficially.

The outcome matrix determines the experiences that the interdependent persons will have in the course of their interaction. Depending on the actions they take, whatever the reasons for them, the outcome matrix specifies what the consequences will be for each of them. Consequently the outcome matrix affects what they might learn from their interaction.

The possible "learnings" are quite varied, including, for example, specific individual actions, joint and coordinated action, preaction communication, and understandings of the contingencies themselves. Thus a given outcome matrix affords the basis for learning to perform, automatically and without thought, a certain action in a specific situation. For recurrent interdependence situations people acquire social habits that enable them to act without analysis and decision. A set of different outcome matrices, representing different contingencies, affords the basis for discrimination learning—learning to vary one's behavior in ways appropriate to different social settings. Also, singly and together, the outcome matrices provide the basis for cognitive learning—for developing an understanding of the types of pattern and the logical relations among them and an insight into the problems they pose for the relationship.

It must be emphasized, though, that when two persons are placed in a given interdependence relationship (as in an experiment) their respective actions and their interaction may not be predictable from the properties of that relationship. One or both may misunderstand their interdependence and therefore make inappropriate decisions and one or both may respond with an inappropriate habit. (The children's game "Simon Says" would be an example of the latter). In the long run, if the inappropriate decision or habit is not deadly, we would expect it to be replaced by one more appropriate. Thus we expect behaviour to be moderately appropriate to the interdependence problem of the moment. The learning tasks here however, are exceedingly complex and difficult, the discriminations to be made are subtle and manifold, and the concepts to be formed are complicated and closely interrelated. Mistakes are to be expected, particularly for the inexperienced and for those whose experience has been restricted to special settings.

It is our working assumption, then, that the *total set* of outcome matrices—those correctly and those incorrectly understood—account for all of social behavior. They account for everything that is or can be learned about social interdependence. Thus in their total effect they are responsible for both the successes and the failures in social interaction—the successes when a specific matrix is recognized for what it really is and is responded to in its own terms and the failures when a matrix is defined and responded to incorrectly. The opposite side of the coin is that any *specific* matrix bears only an imperfect relation to the behavior associated with it. As already described, the behavior occurring in relation to any particular matrix may have little to do with the particular contingencies represented there. In short, when considered as the total set, outcome matrices provide a complete account of social behavior. No single one of them, however, is the sole determinant of action within it.

This book is an analysis of outcome matrices (interdependence matrices). It considers their possible patterns, their antecedents, the problems they pose in relation to their properties, how they can be thought about and provide bases for decisions, and what they make it possible to learn about social life.

THE CONCEPTS OF INTERDEPENDENCE AS DEVELOPED IN THIBAUT AND KELLEY (1959)

To provide a background for our present formulation of a theory of interdependence it seems useful to begin with an outline of the principal concepts that were used in our earlier treatment of the topic (Thibaut and Kelley, 1959) and that serve as the starting point for our present work. To give substance to the meaning and utility of these concepts we choose to begin with a story of courtship and marriage which we subsequently analyze by reference to the concepts presented in the 1959 book. The story is that of Marya and Sergey in Tolstoy's short novel *Family Happiness* (Tolstoy, 1940). We sketch the main episodes in their relationship.

The story is related by Marya, who is 17 when she falls in love with Sergey, a bachelor in his late thirties who lives on a neighboring estate in the country some distance from St. Petersburg. Sergey has loved Marya for a long time and is overwhelmed with joy that she has come to love him. They are married and there is perfect family happiness. Marya describes her feelings:

> The mere sight of him made everything begin to speak and press for admittance to my heart, filling it with happiness. . . . Now I could see what he meant by saying that to live for others was the only true happiness, and I

agreed with him perfectly. I believed that our life together would be end-lessly happy and untroubled. I looked forward, not to foreign tours or fashionable society or display, but to a quite different scene—a quiet family life in the country, with constant recognition in all things of the hand of Providence. . . . his plans for our future life together were just my plans, only more clearly and better expressed in his words.

Blissful months passed and winter came. There were changes that gradu-ally slipped into Marya's feelings.

. . . in spite of his company, I began to feel lonely, that life was repeating itself, that there was nothing new either in him or in myself, and that we were merely going back to what had been before. . . . A new and dis-quieting sensation began to creep into my heart. To love him was not enough for me after the happiness I had felt in falling in love. I wanted movement and not a calm course of existence. . . . I felt in myself a superabundance of energy which found no outlet in our quiet life.

In spite of strong efforts to conceal her feelings Marya's discontent and the basis for it are plainly evident to Sergey. He talks with her about her unhappiness and finally proposes that they spend three months—from Christmas to Easter—in St. Petersburg to attend the theater and ballet and to introduce Marya into society. Sergey has misgivings about this venture and hopes that Marya will reject it. She has had no experience with the city or with society and the idea resonates with her growing need for excitement. They arrive in the city just before Christmas.

From the start nothing has ever been so wonderful for Marya.

I found myself at once in such a new and delightful world, surrounded by so many pleasures and confronted by such novel interests, that I instantly, though unconsciously, turned my back on past life and its plans. "All that was preparatory, a mere playing at life; but here is the real thing! And there is the future too!" Such were my thoughts. The restlessness and symptoms of depression which had troubled me at home vanished at once and entirely, as if by magic. My love for my husband grew calmer. . . . I could not doubt his love; every thought of mine was understood at once, every feeling shared. . . . I also began to realize that he not only loved me but was proud of me.

And Sergey was proud of her, at least for awhile.

Months pass, Easter has gone by and Marya has given herself over to society and to her commitments there, totally enchanted by this glittering life. Sergey observes all of this from the wings; he has gone from boredom to irritation and finally to intermittent jealousy and anger. Marya does not return to the country and, apart from visits to supervise his estate, Sergey remains with her in the city. He holds steadfast in his love for her and in his committed support for all her activities; but he figures only peripherally in her life. Marya:

> . . . I was constantly in society where I did not need him. . . . My whole day, from late in the morning till late at night, was taken up by the claims of society; even if I stayed at home, my time was not my own. This no longer seemed to me either gay or dull, but it seemed that so, and not otherwise, it always had to be.

Three years pass in this way, mechanically. Neither Marya nor Sergey makes any serious move to change their relationship. A son is born and Marya loves him, though it is Sergey who spends time with him. Still, nothing seems to be altered. A summer is spent at Baden, where a goodly sample of fashionable people from the capitals of Europe are foregathered. Here occurs a series of events that causes Marya to feel the futility and emptiness of her life. In this international setting she is outshone and humiliated and she is revolted by the competition for social leadership. Moreover, when she is aggressively courted by an Italian marquis, toward whom she is both primitively attracted and repelled, she becomes frightened by her own feelings and by the thought that she had come so dangerously near to casting her husband and child out of her life. She is overwhelmed with self-disgust. The near-loss of Sergey and her son makes her want to see them very much.

Marya and Sergey return to the country. A second son is born. Nothing much happens, but Marya is ready for a surcease from excitement. The novel ends with a touching scene between Sergey and Marya who is fondling the infant son.

> That day ended the romance of our marriage; the old feeling became a precious irrecoverable remembrance, but a new feeling of love for my children and the father of my children laid the foundation of a new life and a quite different happiness; and that life and happiness have lasted to the present time.

An Illustrative Analysis of the Relationship

We now introduce the main concepts of the Thibaut–Kelley framework through their application to the story of Marya and Sergey as they move through the vicissitudes of their relationship.

Outcomes. The outcomes for any participant in an ongoing interaction can be stated in terms of the rewards received and the costs incurred by the participant, where these values depend on the behaviors produced by the two persons. For some purposes rewards and costs are treated separately, but typically we have assumed that they can be combined into a single scale of "goodness" of outcome. By rewards we refer to whatever gives pleasure and gratification to the person. Costs refer to factors that inhibit or deter the performance of any behavior or segment of behavior—factors such as physical or mental effort or pain, embarrassment or anxiety, and the arousal of conflicting forces or competing response tendencies of any sort. The magnitudes of the rewards and costs experienced by the dyadic members will depend on their needs and values, their skills and abilities in performing the behaviors, and the congruency of the behaviors or behavioral products with their needs and values. Satiation reduces rewards and fatigue increases costs.

In the story of Marya and Sergey the rewards in the early phases of their marriage were based on their need and ability to give love and affection and to receive it. Each found happiness in "living for" the other and happiness in being "lived for." Moreover, their beliefs about the good life and their projects for the future of their lives together were mutually supportive—"his plans . . . were just my plans." For Marya, however, some of these rewards gradually lessened because there was nothing new. Later, in the city, Marya's rewards came not so much from Sergey as from the excitement of being a beautiful woman in an admiring society, but at the end (though it is only briefly sketched) it was again Sergey who became the source of her deepest and best rewards.

At the beginning of their marriage costs were few. They came from the brief periods of separation when Sergey was occupied with the business of the estate—interludes when the demands of the estate competed with their desire to be together. Later, in St. Petersburg, Marya's involvement in society imposed heavy costs on Sergey who would rather have returned to their life in the country but felt obliged to endure a place and a role that he disliked. Still later, during the summer in Baden, it was Marya—humiliated, anxious, and frightened—who experienced the heavy costs.

Evaluation of Outcomes. In evaluating the adequacy of their relationship, the members of a dyad need some kind of standard for gauging the acceptability of the outcomes they receive from it. Two kinds of standard for making such an evaluation have been identified—the comparison level (CL) and the comparison level for alternatives (CL_{alt}). The CL is the standard against which the participant evaluates the "attractiveness" of the relationship or how satisfactory it is. This is the standard that reflects the quality of outcomes that the participant feels he or she deserves. Outcomes falling above CL are experienced as relatively satisfying and those below CL are unsatisfactory. The location of CL on the person's scale of outcomes is determined by all the outcomes known to the member, either by direct experience or by observation of others. The more attainable an outcome, the heavier it will be weighted in forming the CL.

The CL_{alt} can be defined informally as the lowest level of outcomes a member will accept in the light of available alternative opportunities in other relationships. So defined, it follows that if outcomes drop below CL_{alt} the participant will leave the relationship. The location of CL_{alt} depends mainly on the quality of the most attractive of the alternative relationships readily available to the participant. As outcomes in a relationship exceed CL_{alt} by larger and larger degrees the participant becomes progressively more dependent on the relationship as the unique source of his experiences. [For a fuller discussion of CL and CL_{ait} see Thibaut and Kelley (1959), Chapters 6 (especially), 7, 10, and 12.]

The effects of CL on outcome evaluation were particularly striking for Marya. The intense and novel joys of courtship, falling in love, and the honeymoon weeks established a high CL that the ensuing routines of a country household could not equal. "To love him was not enough for me after the happiness I had felt in falling in love." The dissatisfactions that she then revealed to Sergey led him to arrange their sojourn in the city, where a new range of experience for Marya seemed all the more marvelous against the standard of her provincial background. The sheer excitement she felt about her life in society gradually subsided partly (it may be imagined) because satiation set in and partly because her CL rose as it incorporated her recent experiences. "This no longer seemed to me either gay or dull."

As far as we know from Tolstoy neither Marya nor Sergey made any serious effort to break off their relationship. They lived together even through the three years in St. Petersburg, although Marya's dependence on Sergey was sharply reduced: "I was constantly in society where I did not need him." We may guess that, in some degree at least, Marya remained with Sergey because of the high costs of exit (disapproval from kinfolk, friends, church, and the wider society, feelings of guilt about broken obligations, and the hurt to Sergey). These exit costs would serve to depress CL_{alt}. Attractive alternative relationships *were* certainly available to her. But perhaps it was the totality of them and her life with all of that, rather than any other single person, that was attractive to her. When, in Baden, one particular alternative relationship with the Italian marquis was made obtrusively available, she balked and fled—back to her husband and child. It was as though, when her commitment was tested and the irreversible decision was faced, she understood or remembered how much her future happiness depended on them.

Matrix concepts.   The device we have used to represent the various patterns of interdependence in relationships is the outcome matrix. In the simple form in which it is illustrated here the matrix has two columns and two rows. (See Figure 1.1.) The two columns distinguish two mutually exclusive behaviors or behavioral segments (a_1 and a_2) that person A can enact and the two rows distinguish two behaviors (b_1 and b_2) that B can enact. Each of the four cells then represents the intersection or joint occurrence of one of A's behaviors and one of B's behaviors. In each of the four cells the number placed above the diagonal indicates the outcome that A receives, whereas the number below the diagonal indicates B's outcome. Thus, in the relationship summarized in Figure 1.1, if person A enacts a_1 while B is enacting b_1, A receives an outcome of 0 and B an outcome of 2.

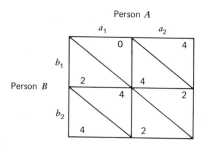

Figure 1.1   Illustration of the 2×2 matrix.

The degree to which outcomes exceed CL_{alt} determines how greatly the person depends on the dyad for favorable outcomes. Accordingly, the numbers entered in the outcome matrix are usually scaled from CL_{alt} as the zero point. The entries in the matrix indicate the degree to which each person is dependent on the dyad, and the pattern of entries thus represents their pattern of interdependence. Each member's dependence constitutes the basis for the other member's power. Thus A's power over B is defined as the range of outcomes through which A can move B, this range being the distance between B's CL_{alt} and the best outcomes A can produce for him.

There are two broad kinds of power. The first we have called fate control (FC). If, by varying his or her behavior, person A can affect B's outcomes regardless of what B does, A has fate control over B. If each has this kind of power, the pattern is one of mutual fate control (MFC). To illustrate this pattern of MFC from the story of Marya and Sergey consider the earliest phase of their marriage. Each wanted above all to give love and consideration to the other; each willingly gave and each happily received "constant mutual love." Figure 1.2 represents this mutually benevolent relationship. When both "give much," both receive their best outcomes and their outcomes are always higher than if the other chose to "give little." Thus the choice of each affects the other's happiness. (Each also derives pleasure from "giving much" to the other; as we show later, this matrix also involves bilateral reflexive control.) The possibility of giving little, which would yield low outcomes to both, no doubt has such low salience that it would scarcely be considered.

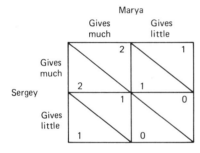

Figure 1.2   Illustration of mutually benevolent relationship with fate control.

A second kind of power is called behavior control (BC). If, by varying his or her behavior, A can make it desirable for B to vary his or her behavior also, then A has behavior control over B. If each has this kind of power, the pattern is one of mutual behavior control (MBC). The behavior of each is conditional on that of the other and coordination of behavior becomes important. In Tolstoy's story Marya speaks of her happiness at the beginning of the marriage that "his plans . . . were just my plans." The *agreement* on a plan was in itself gratifying. Suppose that two plans had been discussed. Sergey's announcement that he liked plan X would have brought Marya to instant accord. She would even have been happy to agree on plan Y and so would Sergey, but neither would have espoused either plan if the other had espoused a different plan. Figure 1.3 shows this pattern of mutual behavior control.

The patterns of interdependence shown in Figures 1.2 and 1.3 reflect the harmony of the early stages of the relationship between Marya and Sergey. Their outcomes are *correspondent*: they are positively correlated

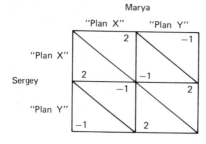

Figure 1.3 Illustration of mutual behavior control.

over the cells of the matrix. What is good for one is good for the other and what is bad is bad for both. They share a common fate. As the story unfolds conflicts began to develop between Marya and Sergey. In the city Marya's commitments to society involved her so exclusively that little was left to give Sergey, who nonetheless "holds steadfast." The pattern of MFC represented in Figure 1.2 then becomes that of Figure 1.4, as Marya's interests shift away from preoccupation with Sergey. Marya's commitments led her to prefer to give little to Sergey, from whom she continued to receive support for all her activities. Conceivably, Sergey could have threatened also to "give little," but as one can see from Figure 1.4 this action would have been quite painful to carry out. The pattern in Figure 1.4 is no longer harmonious: a strong element of outcome noncorrespondence has entered.

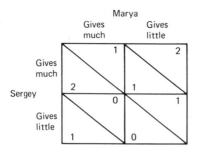

Figure 1.4 Illustration of noncorrespondent relationship with mutual fate control.

Noncorrespondence can also occur, of course, in patterns of mutual behavior control. Suppose that Marya's alienation from Sergey had developed much further. She preferred life in society and he, life in the country. But whatever Sergey did he would have strongly preferred to share with Marya, whereas she would much rather have lived without him. As in Figure 1.5 his best outcome would have occurred if they had lived together in the country and hers would have occurred in society unaccompanied by him. The outcomes of each would have been highly contingent on the other's behavior and noncorrespondently so. [For a more extended discussion of these concepts see Thibaut and Kelley (1959), Chapters 3, 4, 7 (especially), 9, and 10.]

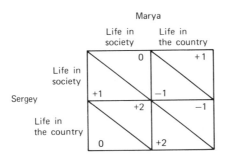

Figure 1.5   Illustration of noncorrespondent relationship with mutual behavior control.

The Status of the Matrix in Our Earlier Work

The view presented in our earlier book took the matrix as being useful in two different ways. For some purposes we assumed that the matrix describes the *subjective* understandings and anticipations of the possible interactions and outcomes, however inadequately they may represent the actual universe of possibilities. Thus employed, the matrix describes the individual orientations of the participants. For other purposes, and more generally, the matrix was intended to be used in the *objective* sense that the values in the cells reflect the actually experienced outcomes when the joint behaviors are engaged in. This use of the matrix thus represents the joint interests of the dyad as a unit. In its subjective form the matrix was said to afford opportunities to make short-run predictions about what behaviors will be performed and whether exploration of the matrix will continue. When the matrix represents the objectively available outcomes (the experiences potentially attainable in the relationship), it could be used to make long-term predictions about the viability of the dyad and, under certain conditions, the behaviors most likely to occur. In its objective form the matrix was intended to have two other closely related uses. It may serve as a bench mark against which to evaluate the degree to which, at any stage in its development, the dyad is realizing the outcomes potentially available, and it may be used prescriptively to make recommendations about the joint behaviors that ought to be performed in the interests of the relationship.

Thus we were aspiring to use the matrix for predicting behavior in the dyad. The subjective matrix was thought to be useful in making short-run predictions about exploratory behavior in the early formative stages of the relationship. The objective matrix was suggested to provide the basis for long-run predictions about patterns of behavior and likelihood of viability of the relationship. Taken together, the two forms of the matrix would then constitute the *effective* matrix from which behavior in the dyad could be predicted.

A THEORY OF THE EFFECTIVE MATRIX

In revising and extending the analysis made in 1959, several avenues of development are open. In an effort to improve the prediction of behavior in interdependent relationships one might be tempted to adopt a psychometric approach. The alternative courses of action persons perceive as available to themselves and to others could be determined and the anticipated consequences of various joint enactments could be measured on preference or utility scales. These assessments and measurements would be used to predict the first response after measurement that each person makes to the situation and, possibly, the first steps of their interaction.

This psychometric approach is part of the strategy adopted by Wyer (1969). Immediately before interacting pairs of unacquainted subjects were asked to fill out a questionnaire that assessed each subject's preference (or utilities) for various combinations of outcomes for himself and his partner. The dyads then proceeded to interact for 50 trials in one of 12 different matrices. The preference judgments taken from the questionnaire responses were used to transform the raw matrix values given to each pair of subjects. These transformed values generated predictions of dyadic behavior that were, in general, quite good and (at least somewhat) superior to those that could be made with the raw matrix values.

Rather than adopting the psychometric approach, we present here a theory about the antecedents of the outcome matrix that is *effective* at the time the behavior occurs—the matrix that is the most immediate determinant of the behavior. To the degree that the theory is correct, comprehensive, and operationalizable, it becomes possible to predict the *effective* matrix from facts about the participants and their situation. The dyadic behavior itself can then be predicted from knowledge of the *effective* matrix.

A valid theory of the antecedents of the *effective* matrix avoids the inefficiencies inherent in the psychometric approach, which stem from the necessity of making *ad hoc* assessments of each situation and each sample of subjects before predicting the behavioral consequences. Such a theory probably also provides a better basis for predicting the longer course or flow of the interaction between interdependent persons. It is likely to imply how the matrix will change as a function of the events of the interaction. At the very least it specifies processes and factors entering into the matrix that are subject to influence and alteration by the interaction itself.

The problems involved in identifying the antecedents of the *effective* matrix are essentially social-psychological in nature and have to do with analyzing the products of social learning—the acquisition of social values and the development of beliefs about social structures and causes of social behavior. Although some of these phenomena have been studied outside social psychology (especially in developmental psychology), their systematic delineation and analysis would seem to be the responsibility of social psychology and not likely to present themselves as problems to other areas of psychology.

There were two main considerations that convinced us of the importance of confronting these problems of the origins of the *effective* matrix. One major impetus to our decision came from our dissatisfaction with simplistic experimentation in which the matrix defined by the experimenter was naïvely assumed to be the effective one. Not only is this assumption erroneous on the basis of everyday observation of individual and cultural differences in what constitutes an incentive but there is much research evidence for its invalidity. The work of McClintock and Messick and their colleagues (e.g., McClintock and McNeel, 1967; Messick and Thorngate, 1967) demonstrates that behavioral choices in response to given matrix values are highly variable across subjects and indeed may be interpreted as measures of the strength of differing social motives. Contextual influences, for example, the subject's comparison level created by the prior level of his outcomes, have also been shown to affect the subject's response to given matrix values (Friedland, Arnold, and Thibaut, 1974). Raw matrix values are simply not satisfactory predictors of behavior.

The second consideration that impelled us to work toward a theory of the *effective* matrix was our concern that the potentialities of outcome matrices have been underestimated and widely misunderstood. The writings of social psychologists abound in references to the narrowly hedonistic assumptions inherent in the use of interdependence matrices and in assertions that such prosocial motives as altruism, cooperation, and the desire for justice are precluded from and inconsistent with an analysis based on these matrices. Our disagreement with the foregoing position is expressed in our theory of the *effective* matrix.

The Given Matrix and the Effective Matrix

The *effective* matrix, as we now construe it, summarizes the set of behavior–outcome contingencies that are operative at the time the behavior occurs. Decisions to act involve choices among the alternatives as defined in the *effective* matrix and are made with respect to the outcomes indicated therein. The postbehavioral assessment of consequences of action are also made with respect to the outcomes in the *effective* matrix. (There are, however, as we argue later, some limits to the participants' exclusive preoccupation with the *effective* matrix.) In short, action is both taken and evaluated with respect to the outcomes in the *effective* matrix.

It is possible to distinguish two sets of factors or processes that contribute to the *effective* matrix. These operate successively in time, the second set acting on the products of the first. The distinction is facilitated by representing the first products in a *given* matrix. Thus we distinguish (a) a set of causal factors that generates a *given* matrix from (b) a set of processes *elicited* by the pattern of that matrix and acting to redefine it. The result of this redefinition is the *effective* matrix.

For introductory purposes we propose to suggest the meaning of the *given* matrix by offering an illustration—the experimenter's game matrix. The experimenter specifies response choices and, in terms of kinds and quantities of incentive, the consequences of various combinations of choice. The local value of each consequence (points, pennies) depends, of course, on the properties of the players. These properties include their needs and concerns, what these lead them to regard as important, their general comparison levels that affect the scaling of the consequences, their marginal utilities, depending on recent deprivation of or satiation with a given incentive, fatigue accumulated through effort required to enact behaviors, and skills determining the costs incurred. The local consequences of interpersonal interferences and facilitation effects are also represented in the *given* matrix.

In general, as in the foregoing illustration, the *given* matrix is determined by environmental factors and institutional arrangements in combination with personal factors (needs, skills, etc.). The matrix is "given" in the sense that the behavioral choices and the outcomes are strongly under the control of factors *external to the interdependence relationship itself*. The outcome in each cell of the matrix—each intersecting or joint behavior—is *given* for the relationship by virtue of the specifications of the social and physical environment and the relevant properties of the two persons.

There is no close causal nexus between the *given* matrix and the behavior it elicits. As we have already observed and as we show more extensively in Chapter 7, outcomes defined locally, cell by cell, as in the *given* matrix, do not account for behavior in interdependent relationships. What the actors often *do* react to is the *pattern* of the *given* matrix; for example, to the disparity between their own and the outcome of the other in a given cell, to the fact that both outcomes are high in certain cells, or to the possibilities of alternating between differentially preferred cells. In effect, by responding to aspects of pattern in the *given* matrix the actors *transform* it into a new matrix, the *effective* one, which is then closely linked to their behavior.

It is to call special attention to this transformation process that we distinguish the *given* from the *effective* matrix. The chain of causal events leading to the *effective* matrix can, we think, be broken to distinguish (a) processes generating a pattern of outcomes, each outcome caused locally, without reference to the others, from (b) processes elicited by that pattern (hence specific to it) and *acting* on it. This is shown in Figure 1.6 in which the arrows at (a) refer to the processes by which each outcome is independently determined and the arrow at (b) refers to the process of recognizing patterns of outcomes and transforming them, that is, the *transformation process*.

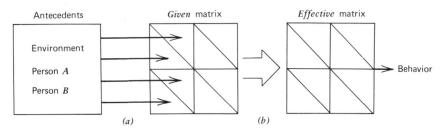

Figure 1.6 The antecedents of the effective matrix.

THE TRANSFORMATION PROCESS

This generates a reformulation or reconceptualization of the matrix with respect to the behavioral choices it affords and to the consequences of various actions. The process works with the facts summarized in the *given* matrix; for example, consider Matrix I in Figure 1.7. Assuming that the

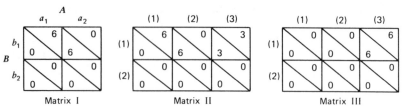

Figure 1.7   Illustration of the transformation process.

interaction is to occur on repeated occasions, the behavioral choices for the two persons may be redefined in the following terms:

Person A: (1) always choose a_1
             (2) always choose a_2
             (3) alternate between a_1 and a_2
Person B: (1) always choose b_1
             (2) always choose b_2

For the *redefined* choices (consisting of policies about courses of action over many occasions) the outcomes can be stated as in Matrix II in Figure 1.7 (the entries being average outcomes per trial). The redefinition of the choices generates a new set of outcomes for the pair, a set in which each person gets something and both get the same outcome. Intuitively, it seems clear that although agreement about what to do would be difficult or impossible in the *given* matrix (Matrix I) it might well be possible in Matrix II. This intuition reflects the fact that certain common social values are available as a basis for agreement in II. Thus A might be heard to say "Don't be foolish and act so that neither of us gets anything," and B might be heard to reply, "That seems reasonable as long as you make it possible for us to share and share alike." This conversation, invoking in simple terms the social values of common welfare and justice, reflects the possibility of applying *criteria of choice* in the matrix (in this case, II) other than those having to do so simply with own outcomes. Consider the extreme case in which each person sets aside his concern exclusively with his own outcomes and focuses instead on two criteria of choice: (a) the total outcomes to the pair and (b) the difference between their respective outcomes. If each person treats the first as a positive criterion (something to be attained and maximized) and the second as a negative criterion (something to be avoided), then Matrix II is transformed to become Matrix III.

In contrast to the original *given* matrix (I) Matrix III provides a clear basis for agreement between the pair. If each could have assumed that both would reconceptualize Matrix I in this manner, explicit agreement would not even have been necessary: each would have known what to do and what the partner would do by virtue of the implicit recognition of their common interest.

Matrix III, which exemplifies the *effective* matrix, results from two successive reformulations of Matrix I: (a) a redefinition of the choices and (b) a shifting of evaluative criteria. The transformation process may involve either or both. These particular transformations change the pattern from one of conflict to one of common interest. Other transformations would have different effects; for example, the relationship could be made more competitive than originally defined. Whereas the transformations illustrated above serve the common interest (if made jointly), others serve just one person's interests. As we shall see, some *given* relationships (described as "mixed motive") can be transformed *either* in ways relating to prosocial goals and values *or* to exploitative purposes and selfish interests.

The concept of "transformation process" affords a way of describing important social determinants of behavior (social values and sociotemporal organization of behavior) and of moving from the level of specific behavior to more complex social phenomena such as the interplay of different orientations to social interaction and systems of rules, roles, and norms. The separation of the analysis of antecedents of the *effective* matrix into pattern–independent and pattern–dependent processes brings into special focus the effects of pattern per se on behavior. This is an especially appropriate focus for social psychology inasmuch as it deals with the social and temporal organization of behavior and the application of social-value criteria to behavioral decision making.

The theme of the transformation process is "taking account of broad considerations." Rather than being viewed *locally*, 'outcomes are considered in the contexts provided by the matrix pattern and by the past and future. The "transforming" person is not content with the matrix as *given* but introduces additional considerations, such as his outcomes in relation to those of his partner and the outcomes he can attain over a long time span. Outcomes are not reacted to one by one and in isolation. They are compared and cumulated. Working within the context of the *given* matrix, the person sees what he can do with it—by planning, reevaluation, and reconceptualization. Note that the transformation process does not involve any direct intervention to change the structure of the *given* matrix. Direct intervention to alter its design is always possible, of course, and would be analogous at the macrosocial level to a distinctive, and perhaps revolutionary, change in the socioeconomic system. Here we are addressing a process that is logically and psychologically antecedent to such a possibility—a process of alterations in the cognitive and axiological significance of the *given* matrix.

The transformation process is precluded by limited information. If the person has too little information to detect the pattern of the matrix, he cannot respond to it in a pattern–dependent way; for example, he may not know what the other's responses are (or how many of them there are) nor the other's outcomes. In this case he would have difficulty ascertaining properties of the pattern. This suggests one approach to a study of the transformation processes. By varying the amount of information given the actors the operation of these processes can be encouraged or discouraged.

The transformation process is subject to change if it is not "working." Ordinarily people are not unconditionally altruistic or just. The "success" of any given transformation depends on what the partner does; for example, a turntaking sequence is practical only if the partner reciprocates. In the absence of reciprocation a different sequential policy will be adopted. The susceptibility of the transformation process to change according to its consequences raises the question of the learning of the components of this process. We now turn to this topic. The general assumption here is that the *given* matrix is, historically and developmentally, the site in which social values and social intentions (plans, rules, and roles) are learned.

The Functions of the Transformation Process

Referring to the example in Figure 1.7, we can see that the actions indicated by the transformed matrix (III) serve not only to yield high outcomes as defined there but also good outcomes to both persons *in the given matrix*. This suggests the first important *function* of transformations and a probable basis for their acquisition. Action within *given* matrices is often unsatisfactory for one or both persons; for example, if in the well-known Prisoner's Dilemma game (PDG), shown in Figure 1.8, each person independently acts in the way that is best for himself, that is, if each chooses his second response, the joint consequence is that both persons receive low outcomes. An appropriate mutual reconceptualization of the interdependence problem, afforded by the transformation process, provides a basis for joint action ($a_1 b_1$) that is more satisfying to both persons *even when evaluated in terms of the given matrix*. In this case one such transformation involves the choice criterion of maximizing their joint score (the sum in each cell), as shown in Figure 1.8.

A *second function* of transformations is that they provide a basis for

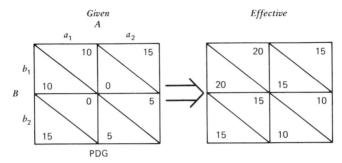

Figure 1.8   The Prisoner's Dilemma game and a possible transformation.

individual action in relation to certain given matrices in which no basis exists; for example, in the *given* pattern in Figure 1.9 (a pattern of simple mutual fate control) neither A nor B has a basis in his own outcomes for deciding what to do. With an outcome transformation that attaches positive value to their joint score each has a reason for choosing his first response. In the transformed matrix a_1 and b_1 are better than their respective alternatives, regardless of what the partner selects.

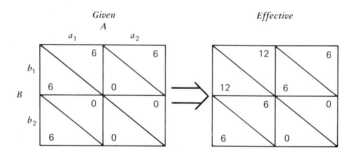

Figure 1.9   Mutual fate control and a possible transformation.

Certain *given* matrices do not require transformation. For these matrices there exists neither of the above reasons for (functions to be served by) transformation. Each person has a basis for action and actions taken on these bases yield satisfactory outcomes. This does not mean that such patterns will not be transformed, for example, as part of some larger "game" or by inappropriate response to their pattern.

Because of the functions they serve, it is reasonable to assume that transformations may be *learned*. The reinforcement for their acquisition has been implied: (a) over the long run they improve the individual's *given* outcomes and (b) they afford a basis for action. The latter may be assumed to be reinforcing via conflict avoidance mechanisms, cost avoidance by avoiding time loss, and/or provision of "unequivocal behavioral orientation" (Jones and Gerard, 1967).

This assumption that the transformational processes are learned raises a number of interrelated questions for analysis and research. For each possible *given* pattern what is possible and likely to be learned? Considering the probable distribution of his experience over the set of possible patterns, what set of transformational tendencies would we expect a person to learn? On what bases does a person learn to discriminate different patterns and contingently apply different transformations? How do the preexisting transformational tendencies of his various partners influence what a person learns? Their tendencies will affect his experience with various approaches to various patterns. His learning does not take place in interaction with equally naïve partners. We must consider the "cultural transmission" of transformational tendencies via experience *in interaction*. (We leave it to others to deal with the "direct" transmission of these tendencies, via moral teaching, propaganda, and so on.)

These transformational tendencies are represented in the mature adult as social and personal values and as rules for good and/or successful social conduct. These values and rules may be prosocial, egoistical, or even antisocial in nature. It is reasonable to assume that because of their functional value these tendencies are acquired not only as instrumentally useful procedures and rules of thumb but also, by association with a broad spectrum of gratifications, as qualities of value themselves. One way of describing this process is in terms of functional autonomy: these tendencies acquire a "life of their own," an independence of their original learning conditions; for example, justice becomes a value to be served without respect to its consequences for the self. Indeed the outcomes evaluated according to the criterion of justice (e.g., minimized difference) may become the only ones operative for the individual. Choices may be based on them, without reference, before or after the act, to own *given* outcomes.

Functional autonomy, however, is rarely absolute. It seems unreasonable to us to assume that the transformation tendencies ever become completely independent of their functional utility. There are several reasons for this. The tendencies are many in number, often somewhat contradictory, and (at least ideally) learned in conditional rather than absolute terms. In order to obtain good *given* outcomes, a person cannot always invoke a particular value, such as justice. He must do so conditionally, depending on the situation and the partner. Indeed, from the point of view of good *given* outcomes, some situations require the opposite (maximizing the degree to which own outcomes surpass the other's). If we assume that the person learns a repertory of transformational tendencies and their conditional application, it seems hardly likely that any one of them will be applied, even to specific situations, without regard to its consequences and without some openness to the different consequences of alternative transformations.

In general, it seems likely to us that the untransformed outcomes in the *given* matrix have, in some final or ultimate way, an impact on the interaction. They cannot, forever and completely, be disregarded even if only because certain of them are basic to the individual's biological survival. This is not to deny that a well-socialized, morally mature person can set aside his own outcomes and act according to purely moral and social considerations with great consistency over long periods of time. However, we find it difficult not to believe that at some level he keeps an account of the consequences of such action for his own personal welfare (i.e., in terms of outcomes in the *given* matrix). [In this connection our analysis shows that the functionally valuable transformations may all have self-interest (own outcomes) represented in them to some degree (as in the foregoing examples). There is no *given* matrix for which the purely altruistic choice criterion of maximizing other's outcomes is more beneficial than the criterion of maximizing joint outcomes.]

THE LOGICAL ANALYSIS

It is possible to identify the major types of matrix pattern systematically. It is further possible to analyze the effect on the various patterns of (a) a set of simple mathematical operations and (b) a set of simple sequences of the behavioral choices. Thus we can develop information of the sort shown in Figure 1.10, specifying for each possible pattern X the patterns $X_1, X_2, X_3,$ and so on, that are generated by applying the various mathematical operations and sequential rules, singly and in combinations, to pattern X.

The relation of this logical analysis to the model of the antecedents of the *effective* matrix (Figure 1.6) is apparent: X corresponds to the *given* matrix and pattern X_1 to the *effective* matrix. The mathematical operations and sequential rules correspond to two important aspects of the transformation process—respectively, the outcome transformations and the sequential transformations.

To facilitate this analysis it is first necessary to examine closely the properties of matrices themselves. Mathematically, the effects of the mathematical operations and sequential rules depend in systematic ways

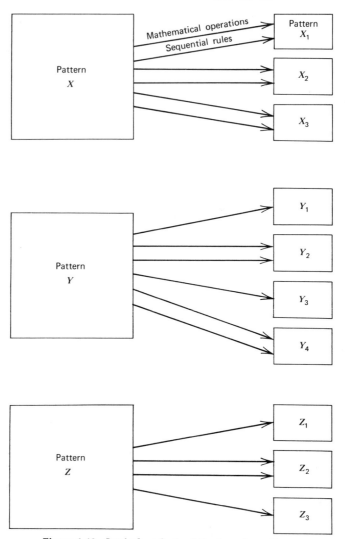

Figure 1.10   Logical analysis of the transformations.

on the properties of the initial pattern. Also the "necessity" for transformation and the "success" of any given transformation depend on
certain properties of the matrices concerned (the *given* and the *effective*
matrices). Finally, the analysis of the pattern of the *given* matrix suggests a
set of specific questions with respect to its antecedents. These are some of
the topics to be considered in subsequent chapters of this book, as
outlined in the following section.

ABSTRACTS OF CHAPTERS

In order to provide a convenient overview of the topics in this book and their sequential development, the abstracts that precede each of the chapters are presented here.

Chapter 2   The Components of Interdependence

This chapter presents an analysis of the basic components that underlie the pattern of any outcome matrix. The analysis is applicable to both *given* and *effective* matrices. These components represent, for each person, his direct control over his own outcomes (*reflexive control*), the direct control over his outcomes by his partner (*fate control*), and the two persons' joint control over his outcomes (*behavior control*). The resultant pattern of a matrix depends on how these components fit together (described in terms of correspondence and concordance) and on their relative magnitudes (*weights*).

Chapter 3   Antecedents of the Given Matrix

This chapter presents a social psychological analysis of the antecedents, both environmental and personal, of the *given* matrix. The analysis is made in terms of the antecedents of the components, the relations in which they stand to each other (their correspondence–noncorrespondence and concordance–discordance), and their relative magnitudes. It also provides a new perspective on the old problems of similarity, complementarity, and compatibility.

Chapter 4   The Domain of 2 × 2 Matrices

This chapter considers the various possible patterns of the simplest matrix (the 2 × 2) and the principal properties of the total domain of such matrices. They are classified with respect to four properties: (a) mutuality of dependence, (b) degree of dependence, (c) bases of dependence, and (d) correspondence of outcomes. Variations in the last property, which reflects commonality versus conflict of interest, are shown to depend in important ways on combinations of the first three properties. Various important patterns and common "games" are identified and located within the domain and in relation to one another. Although it is not possible to consider every possible matrix, the analysis of matrices into components (as described in Chapter 2) and the relation of these components to properties of the domain give confidence in the comprehensiveness of the exploration.

Chapter 5   Properties and Indices of Interdependence Patterns

This chapter proposes indices for the major properties of interdependence patterns and describes how they are related to the components of interdependence. This provides a systematic analysis of what was done intuitively in Chapter 4; namely, a delineation of the links between the properties of the matrix, on the one hand, and the components and their interrelations that underlie it, on the other. The analysis is also propaedeutic to those in Chapters 6 and 7, which show how the properties of the *given* matrix govern the necessity for transformations to be made and how the properties of the *effective* matrix depend jointly on the components of the *given* matrix and the particular transformations made.

The analysis of the bases of correspondence–noncorrespondence reveals the factors underlying the two persons' control over their joint outcomes and over the difference between their respective outcomes, which have implications for the discussion of the bargaining process in Chapter 10. Last, we give systematic attention to questions raised in Chapter 4 concerning the particular combinations of components and their weights necessary for optimal versions of various matrix games.

Chapter 6   Logical Analysis of the Transformation Process

This chapter examines the shifts in matrix pattern generated by applying various mathematical operations and sequential rules to certain *given* patterns. Only certain plausible transformations, corresponding to common values and temporal concepts, are investigated. These include cases in which the person (a) gives some direct weight to his partner's outcomes in his decision-making criteria (outcome transformations), (b) attempts to be the first or second to act on a given occasion out of regard for how the choices are changed for the second actor (transpositional transformations), and (c) adopts a policy governing his successive choices over a series of interactions in the *given* matrix (sequential transformations). The several transformations are analyzed for the effect they have on the patterns of interdependence and therefore on such things as the components of the pattern, the correspondence or noncorrespondence of outcomes, and each person's basis for choice.

Chapter 7   Origin and Evocation of Transformations

This chapter considers the factors that are broadly responsible for the occurrence of transformations. At the outset an analysis is made of the functional value of the transformations described in Chapter 6 as applied to the salient patterns of interdependence identified in Chapter 4. This analysis identifies the functional bases for learning to make, under certain conditions, particular transformations for particular patterns of the *given* matrix. A subsequent section briefly considers the conceptual problems associated with interpreting behavior as providing evidence of transformations. We then discuss the evidence bearing on situational factors that evoke or elicit various types of transformation. A brief review is made of evidence pertaining to the existence of individual differences in transformational tendencies. A final section points to the general theory of self-regulation of motivation that is implied by the present special theory of transformations in contexts of social interdependence.

Chapter 8   Processes of Attribution and Self-Presentation

This chapter analyzes the processes by which the dyadic members learn the nature of the *given* matrix and the transformations that are being applied to it. In discussing these processes, account is taken of the cues presented by each member and the resulting attributions made about the nature of the relationship. In a concluding section the analysis is extended to show how self-presentational and attributional processes operate in the development of trust and intimacy and in the escalation of conflict.

Chapter 9   Interdependence in Triads

An analysis is made of the components of triadic interdependence. This analysis provides the basis for a discussion of the third person's possible effects on the dyad—how the dyad can be strengthened, changed, or disrupted by a representative of the social environment. Attention is then focused on the consequences for the third person of the dyad's behavior, viewed in terms of the power of the dyad over the "outsider." In final sections consideration is given to full-blown, three-way interdependence with special emphasis on some phenomena unique to the triad (relative to the dyad).

Chapter 10   Negotiation and Coalition Formation

This chapter first presents a model of independent and joint action in the dyad that identifies the framework within which negotiation between the members can occur. This framework consists of the various bargaining positions that may be available to the two persons and the settlement points that are viable in relation to the bargaining positions. A distinction is made between two types of bargaining position: (a) those created by each person simply pursuing his own interests and (b) those created explicitly, as threats, for the purpose of imposing on the other person a settlement favorable to the bargainer. The model is then extended to the triad where it forms the basis for an analysis of coalition formation—an analysis of which pair of the three persons, if any, will act in concert against the third. The bases for coalition formation exist in the mutual benefits to the coalition members of working together to create bargaining positions of the two types noted. The possibilities of coalition action are shown to increase the number of possible process and outcome patterns in the triad, compared with the dyad.

Chapter 11 *Epilogue*

This chapter provides a brief interpretive commentary on the theoretical ideas presented in this book. An outline of the kind of theory developed here lists its essential points. Some historical notes relate our central assumptions and orienting ideas to those of Kurt Lewin. A final section highlights several further lines of development of the present theoretical approach.

2

The Components
of Interdependence

ABSTRACT

This chapter presents an analysis of the basic components that underlie the pattern of any outcome matrix. The analysis is applicable to both given *and* effective *matrices. These components represent, for each person, his direct control over his own outcomes* (reflexive control), *the direct control over his outcomes by his partner (*fate control*), and the two persons' joint control over his outcomes (*behavior control*). The resultant pattern of a matrix depends on how these components fit together (described in terms of correspondence and concordance) and on their relative magnitudes (*weights*).*

Person A's control over person B's outcomes may be absolute or contingent. In the first case, by simply varying what he does, A can produce a variation in B's outcomes. We have described this as *fate control* (FC) because A has absolute control over B's fate (Thibaut and Kelley, 1959). In the second case A's effect on B's outcomes is contingent on what B does; therefore they jointly affect B's outcomes. We have described this as *behavior control* (BC) because when A varies his behavior he makes it desirable for B to vary his also (Thibaut and Kelley, 1959). All dyadic relationships characterized by interdependence are based on A's fate control and/or behavior control over B *and* B's fate control and/or behavior control over A. These four elements reflect, respectively, four basic sets of evaluations: (a) B's evaluations of A's actions, (b) B's evaluations of their joint activities, (c) A's evaluations of B's actions, and (d) A's evaluations of their joint activities. Interdependence exists in the relationship *only* if B has differential evaluations (i.e., preferences) in one or both of these respects *and* if the same is true for A. If only A or B have such preferences, the relation is one of unilateral dependence rather than mutual dependence (interdependence).

Two further sets of evaluations play an important role in the pattern of interdependence; namely, each person's differential evaluations of his own behaviors. We refer to them as his *reflexive control* (RC) because as the person varies his actions he has an effect back upon himself affecting his own outcomes. These evaluations have no direct relation to the degree of interdependence but markedly affect the manner in which it is expressed and is likely to be dealt with.

These six sets of differential evaluations, essential to the characterization of any pattern of interdependence, may be conveniently summarized by three matrices, one showing the *bilateral reflexive control* (BRC) component of the relationship, a second showing the *mutual fate control* (MFC) component, and a third showing the *mutual behavior control* (MBC) component; for example, Figure 2.1 shows particular matrices for the three components and the relationship that, in combination, they constitute. Figure 2.1 might reflect the particular facet of a husband and wife relationship that concerns their activities at 5:30 in the evening when he arrives home from work. Each has two salient options: to have a cocktail or to go bicycling. The four cells in the matrix represent the four possible combinations of their respective behaviors, including the cases in which they have cocktails together and go cycling together and also those in which one drinks while the other cycles. The number in the upper-right portion of each cell indicates the wife's outcome for that particular event and the number in the lower-left portion, the husband's outcome. The higher the number, the greater the satisfaction the indicated person derives from that combination of their behaviors.

The BRC component in Figure 2.1 shows that drinking is preferred by the husband as an activity for himself and cycling is preferred (and somewhat more strongly so) by the wife for herself. The MFC component reveals that the wife prefers that, other things being equal, the husband go bicycling. Perhaps she regards it as the healthier thing for him to do; it makes her feel comfortable about his well being. Finally, the MBC component shows that both prefer doing the same activity to doing different ones. Both prefer that they do whatever they do at the same time, as might reflect the satisfactions they gain from undertaking such activities together. The overall pattern of their interdependence with regard to these activities represents a simple summation of the components; the values in each position of the resultant matrix at the right are derived by simply adding up the three values in the corresponding positions of the component matrices.

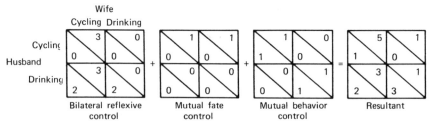

Figure 2.1 Components of hypothetical husband and wife relationship.

Thus the resultant relationship, the overall pattern of interdependence, consists of the three components. More properly, it *may* consist of three components because one may have only zero entries (or the same value in all cells) reflecting a lack of differential evaluation in one or more of the six respects listed. For the relationship to be considered one of interdependence it is necessary that there be variation over the outcome entries for each person in either the MFC component, the MBC component, or both. Within a given component there may be asymmetry between the two persons. This is illustrated in both the BRC and MFC components of Figure 2.1. The latter component shows that although the husband's choice exercises fate control over the wife he has no preference about what she does (except as she does things in conjunction with his own activities—reflected in the MBC matrix). Strictly speaking, there is no *mutual* fate control in Figure 2.1. However, we use the label "mutual fate control" to refer to the component matrix whatever the values occurring there.

Figure 2.1 also illustrates another important property of the components: they may differ in magnitude. It is clear that in this particular part of our hypothetical husband and wife relationship the most important facts are their own preferences about what they themselves do. If we imagine how the two might make their decisions in this situation, the greater magnitude of the evaluative differentiations reflected in the BRC component, relative to those in other components, suggests that this husband and wife will probably be guided by these simple, asocial preferences, each tending to go his own way, she on her Schwinn and he in his Martini.

If our hypothetical pair consistently follows the dictates of its respective reflexive controls, the consequences will be that neither will ever gain the highest levels of satisfaction possible for him or her in this portion of their relationship. Thus the wife will never have the pleasure of her husband's company and the sense of reassurance from his healthful activity that would be possible if they both went cycling together. Similarly, he will never know the delight of her conversation over a drink. To put it another way, if each one is to achieve the highest level of outcome available in this part of their relationship, the other one must make do, at least on that occasion, with rather low outcomes.

This last feature of our example points to an important property of the pattern of interdependence, namely the degree of correspondence versus noncorrespondence between the two persons' outcomes in the various cells. This property determines in crucial ways the problems created for the persons by their interdependence and the process likely to characterize their interaction. The reader will appreciate intuitively the significance of correspondence versus noncorrespondence by realizing that it summarizes how similar or compatible the two persons are and determines how cooperative or competitive their relationship is likely to be. The comments in the preceding paragraph reflect the degree of noncorrespondence of outcomes in the resultant matrix for our husband and wife, a degree partially described by noting that it is not possible for both to attain their maximum outcomes at the same time.

Now let us consider a slight variation in our example. Figure 2.2 presents the same three components as Figure 2.1 but the MBC component is differently oriented. In Figure 2.2 the husband's and wife's evaluations of their joint activities have shifted so that rather than both preferring to do one or the other together both prefer *different* ones. This might be the case, for example, if, on the one hand, she simply cannot stand to watch him drink and he is embarrassed if she does; on the other hand, their joint cycling activities are also somehow mutually unsatisfactory. The result of this different set of preferences is to produce an MBC component more in accord with the dominant BRC component of the relationship; that is, their mutual desire to engage in separate activities coincides with their "reflexive" preferences for different activities. The net effect is to generate a pattern characterized by a higher degree of correspondence of outcomes. In contrast to Figure 2.1 the resultant in Figure 2.2 permits the husband and wife to gain their respective highest levels of satisfaction at the same time.

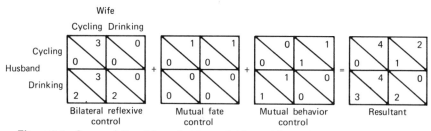

Figure 2.2   Same relationship as in Figure 2.1 but with MBC concordant with BRC.

This example indicates that the pattern of the interdependence depends not only on the three components and their relative magnitudes (to be referred to as weights) but also on their positioning in relation to one another—how they mesh together. We refer to this meshing by the terms concordant and discordant. The MBC and BRC components are concordant in Figure 2.2 and discordant in Figure 2.1. In a similar manner the MFC may be concordant with the MBC when, for example, in their exercise of fate control in a manner favorable to each other's outcome, they also satisfy one of the coordination requirements in the MBC pattern. A discordant relation would exist between MFC and MBC when the actions reflecting mutually benevolent use of fate control converge on cells that are mutually low in the MBC matrix.

Further, BRC may be concordant or discordant with the MFC component—concordant if it is consistent with a person's exercising his fate control in a manner favorable to the other person and discordant if it is consistent with his using fate control to the opposite effect. In our example the husband's RC is discordant with his FC over his wife. As he pursues his own immediate preferences (regarding his own actions) he takes the action less favorable to her. Now it becomes plain why BRC, although having nothing directly to do with *inter*dependence, is an essential ingredient in our analysis. It is in its possible concordant or discordant relations with MFC and MBC that the BRC component affects the pattern of interdependence and thereby the course of the relationship. This is a formal way of expressing the simple fact that the individual's preferences about his own actions affect the manner in which he takes (or is tempted to take) those actions and his exercise of both fate and behavior control over his partner.

One final factor contributes to the overall degree of correspondence—namely, the correspondence or noncorrespondence within the MBC component itself. Our examples have included only highly correspondent MBC components, but the reader can imagine cases of noncorrespondence; for example, the wife might prefer doing things together as in Figure 2.1 but the husband might prefer separate activities as in Figure 2.2. As we shall see, intermediate degrees of correspondence in the MBC component reflect the fact of different strengths of preferences between the two persons in regard to their joint behaviors. The MFC and BRC components do not vary in degree of correspondence. The two sets of entries in each of these matrices vary independently (in the language of mathematics they are orthogonal); so the degree of correspondence (or of noncorrespondence) within the component matrices is always zero.

THE ANALYSIS OF INTERDEPENDENCE

The examples in the preceding section show how we can construct or synthesize various interpersonal relationships. Given certain examples of each component matrix, we can synthesize the resultant relationship by adding the components together. Let us now consider the opposite procedure in which, given a resultant matrix, we analyze it to determine what its components are and how they fit together.

The analysis of rectangular arrangements of numbers such as our outcome matrices is made possible by a procedure derived from what is known in statistics as the analysis of variance. We take for an example a relationship investigated experimentally by Guyer and Rapoport (1970) and described by them as a "threat–vulnerable game." We refer to it simply as a threat game. As shown in Figure 2.3, the relation is asymmetrical. The interaction tends to be one in which A acts as a kind of "allocator" of the outcomes in the relationship (by shifting back and forth between a_1 and a_2 while B does b_1) and B acts as a "threatener," threatening to use his ability to reduce their joint outcomes (as at a_2b_2) to induce A to be fair in his allocation.

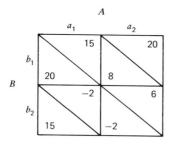

Figure 2.3   Threat game used by Guyer and Rapoport.

The analysis of the relationship in the threat game can be illustrated by first considering only B's outcomes and determining what components contribute to variation in them. Figure 2.4 shows how this analysis is conducted. As a first step the averages are determined for each row and column and are shown arrayed around the total matrix at the left. These averages are then compared to determine how much reflexive control B exercises in this relationship. Because his average outcome for b_1 is 14.0 and for b_2 6.5, his reflexive control is 7.5, the difference between these values. This is indicated by placing 7.5 in each upper cell of the RC component (inasmuch as b_1 is the more valued action) and 0 in each lower cell. Similarly, A's fate control over B is determined by comparing the two averages beneath the game matrix. The difference ($17.5 - 3.0 = 14.5$) indicates how much, on the average, B prefers a_1 to a_2 and this fact is appropriately indicated in the FC component. This reflects the degree to which B is subject to fate control by A's actions. Finally, although A's behavior control over B can be calculated directly, like the first two

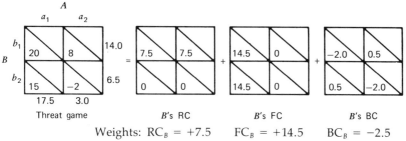

Weights: $RC_B = +7.5$ $FC_B = +14.5$ $BC_B = -2.5$

Figure 2.4 Analysis of components of variation in B's outcomes in the threat game.

components, it is most readily determined as a difference by subtracting RC + FC from the original matrix; that is, for each cell in the BC component we calculate what value must be entered there if the three component values are to add up to the total value. In cell a_1b_1 of the BC component in our example there must be -2.0 in order for the components $(7.5 + 14.5 - 2.0)$ to summate to 20. If the arithmetic is done correctly, all the rows and columns in the BC component will yield the same total (in the example, -1.5).

Below each component matrix in Figure 2.4 we have indicated B's *weight* for that component. This "component weight" simply indicates the magnitude of the difference in B's outcomes produced by each source of control. Thus B's FC weight (FC_B) of 14.5 indicates that he is subject to fate control to the extent of 14.5 units. These weights are given algebraic signs to indicate whether B's outcomes are higher in the upper left (a_1b_1) cell (indicated by a positive sign) or not (indicated by a negative sign). Thus B's RC and FC weights have positive signs because in both cases his high component values occur in the a_1b_1 cell. His BC weight (BC_B), calculated by taking the difference between his high and low values in the MBC component matrix, is given a negative sign because his lower outcome occurs in the a_1b_1 cell. The BC_B weight of -2.5 summarizes the fact that as far as the BC component is concerned B's outcomes are 2.5 units higher in the a_1b_2 and a_2b_1 cells than in the a_1b_1 and a_2b_2 cells.

Following this procedure, we can also analyze the sources of variation in A's outcomes and, putting this analysis together with that of B, we have the complete analysis of the threat game into its components, as shown in Figure 2.5. Each person's component weights, with appropriate signs, are shown below each component matrix.

The essential properties of this relationship are revealed by the analysis. A and B have more control over each other's outcomes than over their own; that is, they have more fate control than reflexive control. The essence of their interdependence is MFC; the bit of MBC is relatively

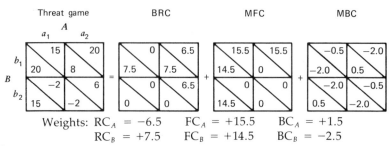

Weights: $RC_A = -6.5$ $FC_A = +15.5$ $BC_A = +1.5$
            $RC_B = +7.5$ $FC_B = +14.5$ $BC_B = -2.5$

Figure 2.5   Complete analysis for both A's and B's outcomes in the threat game.

unimportant. (The small degree of MBC present in the relationship is characterized by noncorrespondence. The reader will note that this fact is indicated both by the pattern in the component matrix and by the opposite signs of BC_A and BC_B.) Additionally, B's RC is concordant with his FC over A but A's RC is discordant with his FC over B; that is, B's RC tends to induce him to take the action that A prefers, whereas A's RC tends to induce him to take the action B does not prefer. (The reader will note that these facts are not only represented in the matrices but are also reflected in the signs of the weights: RC_B has the same sign as FC_A, which is the FC that B exercises over A; and RC_A has the opposite sign from FC_B, which is the FC that A exercises over B.) This combination of concordance and discordance creates the essential properties of the relationship, B tending to the action that is to their mutual advantage and A tending to take the one that is to his own advantage (and to B's disadvantage). The latter creates the situation in which B may have to take his "threat action" (b_2) in an attempt to induce A to perform, at least sometimes, action a_1. Action b_2 is properly called a threat action because B must incur some loss himself in order to reduce A's outcomes. Thus b_2 is something B would rather not do but that he probably will do if he must in order to influence A.

The analysis of a pattern of interdependence made in the manner just outlined has an important property: *it provides a unique analysis for every pattern*. Given a specific pattern of interdependence, the analysis shows us (a) the relative values each person places on his own actions, the other's actions, and their joint actions, (b) the nature of the concordances among the sets of preferences, and (c) the degree of correspondence or noncorrespondence within the MBC component. Thus all the ingredients that go to make up the total relationship are revealed in a precise and unique manner. (However, for a qualification of the uniqueness point see page 42.) Furthermore, the analysis is applicable to every matrix of any size—not only 2 × 2, but 3 × 3 matrices, 5 × 2 matrices, and so on. Important for the consideration of groups larger than dyads is the fact that the analysis also works for 2 × 2 × 2 and higher order matrices. As we show in Chapter 9, however, the number of components increases sharply with the number of persons involved in the interdependence.

This discussion can be summarized by a theoretical statement: all patterns of dyadic interdependence can be viewed as resultants or compounds of the three components BRC, MFC, and MBC. This assertion has analytic and synthetic implications. Analytically, any given pattern of interdependence can be analyzed into a unique set of three component matrices. The analysis reveals the three component weights for each person and how the various types of control fit together (i.e., their concordant–discordant and correspondent–noncorrespondent relations). Synthetically, from different combinations of the three component matrices all possible patterns of interdependence can be constructed. In Chapter 4 we employ the synthetic implication of the analysis to explore the domain of possible patterns and to note the salient types.

THE GENERAL LEVEL OF OUTCOMES: THE GRAND MEAN COMPONENT

In our analyses of matrices so far we have not considered one important property of the matrix, namely, the general level of its outcomes. The most complete way to characterize a resultant matrix is in terms of four sets of values: the magnitude of the BRC, MFC, and MBC components and the two grand means. The magnitudes of the grand means have been concealed by the procedures we have considered so far because they are buried in the pairs of values by which we have chosen to show the BRC, MFC, and MBC components. The grand means are revealed if we use the particular method of analysis shown in Figure 2.6. The pattern, an asymmetrical one, consists of BRC, MFC, and MBC. When the three components are represented by symmetric positive and negative values, as in Figure 2.6, a final matrix with a constant value for each person must be

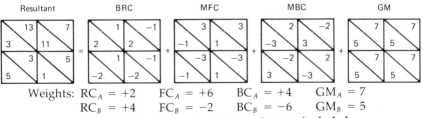

Weights: $RC_A = +2$ $FC_A = +6$ $BC_A = +4$ $GM_A = 7$
              $RC_B = +4$ $FC_B = -2$ $BC_B = -6$ $GM_B = 5$

Figure 2.6   Analysis with grand mean included.

added to account for the resultant matrix. These values are the grand means for each person—28/4 or 7 for person A and 20/4 or 5 for person B in our example. (The calculations are easiest if the grand mean or GM matrix is first determined directly from the averages and the MBC component is found by subtraction in the last step of the analysis.)

The significance of the grand means for the two persons depends on what the matrix represents. In the usual case the matrix describes behavioral choices the two persons make *within* their relationship (as in the example of the husband's and wife's choices between drinking and cycling). The grand means indicate in general how rewarding this portion of their relationship is to them. If each person's outcomes are scaled in relation to his best alternatives (following our suggestion regarding the comparison level for alternatives, Thibaut and Kelley, 1959), his grand mean reflects the general satisfactoriness of this relationship, or the particular portion of it, relative to other alternative relationships. Of course, the grand mean reflects the average of all the person's outcomes in the matrix. Depending on the course of the interaction between the two persons, their average experienced outcomes may be higher or lower than the grand means. The latter reflect only the general level of possibilities in the situation summarized by the matrix.

In a different use of the matrix, one we have not illustrated so far, each person's choices are between being in a relationship with the particular partner or being in some other social location. (A person whose choice to be in this particular relationship is not reciprocated is, of course, left in an uncomfortable limbo to which the alternative location is generally preferable.) In this case the grand means reflect each person's general level of outcomes derived from the particular sort of relationship with respect to which the choices are being made. The outcomes might be scaled according to each person's comparison level for such relationships (Thibaut and Kelley, 1959), in which case the grand means would reflect overall satisfaction–dissatisfaction with this type of relationship.

A different example suggests another role of the grand means in describing interdependence. Figure 2.7 presents three different versions of "Chicken," a pattern consisting of MFC and MBC combined discordantly, the former being the more important of the two. This pattern has taken its name from its alleged correspondence to the contest that pairs of young men have been known to play with their automobiles, racing toward each other at high speed down the center of a highway. The one who first veers to one side in order to avoid a collision is identified as being cowardly or "chicken." In one important respect the patterns reflect this situation: the riskier choice is also the one that enables a person to beat the other. Thus, if A takes the risky choice (D) but B is unwilling to,

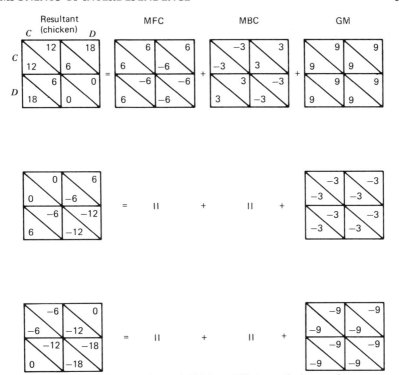

Figure 2.7 Three versions of Chicken differing only in grand mean.

A clearly outstrips *B* in terms of payoff. Thus the relationship provides an opportunity to demonstrate one's willingness to take risk and to outshine another person in this respect. However, another aspect of the real life game of Chicken, the danger, is not well represented unless the grand mean is very low. As shown in Figure 2.7, when the grand mean is high, both persons at worst come out with nothing. Risk exists here only in the sense of variance in possible gains and not in the sense of danger of loss. The versions with negative grand means seem to be more appropriate analogues to the real-life situation, the middle version being the best. With a grand mean of −3 for each person, the relationship is one in which, if both refuse to play the game (i.e., both play C), neither one wins or loses anything. It is only as one insists on gaining some reward from the situation and creates the possible loss for the other one that the interaction runs the risk of leading to large losses for both.

In the comments above we are clearly assuming that the meaning of variability in outcomes depends not only on its magnitude but also on where, within some total range of outcomes, it occurs. Avoiding a loss (to have a zero outcome rather than a −12) is usually different from making a large gain rather then a small one (18 rather than 6). Similarly, to gain a given amount from a zero level (0 to 10) is usually different psychologically from gaining the same amount from a high level (going from 30 to 40). We are referring to the relation between *given* and transformed outcomes and recognizing the nonlinear function and the asymmetries between positive and negative outcomes that sometimes characterize the relation. We have more to say about these matters in Chapter 6.

ALTERNATIVE ANALYSES OF INTERDEPENDENCE

The foregoing procedure for the analysis of interdependence is recommended on the basis of the simplicity of its calculations and the vividness with which it reveals the relative magnitudes of the several sources of variation in the matrix. The analysis, however, is arbitrary in several ways that we now discuss.

Alternative Mathematical Analyses: Decompositions

In our analysis of the matrix in Figure 2.4 we represent B's reflexive control of 7.5 units by entering 7.5 in each upper cell of the BRC component and 0 in each lower cell. To do so is arbitrary. We might, instead, enter *any pair* of numbers in the two sets of cells *as long as they differ by 7.5 units*. Then, depending on the pair of values we use to represent the two levels of RC, B's values in the MFC and MBC components must be adjusted accordingly.

This point is most readily illustrated by Pruitt's study of decompositions of the Prisoner's Dilemma game (1967). This game, shown in the matrix in Figure 2.8, derives its name from a story about two prisoners who are being held in separate cells after their arrest for a major crime. The evidence in the hands of the district attorney is such that they can be convicted only if either one confesses to the crime. The choice of confessing is indicated by D in the matrix and the choice of remaining mum, by C. The outcomes of 6 in the matrix specify the consequences of both confessing and being convicted and the outcomes of 12, the consequences of both being acquitted. If only one confesses, he is rewarded by being set free and having a prior minor charge dropped (indicated by the value of 18). In this case the other one is convicted and given a more severe sentence than if he too had turned state's evidence (an outcome indicated by the 0 payoff). Each prisoner faces the dilemma created by his realization that (a) regardless of what his partner does he himself is better off confessing than maintaining silence, but (b) if both act according to the logic of (a) they will be convicted, whereas with mutual silence they could have been acquitted. (It is perhaps unfortunate that this relationship has become so strongly associated with this particular story. As we shall see, the pattern is characteristic of many types of "exchange" relationship that have nothing to do with crime or penalties.)

Pruitt had some subjects play the PDG shown in Figure 2.8 in its matrix form (Game I). After both subjects had independently chosen C or D the pair of choices was referred to the matrix to determine the outcome of each. In other conditions the game was presented in one of the three decomposed forms shown in Games II, III, and IV in Figure 2.8. The consequences of the C and D choices were shown separately for the self and for the partner and were reported back separately, each person receiving an outcome after his own choice and again after his partner's choice. It can be seen that "your gains" represent the BRC component of the PDG and "other's gains," the MFC component. As shown in Figure 2.9, the three decomposed cases represent three different ways of specifying the BRC and MFC components, Game III corresponding to the method of analysis we have already described. The reader will be able to determine for himself that these are only three of an infinite variety of ways of representing the BRC and MBC components. The only properties that the three cases have in common (and that all such decompositions must have) are (a) that the magnitudes of the differences reflecting degree of reflexive and fate control are, respectively, 6 and 12, (b) that the BRC and MFC components are oriented discordantly, and (c) that the values in

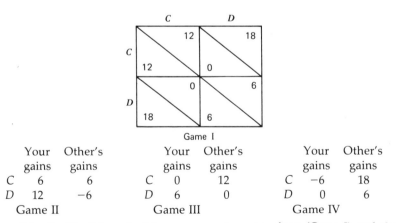

	Your gains	Other's gains			Your gains	Other's gains			Your gains	Other's gains
C	6	6		C	0	12		C	−6	18
D	12	−6		D	6	0		D	0	6
	Game II				Game III				Game IV	

Figure 2.8   Pruitt's Prisoner's Dilemma game in matrix form (Game I) and three decomposed forms (Games II to IV).

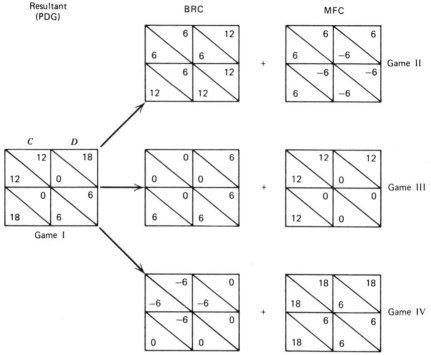

Figure 2.9 Matrix representation of Pruitt's three decompositions of the Prisoner's Dilemma game.

the C,C cell add up to 12 for each person. The first two conditions mean that all three cases in Figure 2.9 have the same component weights for the two persons: $RC_A = RC_B = -6$; $FC_A = FC_B = +12$. The last condition, together with the other two, ensures that all the cell values will add up to those in the resultant matrix.

Pruitt's decompositions make it clear that our analysis of the matrix yields a solution that is unique in a special way. It is unique only with respect to the magnitude of the differences between the values each person places on his own two actions, on the partner's two actions, or on different combinations of their actions; that is to say, it is unique with respect to the component weights for the two persons.

In Chapter 7 we consider the results from Pruitt's studies which show that the particular way in which the PD game is represented has large effects on the resulting interactions. These results are not entirely surprising in view of the different emphases that the several decompositions give to the cost versus reward aspects of the interchange; for example,

Game II highlights the cost that must be imposed on the partner if one is to increase one's own outcomes directly. In contrast, Game IV highlights the necessity of incurring costs oneself if one is to increase the rewards provided to the partner. Thus the different decompositions imply that different psychological bases underlie the resultant patterns. The different bases of component and resultant matrices are considered at length in Chapter 3.

Hamburger (1969) has described the patterns that are decomposable in the manner followed by Pruitt as "separable games." These are patterns consisting only of BRC and MFC components. It should also be noted that games with MBC components are subject to many different minimal–component analyses. Figure 2.10 shows three different analyses for a pattern known as the Battle of the Sexes, which is composed of MFC and MBC, the latter being the larger in magnitude and the two being meshed discordantly. These different ways of thinking about the relationship have not been studied empirically but it seems likely that they would generate different patterns of interaction. They appear to emphasize

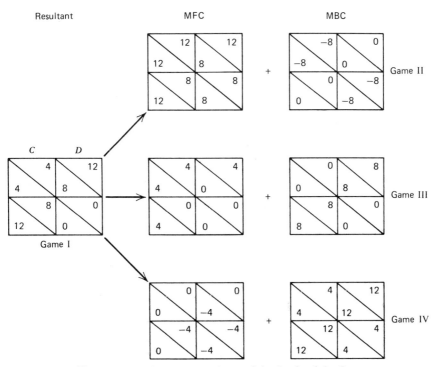

Figure 2.10   Alternative analyses of the Battle of the Sexes.

differentially the importance of helping (or avoiding hurting) the partner and of achieving coordination (or of avoiding incoordination). For this reason they are likely to produce different initial rates of C response and different interpretations of the actions that are taken.

Mathematical versus Social Psychological Analysis

The comments in the preceding section are addressed to the alternative simple mathematical analyses that can be made of a given inter-dependence matrix. Each of these analyses is the simplest possible in the sense that only the minimally necessary set of components consisting of MFC and/or MBC and possibly BRC, is involved. One implication of the preceding discussion is that there are many such simplest analyses and any arbitrary decision about which one to make may fail to represent the analysis the participants make of their own relationship—the way they separate out the issues and values it involves. The present section pursues the distinction between mathematical and social psychological analysis and raises the possibility that none of the alternative simple mathematical analyses may reflect the psychological and social factors underlying the pattern of interdependence. Therefore none of them may capture the components *as the participants think about them*.

Consider the example shown in Figure 2.11 which might characterize

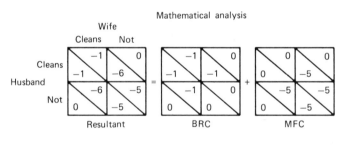

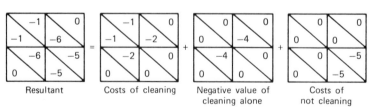

Figure 2.11   A comparison of mathematical and social-psychological analysis of the cleaning example.

the relationship between a young husband and wife in regard to their doing various cleaning chores around their apartment. Let us say that each weekend the choice of each one is between cleaning or not and the consequences are as indicated in the matrix. The mathematical analysis shows that the interdependence involves only two components, BRC and MFC, the latter being more important than the former and the two being meshed in a discordant manner. Each person prefers slightly not to clean and strongly to have the partner clean. (Reference to the preceding section will show that we are again dealing with the Prisoner's Dilemma game.)

An hypothetical social psychological analysis of the relationship is presented in the lower portion of Figure 2.11. This is what might be revealed by asking the couple about the cleaning chores: how much effort it takes to do them alone and together, how each one feels about it if he or she cleans and the spouse does not, and how uncomfortable it is to let the cleaning go altogether. Alternatively, these outcomes might be inferred from a job analysis of the cleaning chores, which might indicate how much mutual interference they involve, and from attitude scales assessing opinions and values about tidiness and fairness. The analysis in Figure 2.11 indicates that the modest costs of doing the cleaning are shareable if both do it, that each one suffers sizable additional costs when he or she does the cleaning alone (e.g., through feelings of inequity), and that the costs of not having the cleaning done at all are even higher.

Several points can be made by reference to this example: (a) the components in the social psychological analysis are themselves complex matrices which can be analyzed into mathematically simpler components. In fact, each of the three components in the lower portion of Figure 2.11 is a mixture of BRC, MFC, and MBC (cf. Figure 2.12). (b) We have identified three social psychological components in this particular example, but in practice the empirical analysis of, any given interdependence pattern might yield any number of such components. This is in contrast to the mathematical analysis that always yields at most the three components (four, if we include GM). (c) Most important of all, the example in Figure 2.11 suggests that the mathematical analysis may not always be useful for understanding the actual elements or components that go to make up certain relationships as they exist in real life. These natural elements are likely themselves to be complex mixtures of BRC, MFC, and MBC. Certainly, when people report to us the factors that underly their interdependence, they are not likely to have them sorted out into the three minimally necessary mathematical terms.

We have more to say about the social–psychological components of interdependence in Chapter 3, in which we consider the antecedents of the *given* matrix. Further, in Chapters 6 and 7, in which we analyze the process by which the *given* matrix is transformed into the *effective* one, we consider how persons may focus selectively on one psychological aspect of the relationship or another (similar to those shown in the lower portion of Figure 2.11), depending on their current intentions and preoccupations.

Analysis of the Given versus the Effective Matrix

The reader may wonder at this point which of the matrices has been subjected to mathematical analysis, the *given* or the *effective*. The answer is that we may analyze one or both, depending on our purposes. We certainly want to analyze and classify interdependence patterns as they are *given*. This analysis is basic to our argument, inasmuch as it identifies the various types of matrix, their properties, and the problems they pose. It affords the basis for identifying the functions that various transformations might serve in solving those problems and consequently for speculating about what transformations may be learned and the conditions under which they are likely to be elicited.

The analysis of the *effective* matrix, identifying its components and their concordances and discordances, reveals how the transformation process shifts the terms of the relationship. As shown in Chapter 6, it is often possible to state the relations systematically between the *given* and the *effective* matrices by formulas that link the components of the two.

Purposes of the Mathematical Analysis

If, as some of the preceding examples (such as Figure 2.11) suggest, the mathematical analysis does not always reveal the social psychological foundations of the interdependence, then of what use is it? At least three answers, some implied in the preceding paragraphs, can be offered at this point. First, as we show in Chapter 4, the components defined mathematically are exceedingly useful in identifying the various types of matrix. Given a classification of matrices, the mathematical analysis of the component weights of a specific matrix is useful for defining or characterizing it so that it can be located in relation to the classes. Second, the mathematical analysis of the resultant matrix points to the kinds of specific problem the pair must cope with if they are to realize to the fullest the potential benefits of their relationship. The relative magnitudes of the three components and their various concordances indicate, for example, the relative importance of developing coordination rules compared with exercising control over own preferences in the interest of helping each other. Third, the mathematical analysis of the natural components constituting a relationship reveals how they fit together, interact, and summate or cancel one another out. This is illustrated in Figure 2.12, which provides the mathematical analysis of the three social psychological components for the cleaning example in Figure 2.11. Comparison of the three analyses shows several important facts. Even though all components involve MBC, they mesh in a manner that cancels out each other's effect, and so the resultant matrix is characterized only by MFC and BRC. The several MFC components are oriented so that they summate, thus producing a strong preference for the partner's doing the cleaning. The BRC components, though individually strong, tend to cancel one another out; the result is a weak BRC pushing each person not to clean. Thus in combination the several social–psychological factors simply yield MFC greater than and discordant with BRC, the Prisoner's Dilemma Game.

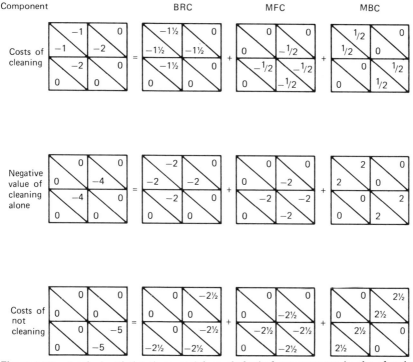

Figure 2.12   Analysis of the three social-psychological components in the cleaning example.

SOME FORMAL CONSIDERATIONS

The analysis of the matrix in terms of three component matrices amounts to making simultaneously two analyses of variance of the matrix, one of A's outcomes and the other of B's outcomes. This is shown in Figure 2.13 for the matrix already described in Figure 2.6. In a 2×2 matrix the sums of squares for each component is simply the square of the difference corresponding to the weight of each component. Thus for A's outcomes in Figure 2.13 the sum of squares for columns is 2^2, for rows, 6^2, and for interaction, 4^2; the total sum of squares is 4 plus 36 plus 16, or 56. The percentage of the total variance accounted for by each component is simply the proportion of the total sum of squares for which its sum of square accounts; these values are 7, 64, and 29%, respectively, for the three components in the example.

We are not the first to suggest the analysis of variance as a means of characterizing interdependence matrices. This possibility has been worked out in various degrees of detail by Wilson and Bixenstine (1962), Wyer (1969), and Wolf (1972). One probable reason why the application of analysis of variance to interdependence matrices has not been fully developed (and one reason why objections will be raised to the present analysis) is that it requires making strong assumptions about the nature of the measurement scales underlying the values in the matrix. Analysis of the variance components requires treating the numbers as if they were taken from an interval scale, that is, a scale on which a difference of n units between any two values means the same thing regardless of what those two values are. Treating the grand mean as an interpretable term requires the further assumption that the numbers come from a scale with a meaningful zero point. Further, when we compare the components for the two persons, as in describing the magnitude of A's RC (RC_A) relative to his FC over B (FC_B), it is necessary to assume that the numbers are comparable interpersonally.

We can admit of little confidence that these assumptions will be justified in the many real-life problems to which interdependence analysis will be applied. We are, however, impressed with the progress that has been made in psychology on similar problems by proceeding as if such assumptions were generally warranted. It seems to be the practical experience in psychological measurement and analysis that limiting oneself to the assumptions that are strictly justified (e.g., of ordinal measurement) is not so productive as being somewhat incautious by accepting stronger assumptions. Furthermore, the stronger assumptions can be made merely for purposes of theoretical analysis. We can simply state that we are assuming that we have numbers from a ratio scale at the outset

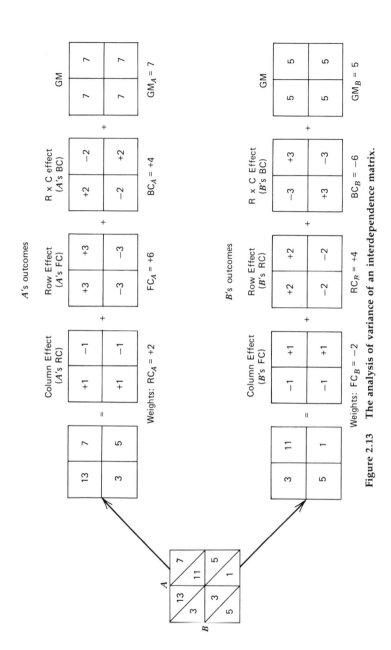

Figure 2.13 The analysis of variance of an interdependence matrix.

of our analysis. Proceeding on this basis permits us to conduct a form of theoretical analysis that is much more powerful and illuminating than an analysis consistent with weaker assumptions would be. The evidence for this last statement may be found in the insights and implications presented in the following chapters, which the reader may judge for himself.

3

Antecedents of the Given Matrix

ABSTRACT

This chapter presents a social psychological analysis of the antecedents, both environmental and personal, of the given *matrix. The analysis is made in terms of the antecedents of the components, the relations in which they stand to each other (their correspondence–noncorrespondence and concordance–discordance), and their relative magnitudes. It also provides a new perspective on the old problems of similarity, complementarity, and compatibility.*

The outcome values in the *given* matrix are determined by features of the social and physical environment or setting in interaction with qualities and states of the dyadic members—their needs and skills. We assume further that the reward and cost values of the outcomes in the *given* matrix will have been affected by each member's general comparison level, by his recent history of deprivation or satiation with a given incentive, by fatigue developed through the effort required to enact behaviors, and by skills determining the costs of behavioral enactments. What we are concerned with in the following pages are the ways in which environmental or situational factors interact with these personal factors of need and skill to determine the components of a *given* matrix and the relationships of the components.

The environmental factors that we consider are those affecting the quality and kinds of resource available to the members and spatio–temporal constraints that may impose coordination requirements on them. We use the term environment very broadly to include natural settings and man-made arrangements and regulations. Hence the environments we refer to may result from the decisions of psychological experimenters, legislators, industrial engineers, union–management negotiations, and parents.

On the side of the personal factors this chapter constitutes an analysis, in interdependence terms, of the personal properties that affect the compatibility of the dyadic members. The classic interpersonal rubrics of "similarity" and "complementarity" are viewed in new terms; for example, an important aspect of similarity is reflected in the analysis of personal factors that produce correspondence or noncorrespondence in MBC between the two persons. One particular form of complementarity exists when the two can, by different actions, reward each other (MFC) and when the RC of each is concordant with the FC he exercises over his partner. The antecedents of compatibility or incompatibility are not exhaustively considered here, however, because some of them have to do with pattern transformations. In Chapter 7 compatibility is viewed from the perspective of social and personal values. We show how, depending on the *given* pattern of interdependence, certain pairings of value orientations are mutually supportive of the relationship and others are disruptive.

A word about terminology: in Chapter 2 we demonstrated the analysis of a resultant matrix into three component matrices. We used the terms BRC, MFC, and MBC to refer to them. At the same time we noted that within a component matrix the weights for the two persons may be equal or different. Thus in the MFC matrix FC_A may be smaller or larger than FC_B in absolute magnitude or they may be equal. (Of course, if $FC_A = 0$ and FC_B is not zero, then, strictly speaking, no *mutual* fate control exists but MFC may still be used to refer to that particular component matrix.) In this and subsequent chapters, when we state that a relationship involves a particular component, say BRC, unless further qualification is added we mean that *both* persons have reflexive control and that the absolute magnitudes of their component weights are approximately equal. Similarly, a relationship characterized by MBC is one in which both persons are subject to about the same degree of behavior control ($|BC_A|=|BC_B|$ and both are greater than zero). The signs of the respective weights (and the relative signs of the weights of different components) are implied by comments about concordance and correspondence.

ANTECEDENTS OF THE COMPONENTS

The components of *bilateral reflexive control* derive from each person's preferences and aversions about performing the various behaviors in his repertory—preferences and aversions that are not contingent on the other person's behavior. By itself, as a pure state of total independence, BRC would develop in any environment in which each of two parties can find something he prefers to do and something he prefers not to do without affecting or being affected by the other. The requirements would appear to be resources adequate for self-sufficiency and barriers to communication, such as physical space or self-absorption.

The component of *mutual fate control* is produced by each person's preferences and aversions for the various behaviors in the other person's repertory—preferences and aversions that are not contingent on variations in his own behavior. Each person can control unconditionally the outcomes of the other and is indifferent in regard to helping or hurting. Pure MFC thus would require an environment in which each controls a different set of resources that are rewarding and/or costly to the other and which are neither rewarding nor costly to himself.

The component of *mutual behavior control* appears when behaviors are selectively interfered with or facilitated by actions of the partner. The consequences of such interference and facilitation produce the BC pattern of rewards and costs. In general—and to oversimplify—interference creates costs and facilitation heightens rewards. Interference is produced by response incompatibility. Responses are incompatible because they simply cannot be performed simultaneously or because they do not in some sense fit together—they create incongruity when performed simultaneously. The inability to perform both behaviors simultaneously often derives from some spatial restriction or scarcity. Two persons cannot depart simultaneously from a room because the exit is too small. In this case the restriction is purely physical. In other cases the scarcity is imposed by a social rule: two persons cannot simultaneously become president of the local Kiwanis Club because a rule restricts the number of incumbents to one. (In these two examples it must be assumed that neither person has a preference for going first: whether exiting first or second or being the first or second president.)

The effects of incongruity on interference are probably largely psychological. In Braithwaite's (1955) example, when Luke plays classical piano while Matthew improvizes jazz on the trumpet, the cacophony is costly to both: it is harder to play and harder to listen. If the incongruity is created by the expression of conflicting opinions voiced on the same occasion by two persons, the interference effects may be reflected in the discomfort or anxiety occasioned by the dissensus. (Again, for the latter example to reflect *pure* MBC it is necessary to assume that the persons do not care which opinions they voice so long as they are not different.)

Another source of incongruity has been pointed out by Foa and Foa (1975) in their discussion of the exchange of different kinds of resource. Although it is entirely appropriate (to say the least) to pay for one's meal at a restaurant, the guest who has been invited to a private home for dinner is expected to depart from the occasion by thanking the hostess and expressing his admiration for her culinary skills; that is, by giving love and status. If, instead, he left a tip and attempted to pay the bill, the embarrassment of the hostess would no doubt be made apparent to him. The interference created by the incongruity between the loving care of the hostess and the guest's commercial response to it would be experienced by both. The general point is that the outcome pattern characteristic of

MBC may reflect the socially defined appropriateness or inappropriateness of various combinations of actions. Qualitative differences in rewards may be identified on the basis of the particular actions or other rewards to which they are most appropriate. Probably no particular rewarding action has the same value, regardless of what the partner does. Even social approval, one of the most generally rewarding actions, suffers in value if the recipient's behavior clearly does not warrant it. One meaning of "economic" transaction is that the resources have fixed inherent values that do not depend on what the partner does (the nature of the "goods" he provides). The MBC pattern generated by considerations of appropriateness is more characteristic of social and affectional exchange.

Response facilitation involves not merely the absence of interference. It may produce a decrement in the costs of producing the behaviors or an increment in their consummatory appreciation. If Luke and Matthew can both play and enjoy jazz, their ensemble playing—whatever the costs—may be an agreeable improvement on the sounds of their solo improvisations. (For this situation to generate pure MBC it must be assumed that they derive as much pleasure when neither plays as when both do.) In this example the efforts to synchronize may impose costs on them; the facilitation occurs only at the level of rewards. Facilitative cost cutting may occur in other settings; for example, when the pooled synchronous efforts of two persons (in building a house, pulling a load) make the task easier for each. A reduction in the costs of making the response and an increase in the rewards for having done so may occur when on the same occasion two persons express similar mutually supportive opinions. (For further elaboration of interference and facilitation see Thibaut and Kelley, 1959, Chapter 4.)

As we noted in Chapter 2, many of the natural *social–psychological components* of interdependence are more complex than the simple mathematical components. This is reflected in several of the parenthetical qualifying remarks in the preceding paragraphs. When Luke and Matthew find that their ensemble jazz playing is better than the solos of either one, the pattern is pure MBC only if they also derive equal net satisfaction when neither plays. A more common version of this situation is shown in the conjunctive pattern in Figure 3.1, where the rewards are derived only when both play. A noncorrespondent version of the conjunctive pattern is the "turn-taking" game in Figure 3.1. Luke may prefer that both play and Matthew, that neither play. In each case the reward for each person requires that both persons make a certain response. The turn-taking game is generated by spatial restriction or scarcity (as in the examples of leaving an area through a narrow exit or attaining the club presidency) *plus* preferences regarding which person takes which action (leaves or becomes president). (In terms of the analysis of Chapter 2 these particular patterns involve all three simple mathematical components, combined in equal proportions.) The "complement" of the conjunctive pattern is the disjunctive one (Figure 3.1) in which rewards are high (or costs low) if either person makes the appropriate response. Put another way, the low outcomes are received only if both persons act improperly. This pattern often reflects an intersubstitutability between the actions of the two persons, as in Deutsch's cooperation condition in which the entire group is graded well if any of the members attain a good problem solution (1949).

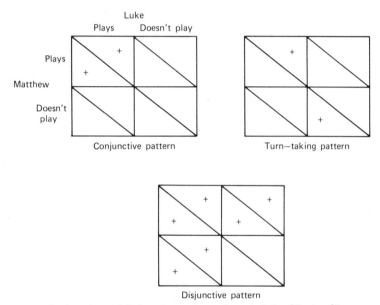

Figure 3.1 Conjunctive and disjunctive patterns characteristic of "natural" components.

ANTECEDENTS OF CORRESPONDENCE

The discussion of correspondence in Chapter 2 suggested that this property of interdependence is determined by the degree of correspondence in the MBC component, by the concordant or discordant relations between the BRC and MFC terms, and by the concordance of MBC with either BRC or MFC. The correspondence or noncorrespondence of a matrix relates to the amount of conflict the pair will experience. The analysis thus points to several different sources of conflict and suggests new ways of looking at the determinants of compatibility or incompatibility between two persons. As the reader will anticipate, the factors contributing to correspondence or noncorrespondence define different respects in which psychologically the two persons are similar or dissimilar and complementary or anticomplementary.

Correspondent versus Noncorrespondent MBC

The dyadic pattern of *correspondent* MBC results when the two persons are affected in the same way by facilitation and /or interference. In some cases both persons have the same behavioral choices, as in the example of Luke and Matthew (Figure 3.1), each of whom had to decide whether to play his instrument. In these cases the symmetry of effect constituting correspondence may reflect either mutual preferences for similar behavior or mutual preferences for different behaviors. Thus both correspondent MBC matrices in Figure 3.2 show that persons A and B are facilitated and/or interfered with by each other's behavior in the same way, but in the left matrix this symmetry results from a mutual preference for similar behaviors and in the matrix on the right, from a mutual preference for different or complementary behaviors. To suggest some examples, in the left matrix C versus D might refer, respectively, to (a) reading versus watching TV (in a small apartment), (b) talking versus being contemplative, (c) discussing politics versus discussing art, or (d) playing classical music versus jazz (as in the earlier example). In the right matrix, in which similar behaviors are mutually interfering and/or different ones are facilitative, C versus D might refer, respectively, to (a) going first versus second through a narrow doorway, (b) taking the initiative versus being submissive, or (c) talking versus listening (in a fine-grain analysis of conversation). Of course, we must assume in all the foregoing examples

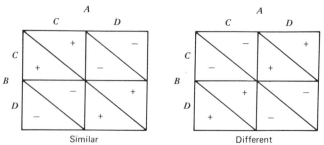

Figure 3.2   Correspondent MBC involving similar or different behaviors.

for both matrices that there is no unconditional (RC) preference for either of the two actions; for example, talking versus listening.

Noncorrespondent MBC results from asymmetry of interference or facilitation. As shown in Figure 3.3, behavioral combinations that are facilitative for one person are interfering for the other and vice versa; for example, A and B might be a teenage boy and girl on their first date and 1 and 2 might correspond to the benches on the two sides of a table in a rear booth at the soda fountain. The boy, A, having an interest in hugging and physical contact, prefers them to sit on the same bench and doesn't care which. The girl, B, interested in conversation and finding out more about this fellow, prefers them to set on opposite sides of the table. (The reader can easily imagine that with similar interests both would prefer either the same bench or opposite ones.) The asymmetry here derives from the different goals the two have with respect to their interaction. A similar example might be provided by Braithwaite's musicians, both of whom can play either piano or strings. Person A (Luke) enjoys it when both play piano (behavior 1 in Figure 3.3) and he also enjoys their both playing strings (behavior 2). Person B (Matthew) is presently studying music in which a piano accompaniment is provided for a string instrument. Hence he tries to play piano (behavior 1) when A is playing the violin and tries to play the violin (behavior 2) when A is playing the piano. Sometimes, however, Matthew misjudges and finds that he is playing the same instrument as Luke. The same outcome pattern would emerge if Matthew were trying to have an interesting debate on the merits of two political candidates and Luke's intention was to reach consensus on one or the other. Matthew would be pleased when he succeeded in disagreeing with Luke but sometimes would miscalculate and find himself agreeing (or perhaps be reluctantly forced to agree by the weight of evidence.)

Noncorrespondence also stems from individual and cultural differences in preferences for similarity versus difference. Suppose that individuals vary in their preferences for discrepancy between their own and other persons' opinions. In the extreme case one person would prefer

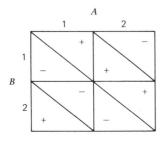

Figure 3.3   Noncorrespondent MBC.

the expression of similar opinions and the other, the expression of different opinions, the resulting matrix (for the expression of attitudes on a given issue) being one of high noncorrespondence. As the last example suggests, this might reflect different motives—one person seeking opinion validation and the other, a stimulating exchange of ideas. (It should also be noted that the expression of attitudes generally involves RC and FC components inasmuch as most persons have certain attitude positions they prefer to state and to hear stated.) Cultural differences in preferred interaction distances would also generate a noncorrespondent MBC pattern, similar to that described for the teenagers on their first date. Neither person cares just where the interaction is but one prefers closeness (the same spot) and the other, distance (different spots). These differences do not reflect different motives but rather different interaction habits that are facilitated or interfered with by different sets of cues.

Concordance between BRC and MFC

Whereas the crucial factor in the preceding discussion is whether the two persons are affected in the same or different ways by *combinations* of their actions, here the central question is whether they are affected in the same or different ways by their respective actions considered *singly*. Each of the two persons may have preferences about what he and the other person does. If each person wants to do what the other wants him to do, BRC and MFC are concordant. This may be true for reasons of reward or cost factors or both. (In the following examples to simplify the story we speak of the concordance resulting from both persons' preference for the behavior of only *one* of the pair.) Both A and B may get reward from A's behavior 1; or A may get reward from it whereas B avoids the costs produced by behavior 2; or both may find the costs of behavior 1 to be lower than if A performs behavior 2; and so on. In the case of moderate concordance (i.e., concordance generating moderate correspondence) A prefers to some degree to do what B prefers very strongly; for high concordance both have preferences of similar strength regarding A's behavior.

Socially and psychologically, this concordance can be traced to learning conditions that result in a person performing, at low cost and/or high direct gratification, actions that other persons value. In the extreme case the person finds joy in the very activities that help or please others. This would be illustrated by the story teller who enjoys his own stories and who pleases his audience, the parent who takes pleasure in building the treehouse that the child wants, or who enjoys making clothes that the offspring enjoys wearing. In most such instances the actor would also get rewards from the other person's *responses* to his help or even from the knowledge that the other person is pleased (which would involve a value transformation, Chapter 7), but we mean here to emphasize the *direct* satisfaction the actor gains from the behavior that the other enjoys. The case in which the costs of behaving in the manner the partner prefers are lower than the costs of alternative behaviors might be illustrated by the exchange of favorable evaluations. Under certain conditions, for example, when each person's behavior is within the general zone of acceptability, to be critical or even to say nothing might be more costly than to be complimentary. If each is pleased by receiving the other's compliments, then this pleasure is concordant with the cost-savings aspects of delivering the compliment. Concordance derived from mutual cost reduction might occur for a pair of recently introduced persons, neither of whom is yet ready to discuss personal matters. For cost-cutting reasons each would prefer not only to talk about other matters himself but also to have his partner speak of other matters.

The discordant relations between BRC and MFC reflect a conflict between what the person prefers to do and what his partner wishes him to do. The action desired by the partner (for reasons of reward attainment or cost avoidance) is either less rewarding for the actor than the alternative action or more costly. If we focus on the costs for the actor (or the rewards he forgoes) in completing the "helpful" action, the BRC–MFC discordance represents the essential condition of social exchange. Exchange implies giving up something in exchange for receiving something. Although one may speak of "exchange" in the concordant case, in which each one directly appreciates what the other also prefers, exchange is not necessary for the relation to have benefits for both. The dependence may be unilateral, as with the story teller or helper in the concordant examples given above. In contrast, with discordance an exchange is necessary if there is to be mutual satisfaction. Each person produces at some cost to himself an action that is valuable to the other. For the exchange to be mutually profitable the costs to self must be lower than the rewards to the partner. Thus true social exchange occurs when the MFC component is more important than the BRC component with which it is discordantly associated. (When the two components are equal in magnitude, a strict conflict of interest obtains.)

The reader will think of numerous examples of exchange with discordant MFC and BRC. Youngsters can trade baseball cards when each has a card that costs less to give up than it is worth to the partner. (Although this may seem to imply an interpersonal comparison of costs and rewards, no such implication is necessary. Exchange will occur if each child makes the judgment that he prefers the other's card to his own.

Thus only intrapersonal comparison is involved.) Exchange may be based on complementary skills, for example, when both persons desire both products 1 and 2 but A is more skillful at fabricating product 1 and B is more skillful with product 2. Mutual interest in cost cutting provides the basis for specialization of production activities.

The analysis of Foa and Foa (1975) implies that RC's concordance or discordance with FC depends on the nature of the resource that is being exchanged. The implication is that discordance increases to the degree that giving up a resource depletes the giver's supply of that resource. If the act of giving does not diminish the giver's supply of the resource, the FC–RC relationship will be neither concordant nor discordant, as in giving information to another (although the costs of *communicating* the information may contribute some discordance). The components will be concordantly related if the act of giving increases own outcomes, as in the giving of love. For two lovers in sexual embrace, to use an example from Foa and Foa, the BRC is concordant with the MFC.

Concordance between BRC and MBC

Both this and the MFC–MBC concordance reflect no simple similarities or differences between the two persons but rather the relation of the convergence between their respective RCs (or FCs) to the coordination requirements of their MBC matrix. Concordant BRC and MBC reflects the situation in which, when each person takes his most preferred action, the pair is brought to a cell that is rewarding from the point of view of behavioral facilitation. Two cases can be distinguished, depending on whether their MBC component requires similar or different behaviors. In the first case concordance would require that the two persons prefer the same action; for example, in our earlier example of the activities of a husband and wife at 5:00 PM the mutual preference for acting together would have been promoted by their preferring, in terms of direct rewards, the same activity, either drinking or cycling. If the MBC coordination requires different actions, then different reflexive preferences are concordant; for example, if for its most effective performance a task requires that one person take the initiative and the other follow, the necessary coordination is achieved by two persons whose preferences regarding their own dominance or submission are different. Another example is provided by the two persons at the start of an automobile trip. Person A prefers to drive and person B prefers being the passenger. The coordination requirements of the task are thus satisfied by their divergent preferences. (The more distal antecedent of this coordination requirement is, of course, the decision of the automobile designer who provided only one driver's seat. The designer, in turn, was responding to certain obvious physical and psychological facts relating to the human control of machines.) These examples make clear that similarity in reflexive preferences promotes certain types of coordination but a complementary difference in such preferences promotes other types. In both cases the concordance reflects the fact that the preferences of the two persons for their own behaviors are such, either similar or different, that they readily satisfy coordination requirements.

If in the discordant case both persons follow their preferences with regard to their own behavior, they act jointly in a manner that fails to satisfy their preferences regarding combinations of their behavior. It is necessary for one person to override his reflexive control if the benefits of coordination are to be realized. Again two kinds of discordance can be distinguished: (a) the MBC requires the same behavior of each but each prefers different ones, and (b) the MBC requires different behaviors but each prefers the same one.

Concordance between MFC and MBC

Here the ruling factor is the meshing between the mutually beneficent exercise of fate control and the MBC coordination requirements. Discord is illustrated by the game known as the Battle of the Sexes in which, for example, each person wants the partner to do a different thing (the wife wants the husband to dress in a "mod" fashion and he wants her to dress conservatively), but the rewards are highest when their behaviors are similar (they appear well together with a similar mode of dress, whichever one it is). Again, this case, in which the different desires for the partner's behavior conflict with MBC requirements of similarity, can be distinguished from the case in which similar desires for the partner's behavior conflict with MBC requirements of difference; for example, in a mismatched couple each desires submissiveness from the partner, but their tasks are predominantly those that require a pairing of leadership with followership. The game known as Chicken involves a similar discordance: each person has a strong preference for the other one to back down. This makes difficult the coordination on different behaviors that is specified by the MBC component of the game.

Concordance is present when what the two persons want of each other is consistent with what they want in the way of joint behavior. Their desires for the same behavior from each other may be concordant with MBC coordination that requires matching behavior or their desires for different behavior from each other may be concordant with a coordination requiring complementary actions. As an example of the latter consider A and B, both of whom can play trumpet and piano with equal facility and enjoyment. If their ensemble playing sounds better when one (no matter which) plays the piano and the other, the trumpet, this advantage will be concordant with A's liking to hear B on piano and B's liking to hear A on trumpet.

Similarity versus Complementarity

In many of the preceding examples it has been reasonable to assume that the behavioral alternatives are identical for the two persons. Under these circumstances we have seen that correspondence can reflect either similarity or complementarity between the two persons; for example, although both matrices presented in Figure 3.2 describe correspondent coordination problems, in the one case, if the behavioral choices are the same for A and B, they must enact similar behaviors, whereas in the other they must enact different ones. As summarized in Figure 3.4, the same distinction can be made with respect to each of the concordances relevant to the degree of correspondence of the relationship. This figure describes the circumstances and preferences that must exist if each of the four factors contributing to correspondence is to reflect a case of similarity or complementarity.

The matrix analysis is indifferent to the distinction between similarity and complementarity, being sensitive only to differences in pattern that

Figure 3.4   General antecedents of outcome–correspondent types of interdependence.

	Similarity	Complementarity
Correspondent MBC	Similar behaviors produce coordination. Similar behaviors are symmetrically facilitative and/or dissimilar behaviors are symmetrically interfering.	Different behaviors produce coordination. Dissimilar behaviors are symmetrically facilitative and/or similar behaviors are symmetrically interfering.
Concordant BRC and MFC	Each prefers to perform the same behavior and this is the behavior the other prefers him to perform.	Each prefers to perform a different behavior and this is the behavior the other prefers him to perform.
Concordant BRC and MBC	Each prefers to perform the similar behavior that produces coordination.	Each prefers to perform the dissimilar behavior that produces coordination.
Concordant MFC and MBC	Each prefers the other to perform the same behavior and these similar behaviors produce coordination.	Each prefers the other to perform a different behavior and the dissimilar behaviors produce coordination.

are not attributable to a particular identification or labeling of the behavioral alternatives available to each person. The distinction, however, is an important one for the application of the analysis to social psychological problems; for example, it seems probable that similarity or matching MBC requirements are easier to identify and learn than the complementary. The similarity requirements may also in general be easier to manage on the spur of the moment; it is usually easier for one person to imitate the other than to complement his action (as by doing the opposite or making a compensatory adjustment.) Some of the common complementary MBC problems are handled by rules that constrain all interactions to one of the two +, + cells (e.g., rules of the road: driving on the right side of the road and yielding right of way at an intersection to a vehicle on one's right).

In exchanges involving BRC and MFC the similarity pattern requires not only that *A* derive direct reward (or cost cutting) from his own performance of a given behavior but also that he gain *additional* benefits from the same behavior in *B*. This is often characteristic of social activities among peers such as singing and telling stories. Complementarity in the BRC and MFC combinations is more common in role-differentiated relationships such as a husband–wife pair; for example, according to stereotyped role conceptions, he prefers to take out the garbage and have her wash the dishes and she prefers to wash the dishes and have him take out the garbage.

Many relationships cannot be characterized in terms of similarity versus complementarity because the two persons' behavioral choices are not the same. Consider, for example, the PD game. (Although this involves discordant rather than concordant BRC and MFC, the discordant BRC is not so great that it precludes a mutually rewarding exchange.) In the experimental version each person has the same choice between the C and D responses. Perhaps the most common close parallel in real life is the relation between two sellers of a given product to the same set of buyers. Under certain conditions of demand their respective decisions to set a high or low price (each one facing the same choice) yield outcomes corresponding to the PD pattern. Probably more common examples of the pattern in economic exchange are those in which different behavioral alternatives exist for the two persons: buyers and sellers exchanging goods and services, different goods, services for money, and so on.

ANTECEDENTS OF COMPONENT WEIGHTS

To repeat, when more than one component is involved in an interdependent relationship, they may be combined concordantly or discordantly—and the psychological antecedents of the paired components will differ accordingly. In addition, as described in Chapter 4, it is necessary to take into account the relative weights of the associated components. Thus true "social exchange" occurs only when the MFC term is larger than the BRC term with which it is discordantly paired. We now turn to a discussion of the antecedents of differently weighted combinations of the paired components.

MFC > BRC.   As in all unequally weighted pairings, the inequality can result from one component's being very large or from the other's being very small (or for both reasons). In the *discordant* case that produces "social exchange" each person can at small cost to himself greatly advantage the other. In the earlier example of trading baseball cards it might be assumed that a boy with duplicate cards will not greatly hesitate to exchange one of his duplicates for a card that he has not yet acquired. More generally, this trading relationship might be expected to develop when each has a relatively large supply of a different resource that the other strongly values. It may also develop when two persons are differentially skillful at providing two services or goods that both of them value. The skills of each make the costs of providing a particular reward less than its value to the partner. This pattern of discordance is exemplified by the Prisoner's Dilemma game. In the *concordant* case each has only a slight preference to do what the other strongly wants him to do. The Matthew–Luke duo remains intact because each greatly enjoys hearing the other play, although neither receives more than slight pleasure from his own performance. (This pattern of concordance is illustrated by the Maximizing Difference game; see Chapter 4.)

BRC > MFC.   In this combination preferences about own behavior are more important than those concerning the behavior of the other. In the *discordant* pairing each strongly prefers not to do what the other slightly prefers him to do. This might be exemplified by the strained relations between two diplomats from rival countries: each finds it personally quite costly to give the other the compliment each mildly feels he deserves out of respect for diplomatic protocol. A general case would be an attempt by two persons to exchange different resources, each giving something of which he has a smaller supply than his partner; or they might attempt to exchange mutually valued services that neither one is expert in performing, the costs being too high to be offset by the reward value to the partner. The *concordant* case implies that each strongly prefers to do what the other only slightly prefers him to do. Thus Luke and Matthew may strongly prefer to play the guitar (rather than, say, being quiet) but experience only a marginal increase in pleasure from one another's playing.

MBC > *BRC*. In general, coordination is more important than reflexive preferences. In the *discordant* case two behaviors meet the strong coordination requirement, but both persons are somewhat inclined to prefer the behavior that leads to incoordination. In the example of the automobile trip both persons may mildly prefer to be the driver or both may have inclinations to be passengers. In the *concordant* case again two behaviors meet the strong coordination requirements, but the behaviors are so similar that there is little basis for personal preference (as in sitting on one or the other end of a teetertotter). If the behaviors are quite different, the persons' preferences for them are weak: one weakly prefers to drive the car and the other mildly likes being a passenger.

BRC > *MBC*. Now, coordination becomes less important than preferences about own behavior. In the *discordant* case the two behaviors or roles that satisfy the weak coordination requirement are so strongly relevant to the persons' needs or abilities that each strongly prefers to perform the behavior leading to incoordination. If the two persons in the example of the activities of husband and wife at 5:00 p.m. (Chapter 2) have strong and different preferences for the two activities of drinking and cycling, they will not meet the coordination requirement (weak in this version of the example) of doing things together. The *concordant* case is similar except that the strong preferences for own behavior lead to satisfaction of a weak coordination requirement. Both husband and wife prefer martinis to bicycles and enjoy martinis even (somewhat) more when together.

MBC > *MFC*. Here, in general, coordination is more'important than preferences about the other's behavior. (Battle of the Sexes, Chapter 4, exemplifies the *discordant* version of this unequally weighted combination of MBC and MFC.) In the example of the automobile trip there is a strong coordination requirement that one drive and one "ride." Although neither person has a preference with regard to his or her own driving or sitting, the discordant case is produced if each is slightly afraid of the other's driving. *Concordance* occurs when both persons have mild preferences for the other's behavior that lead to meeting a strong coordination requirement. Two musicians sound much better when one plays trumpet and the other, piano. Both play trumpet and piano with equal facility and enjoyment but *A* mildly prefers to hear *B* on trumpet and *B* has an equally small but real preference to hear *A* on piano.

$MFC > MBC$.   The coordination requirement is relaxed. *Discordance* is well illustrated by the game of "Chicken" for this unequally weighted combination. Each person in the game has a strong preference for the other one to back down, such preference outweighing the coordination requirement. The *concordant* case is realized when strong preferences for particular behaviors from each other support the weak coordination requirement. Two musicians sound somewhat better when one plays trumpet and the other plays piano, and A strongly prefers to hear B on trumpet, whereas B strongly prefers to hear A on piano.

ANTECEDENTS OF THE GRAND MEANS

We assume that each person scales his outcomes in relation to a comparison level (CL). (In Chapter 6 we consider the consequences of possible nonlinear effects in this scaling.) Therefore the average level of each person's outcomes in the matrix (his GM) reflects the magnitudes of the rewards to be enjoyed and costs to be incurred in relation to his CL. As described more fully in Thibaut and Kelley (1959), the CL is the level of outcomes the person feels he deserves on the basis of his experience in other similar relationships and his understanding of the satisfaction persons in such relationships should and do enjoy. The outcomes in the particular matrix are positive if above CL and negative if below it, the person being satisfied or dissatisfied, respectively. His GM does not, of course, necessarily reflect the level of outcomes the person typically attains within the dyad. If the pattern is sufficiently correspondent and if the two persons succeed in attaining the high outcomes and avoiding the low, each person's outcomes may be considerably higher than his GM. Alternatively, if the two persons become trapped in a cell with low outcomes, their outcomes may be considerably lower than their GMs. (The superiority of the attained outcomes relative to the GMs might be used as an indicator of the efficiency of the dyad.) To simplify the following discussion, however, we assume that the attained level of outcomes for each person is approximately equal to his GM in the matrix.

Assume, then, that the GM reflects the person's general level of satisfaction or dissatisfaction with the interaction summarized by the interdependence matrix. Would a person continue interaction if his outcomes were generally negative? The answer is found in the nature of his alternatives to the present interaction. The specific matrix may be only part of the total dyadic relationship, and one person may accept negative outcomes in it as part of an extended trading process in which they are offset by positive outcomes in other domains of the relationship. (In this case we might wish to expand the matrix to incorporate all the significant parts of the relationship, the positive as well as the negative.)

If the person's outcomes within the total realm of the dyadic interaction are generally negative and if, nevertheless, he continues the interaction, it is presumed that his alternatives to being in this dyad are even worse. More generally, each person is assumed to have a comparison level for alternatives (CL_{alt}) for each relationship. This is the level of outcomes he believes he can obtain from interactions and activities (including solitary ones) that are available to him as alternatives to the present interaction. When outcomes in the latter drop below the CL_{alt}, he (sooner or later) leaves it and moves to his alternatives. According to this logic, if he believes those alternatives to yield poorer outcomes than the present relationship, he will remain in it even if it is not producing outcomes he regards, in relation to the CL, as satisfactory. The antecedents of this situation, in which his GM is negative, are found in experiences and conditions that produce a gap between his CL and his CL_{alt}. In one common case more attractive relationships are highly salient for him and his CL is high. However, he is required to remain in the present less rewarding relationship because the social, emotional, or legal costs entailed in moving to the better alternatives are too high (his CL_{alt} is low).

This is an appropriate place to consider the interdependence implications of the GMs and CL_{alt}s of the two persons. Any relationship can be considered in terms of the behavior alternatives shown in Figure 3.5, in which each person's choice is between being inside or outside the relationship. "In" refers to being oriented to the dyad—desiring to continue (or resume) it. "Out" refers to moving into the best available alternative relationship. When both persons choose "in," they interact within the dyad and each person receives a level of outcomes we assume (see before) to be approximately equal to his GM. When either person chooses "out" (i.e., to leave this dyad and pursue his alternative sources of reward), he moves to the level of outcomes represented by his CL_{alt}.

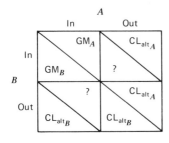

Figure 3.5   The interdependence pattern for being inside or outside a relationship.

When one person chooses "out" and the other chooses "in," the latter is cast into a state of limbo. Because the relationship does not exist and interaction cannot take place unless both persons are "in," he is caught somewhere between the dyad and his alternative. The question mark for his outcomes reflect uncertainty about the consequences of this in-between status. It is probably less satisfactory than the CL_{alt} (as indicated by the connotations of unrequited love and rejected offer of friendship) and the person will probably eventually move to his alternative. The in–out cell is probably also somewhat uncomfortable for the person who is "out"—if he or she knows that the partner desires to resume the relationship. (If the person is completely "out," the partner's orientation may not be apparent.) In sum, the pattern of outcomes for an ongoing relationship is probably similar to one of the two patterns in Figure 3.6. Case I illustrates symmetrical dependence. A person's dependence is a function of how much his GM exceeds his CL_{alt}. In Case I the two persons are equally dependent on the existence of their relationship. The components of the interdependence are primarily MBC—each person wanting to match the partner's "in" or "out" choice—and MFC—each one wanting the partner to be "in" rather than "out." In Case II B's dependence is far greater than A's. According to the principle of least interest, A can be expected to exercise greater power within the relationship than B: "That person is able to dictate the conditions of association whose interest in the continuation of the affair is least" (Waller and Hill, 1951, p. 191). As we show in Chapter 10, A's high CL_{alt} (high in relation to his outcomes in the A–B dyad) affords him a bargaining position from which he can make a strong case for receiving his higher outcomes within the relationship; that is, among the pairs of outcomes available within the A–B dyad (which are summarized by the two GMs), A can lay claim to those that yield his higher outcomes even if they happen to yield B rather low ones. Up to a point (at which he is not realizing the good outcomes reflected in GM_B

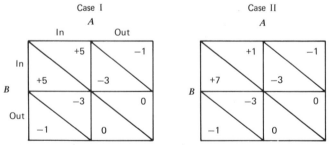

Figure 3.6   Typical outcome patterns for the in/out choice matrix.

and is being pushed too close to his CL_{alt}), B will be willing to honor A's claims in order to ensure the continuation of the dyad.

The antecedents of dependence are, of course, found in conditions that result in high rewards being uniquely available in the particular relationship. Individuals whose personal properties (e.g., attractiveness, skills) enable them to attain good outcomes in a number of different dyads are not greatly dependent on any given dyad. A person who derives a highly unique kind of satisfaction from the partner and who therefore finds the partner irreplaceable is, of course, highly dependent on that partner. Two persons who manage to please each other in ways they have never experienced with other partners and do not expect in other relationships have the basis for strong mutual dependence. Social and personal rules that delimit certain highly rewarding activities (e.g., sex, personal intimacies) to a given dyad serve to heighten and maintain the interdependence of that dyad.

4

The Domain of
2 × 2 Matrices

ABSTRACT

This chapter considers the various possible patterns of the simplest matrix (the 2 × 2) and the principal properties of the total domain of such matrices. They are classified with respect to four properties: (a) mutuality of dependence, (b) degree of dependence, (c) bases of dependence, and (d) correspondence of outcomes. Variations in the last property, which reflects commonality versus conflict of interest, are shown to depend in important ways on combinations of the first three properties. Various important patterns and common "games" are identified and located within the domain and in relation to one another. Although it is not possible to consider every possible matrix, the analysis of matrices into components (as described in Chapter 2) and the relation of these components to properties of the domain give confidence in the comprehensiveness of the exploration.

In this chapter we consider the different patterns of interdependence that are generated by the many possible combinations of components as they vary in their relative magnitudes and in their correspondence and concordant–discordant orientations. For practical purposes we limit our exploration to 2 × 2 matrices.

As noted in Chapter 2, the analysis of components and patterns applies equally to the *given* and the *effective* matrix of interdependence. Thus the taxonomy of patterns presented here could be used for classifying a set of *given* or a set of *effective* matrices. In Chapter 7 we use the present taxonomy as a basis for identifying the main examples of *given* matrices that have certain properties. We examine them systematically for what they imply to be functionally useful transformations of the *given* matrix into the *effective* one. The present classification system gives us assurance at that crucial point that our sample of matrices is comprehensive and consequently that our analysis is well founded.

The major purpose of our exploration of the 2 × 2 domain is to identify the properties or dimensions with respect to which interdependence patterns differ. These will provide us with a framework for locating patterns relative to one another and for imposing a rough classification on them. At the conclusion of this effort we will have an understanding of the attribute "space" that characterizes interdependent relationships and this in turn can be examined in relation to the classification of relationships provided by other theoretical perspectives or by analyses of the layman's perception of social relationships. In Chapter 5 we analyze the major properties more systematically, suggest quantitative indices for them, and determine exactly how they relate to the components and their intermeshing.

Beyond our special purposes in exploring the domain of 2 × 2 matrices, the reader will find this chapter useful in calling his attention to various important patterns that, because of their special properties, he may wish to remember. There is, of course, an infinite number of patterns. Within this universe, however, there is a limited number of noteworthy patterns—some 20 or 30. These patterns are special for different reasons—some because of their simplicity, others because of a property they represent in an extreme degree, and others because they face the interdependent person with sharp dilemmas of choice.

STRATEGIES FOR EXPLORING THE DOMAIN

In principle, all possible patterns of interdependence can be constructed by combining the three components in all possible sets of magnitudes and concordances. In practice, the number of matrices generated in this manner is endless and, because they vary continuously rather than discretely, the task of distinguishing among them becomes difficult. An alternative approach is to consider the domain of all possible patterns as a large terrain to be explored while the salient features and landmarks along the particular trails followed are noted. Because we can select these trails in a systematic manner (by selecting certain discrete values of the components) and because the terrain has regular features (due to its combinatorial genesis), we can more or less fill in the unexplored portions of the map by extrapolation from our limited observations. There are, however, a number of ways to explore the domain and, as we show, what one discovers on his journeys depends on the particular constraints he places on his search process.

Rapoport and Guyer (1966) restricted their analysis of 2 × 2 matrices to those in which each person's four outcomes are completely ranked, the most desirable having a value of 4, the second most desirable, a value of 3, and the least desirable, a value of 1. Then all possible configurations of such matrices were identified and the 78 unique configurations were classified. Whereas the Rapoport and Guyer procedure distinguishes four levels of outcome for each person and requires that each level occur only once in the matrix, we begin with a simpler approach in which we distinguish only two levels of outcome for each person, that is, high and low, and then identify all their possible combinations and configurations; for example, we distinguish all the different patterns in which one person has two high and two low outcomes, the other person, one high and three low outcomes.

A second strategy for identifying and classifying various matrices is provided by the component analysis. The general approach is to consider all possible combinations of components of various magnitudes and to combine them in all the different ways possible. Because of the extremely large number of possibilities, this is feasible only if certain constraints are placed on the sets of components chosen for combination. Later we consider patterns based on symmetric components. Components are symmetric when the two persons are subject to a given type of control, whether reflexive, fate, or behavior control, to *the same degree*.

Several observations can be made about these two strategies for exploring the domain of matrices. First, the second strategy is the more general and subsumes the first under it. Thus the exploration of the matrices defined by various levels of outcome can be described in terms of combinations of particular values of the components; for example, by applying the component analysis to the Rapoport and Guyer matrices we find that very special sets of components are involved. (If the reader objects to applying the analysis of variance to the rank-ordered outcomes, he need only be reminded that we are doing this simply to characterize this particular set of matrices and to relate them to the larger universe of matrices.) The Rapoport and Guyer matrices are restricted to the sets in which each person has component weights of 2, 1, and 0, which are distributed in all possible ways over his RC, FC, and BC terms. The same observations can be made about the two-outcome-level matrices to be considered later. Identification of all possible patterns of two-outcome levels amounts to considering all possible combinations of *certain* sets of weights for the two persons.

Second, the matrices one "sees" in his exploration of the domain depend on the particular constraints he places on his exploration process; for example, because the Rapoport and Guyer strategy implicitly restricts our purview to patterns in which each person has weights 2, 1, and 0 distributed over his three components, it does not permit us to identify matrices such as pure MFC, pure MBC, the simple FC–BC pattern, or combinations of all three weighted equally. Similar limitations exist for the sample of two-outcome-level matrices. The sample does not include symmetrical component patterns found in the Rapoport and Guyer sample, such as those of PDG, Chicken, and Battle of the Sexes.

The fact that the patterns of interdependence depend on the number of outcome levels distinguished has an interesting social–psychological implication; that is, the kinds of relationships interdependent persons experience will depend on how discriminating they are among their outcomes. Persons who, in 2 × 2 cases, distinguish only high and low levels, will never be faced with the subtleties of the Prisoner's Dilemma or similar patterns requiring finer discriminations. This might be true for the infant who knows only that he is comfortable or uncomfortable or for the newcomer to a foreign country who, for reasons of language or cultural handicaps, can distinguish only that other persons are being friendly or unfriendly toward him.

One might question the wisdom of considering matrices involving only gross distinctions in outcome (e.g., only high and low). It is not easy, however, to know how fine a scaling of outcomes the actors are capable of. This ability undoubtedly varies as a function of their experience, knowledge, freedom from time pressure, and the nature of the specific consequences represented in the matrix (their complexity and commensurability). In the absence of specific evidence on this point we believe it is desirable to conduct the analysis at different levels of fineness. Certainly, there is a strong esthetic appeal in the simplicity of the two-outcome-level analysis in which minimal assumptions are made about the valuational skills of the actors.

For reasons implied—that we want to see all the major types of possible pattern including those available to highly discriminating persons as well as those who make only gross distinctions—we decided to use several different exploration strategies.

PROPERTIES OF THE DOMAIN

We have chosen to differentiate the various matrices on the basis of their properties—the configurations, patterns, and components they display. Although we often speculate about the behavioral consequences of different matrices, these comments are intended merely to suggest the social and behavioral implications of the matrix analysis. We have tried to avoid relying on such speculations as the basis for description and classification. This reliance seems to us to blur the distinction between the *structure* of interdependence and the interaction *process* of which structure is only a partial determinant.

Our approach is to be contrasted with that of Rapoport and Guyer (1966). They analyzed the ranked-outcome patterns in terms of (a) what outcomes each person will receive as a consequence of their making simultaneous and independent choices and (b) what a person who is not satisfied with the initial results can do, anticipating a second choice occasion, to improve his outcome. The assumptions concerning the basis of these choices follow those of game theory as closely as possible. Each person is assumed to have complete knowledge of the matrix. The criteria used in making the initial choices generally involve attempts to maximize one's own outcomes. There is no assumption that the persons are able, on successive occasions, to work out collusive turntaking arrangements. As we detail in Chapter 6, such arrangements change the game and therefore are viewed from the game theoretical perspective as irrelevant to the characterization of a given pattern.

In contrast, our general theoretical perspective is one of problem solving. *Given* matrices (*given*, in the technical sense defined in Chapter 1) are viewed as problems to be solved rather than as final, fixed causes of behavior. The problem-solving analogy implies that the reactions to a particular *given* matrix will be diverse, themselves characterized by pattern and structure, and even involving redefinitions of the problem. In the classic game theoretic view, illustrated by the Rapoport and Guyer analysis, the game matrix represents the final definition and distillation of the social situation to be used with narrow choice criteria in prescribing what each player should do. This meaning of the matrix corresponds to our conception of the *effective* matrix as being the definition of the relationship most closely linked to behavior. Because of our central interest in both *given* and *effective* matrices and in the links between them, we must characterize them in the same terms. This precludes classification in terms of their behavioral consequences and limits us to the use of matrix properties as such.*

Excluding the case of perfect independence (the matrix of bilateral reflexive control), 2 × 2 matrices can be classified in terms of four major properties: (a) *mutuality of dependence*: whether there is mutual dependence (to be referred to as *interdependence*) or unilateral dependence (to be referred to simply as *dependence*); (b) *degree of dependence*: the degree to which the one or two persons are dependent on their partners; (c) *bases of dependence*: whether the dependence in the relationship involves fate control, behavior control, or some combination of the two; and (d) *cor-*

---

* Our use of the term behavior control to characterize a particular pattern in the matrix may seem inconsistent with this point. It implies a simple scenario of interaction, namely, if B is subject to BC and A varies his behavior, B is likely to vary his as well. However, we intend that the term simply refer to the fact that when A varies his behavior it is desirable for B to vary his also. Whether B does so is another matter, determined by other factors. In retrospect it might have been wise to adopt terms more descriptive of the matrix pattern than are fate control and behavior control. It seemed simpler and we found it more natural to continue using those terms that we had adopted earlier (Thibaut and Kelley, 1959).

respondence of outcomes: degree to which the outcomes of the two persons are correspondent or noncorrespondent. Figure 4.1 presents a convenient way for locating matrices with respect to the first three of these four properties. It is, in a sense, our basic road map of the 2 × 2 domain.

The central orienting point in Figure 4.1 is the state of independence. The matrix there is characterized by bilaterial reflexive control (BRC). Above this central point is the realm of interdependence. As we move upward, each person's dependence increases so that patterns of total interdependence are at the top of the map. Along the first branch these are characterized by mutual fate control (MFC), along the third branch, by mutual behavior control (MBC), and along the second and fourth branches, by mixtures of fate control (FC) and behavior control (BC). Two kinds of mixture can be distinguished, namely, those at the end of the second branch in which each person is subject to both FC and BC and those at the end of the fourth, dotted branch in which one person (person A) is subject to FC and the other person (person B) is subject to BC. (Throughout what follows A is used to designate the person whose behavioral choices are represented by the columns of the matrix and B, the person whose choices are represented by the rows.)

Intermediate degrees of interdependence, between the extremes of no interdependence at BRC or of complete interdependence at the top of the domain, are located at intermediate positions along the upward branches of the map. As we move upward along a branch the reflexive control is reduced for each person and replaced by FC, BC, or their combination, depending on the particular branch being followed. Other possible

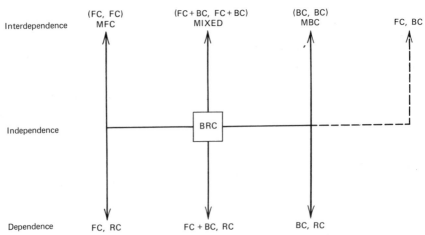

Figure 4.1   Map of variations in dependence and bases of dependence.

branches, not shown, are intermediate between those in Figure 4.1. These would involve mixtures of FC and BC but with the predominant component being one or the other. To avoid confusion these and other intermediate branches of the map are omitted.

The lower part of Figure 4.1 shows matrices of unilateral dependence. At the level of total dependence the dependent person (it will be person A) is subject wholly to FC, BC or some mixture of the two, but the partner (person B) is subject only to RC. Again, intermediate degrees of A's dependence are located at intermediate positions along the appropriate branch. As we move downward from BRC, person A's RC is reduced and replaced by FC, BC, or both, depending on the branch.

Figure 4.1 provides a means of locating matrices with respect to mutuality, degree, and bases of dependence. The fourth property, correspondence of outcomes, can be plotted orthogonally to each branch of the figure. In this way we can see how variations in the degree and type of interdependence affect the degree of commonality of interest between the two persons. This is shown in Figure 4.2, which is explained in the following section.

DISTRIBUTION OF MATRICES

We now proceed to explore this domain of 2 × 2 matrices. We shall determine how the important fourth property of matrices, their correspondence or noncorrespondence, is related to the other properties. We first show the locations of various two-outcome-level (TOL) matrices and some of the ranked-outcome (RO) matrices classified by Rapoport and Guyer. These matrices, supplemented by other cases, will give us a view of the general outlines of the domain.

Two-Outcome-Level Matrices

It is possible to construct 30 different matrices by defining two outcome levels, high and low, for each person. Each person may have zero to four high outcomes in a 2 × 2 matrix but the extreme cases, 0 and 4, are of no interest to us because the person's outcome does not vary. Thus it is necessary to consider only those possible patterns in which each person has one, two, or three high outcomes. The reader can determine for himself that there are three different patterns in which each person has only one high outcome; six different patterns in which one has one high outcome and the other has two; four patterns with one and three, eight with two for each, six with two and three, and three with three for each. In developing these possibilities, it must be kept in mind that a pattern is unique only if it is not possible by relabeling the rows and/or columns or by interchanging the labeling of persons A and B to convert it into one of the other patterns in the set. (In practice, the process of identifying all the unique patterns by drawing up matrices and comparing them with others already identified is rather cumbersome and subject to error. One of the benefits of the component analysis is that it provides a more systematic and foolproof procedure for identifying all the possible matrices.)

The locations of some of the two-outcome-level (TOL) patterns are indicated in Figure 4.2 by Ts. (The Rs in the figure indicate the locations of ranked-outcome matrices, discussed later.) Along each branch of the figure we have introduced correspondence of outcomes as an orthogonal variable. Patterns of extreme correspondence are located at the right edge of each small table and those of extreme noncorrespondence, at the left edge. Patterns in the center of each small table are characterized by neither correspondence nor noncorrespondence of outcomes. (Correspondence is indexed here according to the formula given in Chapter 5.) An extra small table at the top of Figure 4.2 displays the patterns of total interdependence. They have no RC for either person and reflect different combinations of FC and BC but are of special interest because of the high degree to which the two persons are interdependent.

Twenty-two of the 30 possible TOL patterns are located at the 14 positions shown in Figure 4.2. (Several patterns are located at certain of the positions. Also, the reader will note that BRC is repeated in each small table, whenever appropriate.) Varying degrees of correspondence occur at most points in the domain; for example, four different degrees of correspondence are represented by the mixtures of FC and BC at the intermediate level of interdependence. The reason, of course, is that these components can vary in their concordance and, when MBC is involved, in correspondence.

The remaining eight TOL patterns constitute mixtures of interdependence and dependence. All involve some asymmetry in dependence even though each person is, to some degree, dependent on the other. If the reader can imagine folding Figure 4.2 lengthwise along the horizontal line of independence, these eight patterns would be located at positions intermediate between the upper and lower levels of the fold.

An examination of the distribution of the TOL matrices in Figure 4.2 shows that these simple matrices cover a considerable portion of the 2×2 domain. A good deal of the possible variety in patterning is captured by matrices in which only high versus low outcomes are distinguished. On the other hand, it is clear that some parts of the domain are not represented by TOL matrices. This is certainly true with respect to

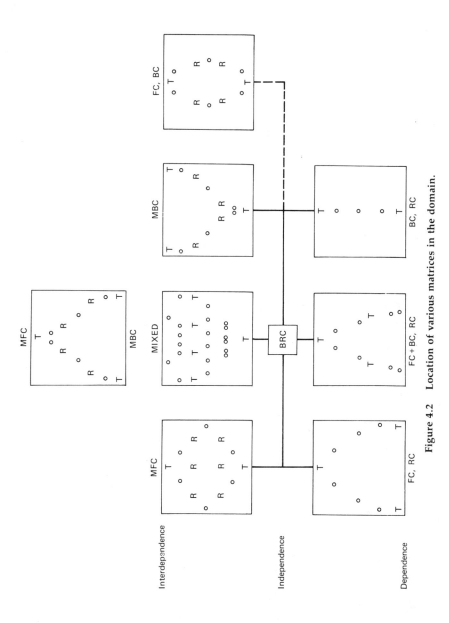

Figure 4.2 Location of various matrices in the domain.

intermediate degrees of interdependence, which are represented among the TOL matrices only by patterns involving mixtures of FC and BC, and the same is true for intermediate degrees of dependence.

The Rapoport and Guyer Matrices

As noted earlier, in basing their taxonomy on matrices in which each person's four outcomes are defined in terms of rank orders, Rapoport and Guyer limited themselves to matrices in which each person's three component weights are in the ratio $2:1:0$. This is without respect to order, so one person's RC, FC, and BC component weights may be in the ratio $1:0:2$, respectively, whereas another's may be in the ratio $0:2:1$. The component analysis affords a convenient method for determining how many such matrices there are and for generating a complete list of them. Seventy-eight different patterns can be generated with the $2:1:0$ ratio of components.

In Figure 4.2 Rs show the locations of 26 of the ranked-outcome (RO) patterns on our map of the 2×2 domain. (Two patterns are located at each of eight locations in the figure; therefore only 18 locations are indicated.) These 26 are the only ones among the 78 possible RO patterns that can be located directly on the branches of the domain. Because of the required ratio of the components, the remaining patterns fall either in the "fold" between dependence and interdependence (48 patterns) or between the mixed and the FC, BC interdependence patterns. Thus there are no pure cases of unilateral dependence. With the $2:1:0$ weights A may be totally dependent on B but the latter is always partly dependent on A. The only cases of mixed interdependence are those at the level of total interdependence. Mixtures at lower levels of interdependence require that all three components be greater than zero for both persons.

Outlines of the Domain

The locations of the TOL and RO patterns in Figure 4.2 begin to reveal the outlines of the 2×2 domain; but even together they show only part of the picture. Using the components analysis, it is a simple matter to construct other matrices to fill out the gaps in Figure 4.2 and to determine their correspondence. The locations of these additional patterns are shown in Figure 4.2 by small circles.

Figure 4.2 makes it clear that the entire range of correspondence–noncorrespondence does not occur at all points along the branches of the "map" (i.e., for all combinations of mutuality, degree, and bases of dependence). Among the patterns of interdependence, in the upper part of the figure, the maximum range occurs at intermediate degrees of interdependence when it is based on MFC but at maximum interdependence when it is based on MBC. Correspondence and non-correspondence never become extreme when the interdependence is based on one person's FC and the other's BC.

Among the dependent patterns correspondence is always neutral for the BC, RC combinations. The maximum range of correspondence–noncorrespondence occurs only for combinations in which the dependent person is subject, wholly or in part, to FC, and the maximum range occurs only at the most extreme degree of dependence.

PATTERNS BASED ON SYMMETRIC COMPONENTS

Our final foray into the domain of 2 × 2 matrices is limited to patterns based on symmetric components. These are the patterns in which the two persons are affected by each type of control to the same *degree*; that is, A's component weight for RC is of the same magnitude as B's and the same is true, respectively, for their FC and BC weights. In short, $|RC_A| = |RC_B|$, $|FC_A| = |FC_B|$, and $|BC_A| = |BC_B|$. Therefore, when we refer to an MFC component of 4, we mean that each person's weight for FC has a value of 4. The sign of each FC weight may be positive or negative and is reflected in the concordant–discordant relations between the MFC component and the other components.

We now consider not only the distribution of patterns over our map of the domain but also the details of the patterns themselves. This will give us a close look at the details of the interdependence portion of our map (with the exception of the FC, BC part). In particular, we will have an opportunity to note the location of certain classical patterns such as the Prisoner's Dilemma, Battle of the Sexes, and Chicken. First we examine combinations of pairs of the components and then combinations of all three.

Combinations of MFC and MBC

Figure 4.3 presents the set of patterns generated by combining MFC and MBC in various proportions, as indicated along the vertical axis of the figure. For each ratio of MFC to MBC the components are combined in all possible concordant and discordant relations. BRC being absent, these patterns represent cases of total interdependence. Thus Figure 4.3 constitutes an exploration in detail of the uppermost chart in Figure 4.2. As there, noncorrespondent and correspondent MBC define the extremes of

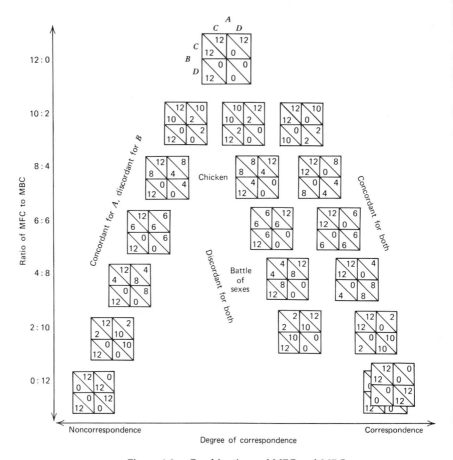

Figure 4.3   Combinations of MFC and MBC.

the correspondence dimension and MFC provides a definition of its midpoint. The distribution of the patterns in Figure 4.3 shows that with increasing preponderance of MFC the mixtures approach the middle of the correspondence–noncorrespondence dimension. (The two columns of matrices on the right of the figure share the same correspondence values. Those on the right, however, are more correspondent when a correction is made in the index of correspondence to take account of the shape of the "frontier." This correction is discussed in Chapter 5.)

The patterns in Figure 4.3 reflect the relations between actions necessary to exercise benevolent fate control and the pairs of actions necessary to satisfy coordination preferences or requirements. The BRC component being absent, these patterns have the important property that the person has no behavioral choice that he prefers regardless of what the partner does (often referred to as a dominant choice). Moreover, the person's two alternative behaviors present him with a relatively risky versus a relatively safe choice. Depending on what the partner does, one action affords sharply different possible outcomes (e.g., 12 versus 0), whereas the other action provides more similar ones (e.g., 8 versus 4). The degree to which this is true increases as the MFC and MBC components become increasingly *equal* in magnitude, the outcomes for the equal case being 12 versus 0 compared with 6 versus 6. Thus each person has no RC basis for choice (his two actions yield him the same average outcome), but he is given the possibility of choice on the basis of perceived riskiness (differences in variability of possible outcomes).

Among the occasions on which the two persons have the same preferences regarding their joint outcomes (correspondent MBC) the MFC can be either concordant or discordant with these preferences. The concordant patterns, shown along the right side of Figure 4.3, have relatively high correspondence and in all cases there is a mutually preferred joint activity, CC. For each person action C is the one that both helps the partner and involves the greatest risk. Thus successful accommodation here probably requires willingness to help the partner in the confidence that he will reciprocate. This problem seems to become most severe with intermediate ratios of MFC to MBC, the patterns in which the fate control over the partner is considerable but enough MBC is present that the combination involves considerably greater risk for the helping action.

Two of the discordant patterns, differing only in the relative magnitudes of MBC and MFC, have been referred to as Chicken and Battle of the Sexes. The Chicken pattern provides an opportunity to demonstrate one's willingness to take risk and in doing so to outdo the other person. For this to be true Chicken must be located at an appropriate intermediate position between pure MFC (where there is maximum ability to reduce the other's outcomes and to maximize one's potential advantage over him but no difference between the choices in their riskiness) and MFC = MBC (where D is, to a maximal degree, the riskier choice, but the difference in possible scores is not very great, correspondence being rather considerable). In Chapter 5 we discuss more systematically the question raised here of the optimal ratios of components for certain patterns. The irony of Chicken lies in the fact that although CC yields good outcomes for both persons the pull of competition and risk-taking motivation moves the two persons away from that cell to the mutually least advantageous. This is to be contrasted with the Prisoner's Dilemma in which the same effect is achieved by virtue of each person's pursuit of his RC and, possibly, a competitive advantage.

Battle of the Sexes refers to the problem a husband and wife often have in coordinating their activities because of their preferences for what each other does; for example, they both strongly prefer that one play the piano while the other sings rather than have both attempt either activity. Yet each (less strongly) prefers to hear his partner play the piano rather than sing. The predominance of the MBC factor means that coordination is the salient feature of the Battle of the Sexes relationship. The discordant MFC component creates a situation in which the strong coordination preferences are best satisfied only by an alteration procedure in which each person temporarily permits the other to act in a way the former does not prefer. These properties, characteristic of the Battle of the Sexes relationship, are present over a range of MFC to MBC ratios, but it seems intuitively clear that the conflict between the coordination requirement and the MFC preferences becomes sharpest for ratios of MFC and MBC in the neighborhood of 4:8. It is here that it is highly important that the pair coordinate on one or the other of the two cells with high totals and, because the difference in payoffs is fairly large in these cells, that the pair alternate between them. Again we encounter the problem of the optimal ratio of components for a given pattern, a problem to be considered in Chapter 5.

The combinations of MFC and noncorrespondent MBC are all asymmetric games. (Compare the symmetry of outcomes around the major diagonal of the matrices on the right of Figure 4.3 with the asymmetry in the matrices on the left.) In the patterns in Figure 4.3 the MFC is concordant with A's coordination preferences and discordant with B's. This asymmetry is reflected in two properties of the pattern. First, the maximum total outcomes (often referred to as maximal joint payoff or MJP) are attained only by a joint action that favors A. Thus, if equal outcomes are to be attained by some sort of alternation, something less than MJP must be acceptable for the pair. This irreconcilability between MJP and equal division appears to be most severe with patterns in the region of 4:8 to 6:6. It is for these patterns that (a) B is greatly concerned about his small share of the MJP cell and (b) the joint profit is greatly reduced by adopting a procedure that permits equal shares. This irreconcilability is potentially important to the pair because it places in contraposition two common social values, namely, the general (total) welfare versus justice (equality).

Second, although turn taking is necessary to approach equality of outcomes, exact equality requires a special ratio of turns favoring A over B; for example, for equality to prevail in the 4:8 pattern there must be a 3 to 2 trade off between the 12, 4 (CC) and 0, 12 (CD) cells. The resulting average joint score of 14.4 is to be compared with 16 in the MJP cell. (It is a simple mathematical fact, but perhaps of social psychological importance, that the most efficient turn taking is one that involves a trade off between the MJP cell and another cell in which the person disadvantaged in the MJP cell has the greatest advantage. So for an equal-share, optimal joint-profit exchange the party favored in the MJP cell must be willing to move to another cell that he likes least, that is, from the 12, 4 cell to the 0, 12 cell rather than to the 4, 8 cell in the 4:8 pattern in Figure 4.3.) As the MFC component becomes relatively more important, the need for turn taking as a means of approaching equality is reduced and, of course, with high MFC each person needs only induce his partner to exercise his fate control benevolently.

Combinations of BRC and MBC

With the addition of MBC to BRC shown in Figure 4.4 we generate patterns that vary in the degree of interdependence. Interdependence is maximal at the top of the figure where the BRC is minimal, whereas at the bottom of the figure, with pure BRC, there is, of course, no interdependence at all. The pure BRC pattern, like the MFC, has an intermediate degree of correspondence. Figure 4.4 will be recognized as corresponding to the MBC branch of Figure 4.2. (Again the two right columns of matrices share the same correspondence values. Their relative positions in the figure reflect a correction for the frontier values, described in Chapter 5.)

On the right side of Figure 4.4 are patterns based on correspondent MBC in which the two persons have the same preferences regarding their joint activities. The various patterns reflect whether the BRC preferences promote the commonly desired coordination by concordance with the MBC pattern or whether they interfere with it because of a discordant fit. It can be seen that all the concordant combinations contain one mutually preferred cell and that the advantage of this cell in relation to the next best one (in terms of mutual preference) increases with increasing BRC. Thus with increasing magnitude the BRC component reduces the necessity for the pair to coordinate between two good, mutually preferred sets of activities. For lower degrees of BRC (upper portion of the figure) it provides a means of solving the coordination problem by having each person follow his own RC preferences. There is probably some low ratio of BRC to MBC, perhaps 2:10, where there is an optimal "mix" of these two properties; that is, where there is enough BRC to afford a dependable basis for coordination but enough MBC to make coordination important to the pair.

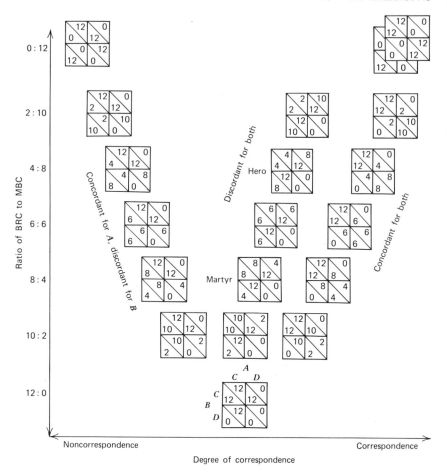

Figure 4.4   Combinations of BRC and MBC.

With small magnitudes of BRC the *discordant* fit reduces the degree of correspondence and thereby increases the need for alternation between diagonal cells if equal and good outcomes are to be attained. Following the BRC brings the pair to mutually low outcomes. Thus with weak preferences regarding own behavior that conflict with coordination requirements it is impossible for both persons to attain maximum satisfaction at the same time. Good outcomes can come only by alternation which requires selective inhibition of the RC factors. This relationship has been called Hero by Rapoport and Guyer (1966) for the reason that when both persons are acting according to their RCs a person who then foregoes his RC advantage (moving from C to D) improves the outcomes for both but more so for the other person than for himself. As shown in Figure 4.4, with increasing relative magnitude of the BRC component this problem disappears and maximum joint outcomes (MJP) become available if each person simply acts on his RC preferences. Once again there appears to be some low-to-intermediate ratio of BRC to MBC in which the psychological properties of Hero are optimal. In the neighborhood of 4:8 there is, on the one hand, a fairly strong basis in RC for each person to make the C choice and, on the other, sizable negative consequences for both person's doing so (MJP cell versus next best cell is large).

When the MBC component is noncorrespondent, the BRC component will be concordant for one party and discordant for the other. In Figure 4.4 the concordance has been created for person A who controls the columns. If both persons follow their RC preferences, their actions converge on the outcome A prefers. Like the comparable patterns of MFC and MBC in Figure 4.3, these noncorrespondent patterns are characterized by irreconcilability between maximum joint outcomes and equality of outcomes. As in the MFC + MBC patterns, this conflict between MJP and equality is sharpest for patterns with ratios around 4:8 to 6:6. The difference between the two sets of patterns is in which person is in a position to shift the pair between the two cells providing optimal tradeoff. Here it is the person who is advantaged in the MJP cell, whereas for the patterns in Figure 4.3 it is the disadvantaged person. (In asymmetrical MBC patterns with noncorrespondence, also characterized by this irreconcilability, *either* party can make the move necessary for optimal tradeoff. In the BRC + MFC asymmetrical combinations in Figure 4.5 that are characterized by irreconcilability it is the advantaged person who must provide the optimal tradeoff.)

Combinations of BRC and MFC

Some of the specific patterns generated by combining MFC with BRC in various degrees and ways are shown in Figure 4.5. The ratio of BRC to MFC decreases as we move toward the top of the figure. Figure 4.5 corresponds to the MFC branch of Figure 4.2. With symmetric components MFC can be combined with BRC in only three ways. The results are shown from left to right for the combinations discordant for both A and B, concordant for A but discordant for B, and concordant for both.

The two patterns at the extreme left and right are those in which the two components are equal. In the left pattern, which is one of perfect noncorrespondence, the degree of BRC (cost to each person) is just sufficient to offset the degree of MFC (reward he delivers to his partner). This yields

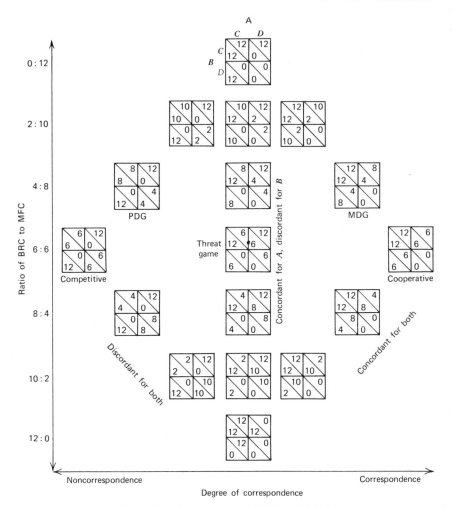

Figure 4.5   Combinations of BRC and MFC.

a "constant-sum" relationship; whatever one person can do for the other by the benevolent use of his fate control is exactly counterbalanced by rewards he has to give up or costs he must incur in order to do so. Thus the total outcome to the pair is constant over the entire matrix. (Obviously if appropriate values are used the relationship is "zero-sum," the net outcome to the pair—the gains of one less the losses of the other—always being zero, no matter what they do.) This kind of perfectly competitive relationship is to be compared with noncorrespondent MBC (e.g., Figure

4.4), in which case the two persons have similarly strong preferences regarding the joint activities of the pair but these preferences are totally in disagreement. Rather than the conflict of interest being caused by the incompatibility between each person's RC and his partner's FC, it arises from the incompatibility between their BCs. A comparison of the two reveals that the different patterns have different consequences; for example, they differ with respect to the manner in which equal outcomes can be achieved. Cells of moderate outcomes exist in the MFC plus BRC patterns, whereas these outcomes can be obtained only by a regular alternation procedure in the noncorrespondent MBC pattern.

Similar observations can be made regarding the two types of perfectly cooperative relationship, the one arising from a concordance between each person's RC and the partner's FC (Figure 4.5) and the other, from correspondent MBC. The former yields only one jointly best outcome, whereas the latter involves two such points. This results in different problems for the pair if they are to attain maximum joint outcome. With BRC + MFC this requires merely that each one follow his RC, but in the case of correspondent MBC a joint coordination on one of the best points is necessary.

The patterns in which MFC is greater in magnitude than BRC are among the most thoroughly investigated in game research, the bilaterally discordant one being the Prisoner's Dilemma game (PDG) and the bilaterally concordant, the maximizing difference game (MDG). In both (as in all the patterns in Figure 4.5 in which BRC is greater than zero) each person has a "dominant" response, that is, an action that, because of the RC factor, yields him better outcomes no matter what the other person does. In the case of the PDG pattern, if both choose these dominant responses, the total outcomes for the pair are the lowest in the relationship. It is the irony of this type of relationship that as each person pursues his own interest the general welfare of the pair suffers. This aspect of the pattern seems to be most marked for some ratio of BRC to MFC intermediate between 6:6 and 0:12, a point we discuss in Chapter 5.

A further property of the PDG is that the dominant response yields the possibility of gaining a higher score than the other person, which might be important for someone competitively motivated. The MDG pattern separates this consequence from the dominant response. In the MDG pattern the dominant response (C) serves to yield the best possible outcomes for the pair and the individual but not to maximize the difference between one's own score and the partner's. If a person wishes to try to maximize this difference (i.e., to best his partner), he must incur a loss to do so, this being equal to the RC. With increasing magnitude of RC the degree to which he can surpass the partner decreases so he must expend more cost for a smaller difference. Thus the set of patterns over the range of 6:6 to 0:12 provides a means of assessing the person's desire to surpass his partner. Their joint use permits an answer to the question: How much loss will this person undergo possibly to gain more than his partner? (It is not apparent in Figure 4.5, but by varying the magnitudes of the two components independently (rather than relatively) the cost can be held constant and the possible difference varied or the size of the possible difference can be held constant and the cost varied. The former is accomplished by holding BRC constant and varying the MFC component, the latter by varying both components simultaneously.)

When BRC is concordant with MFC for one person but discordant for the other, we have the threat game. This has already been discussed and a version of it, used in research by Rapoport and Guyer, is described and analyzed in Figure 2.3. In the center column of Figure 4.5 RC is concordant with FC for B (the row player) but discordant for A (the column player). His RC makes it desirable for B to make the C choice which is to their mutual advantage. A's RC, however, makes it desirable for him to make the D choice which results in a large outcome for himself and a relatively small one for B. This, of course, raises the question of equity and B's ultimate response to inequitable treatment is to *threaten* to make his D move (hence the name of the game). In short, the pattern creates an asymmetry of roles between A and B. The attainment of high outcomes is dependent on B's continuing to play C, whereas the fair division of those outcomes requires A to alternate in some fashion between his two actions. Thus in a schematic way the pattern portrays the problem of managing an exchange of B's loyalty to the mutual interest for A's just treatment of him. This problem has been studied extensively by Thibaut and Faucheux (1965) in what is essentially an expanded version of the 2 × 2 threat game.

The properties of the threat game, already described, are obviously most strongly present at intermediate ratios of BRC to MFC. Person A's temptation to exploit B increases with decreasing MFC but B's unhappiness with such treatment decreases as we move down the scale. Person B's ability to threaten effectively probably declines as we move down the scale inasmuch as there is a decrease in the magnitude of his FC effect on A and an increase in the RC counter to the negative use of his FC. The optimal mix of conditions, entailing A's temptation to be unjust and B's ability to pose an effective threat, probably occurs in the range of 4:8 to 6:6 ratios of BRC to MFC. It may be noted that Rapoport and Guyer used approximately a 1:2 ratio.

Combinations of All Three Components

So far we have considered all possible configurations of *pairs* of symmetrical components, meshed together in all possible orientations. There still remain to be explored the combinations of symmetric components taken three at a time. It may be helpful to show how these three-component patterns relate to those we have already considered and at the same time give the reader a more general view of the dimensions and shape of the subdomain of symmetric-component patterns.

The general outline of the subdomain is shown in Figure 4.6. The three preceding figures are placed together to form a solid. Figures 4.4 and 4.5 are joined at the pattern they share (BRC), Figure 4.5 forming the near surface of the solid and Figure 4.4, the far surface. Then Figure 4.3 is joined to Figure 4.4 at the two patterns they share (correspondent and noncorrespondent MBC) and Figure 4.3 is joined to Figure 4.5 at the MFC pattern. The reader will understand that we are forming a three-

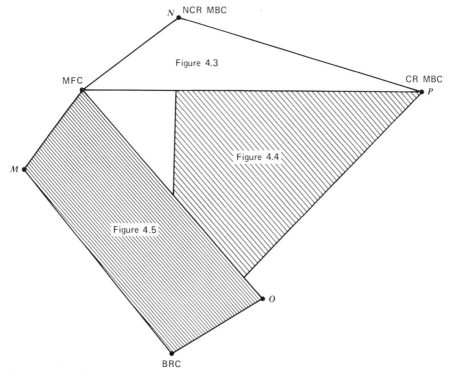

Figure 4.6   Space defined by symmetric component matrices.

dimensional figure with three of the charts in the interdependence portion of our map of the total 2×2 domain (cf. Figure 4.2). The MFC branch forms the near surface, the MBC branch forms the far surface, and the chart of the total interdependence patterns forms the top surface. This inverted solid, nearly pyramidal in shape, is balanced on the BRC tip. Minimum interdependence exists in the lower portion of the solid and total interdependence exists on the top surface.

Our present interest is in combinations of all three components which exist in the interior of the solid and are represented on the "mixed" branch of our map of the domain. One important fact about these combinations can be observed in Figure 4.2. They include perfectly correspondent and noncorrespondent patterns. In general, if we start with the combinations of MFC and MBC shown in Figure 4.3 and add a degree of BRC equal to the MFC component and either discordant or concordant with it, we generate sets of perfectly correspondent and noncorrespondent patterns. If BRC discordant with and equal to the MFC component is added to the left-hand sets of MFC plus MBC (Figure 4.3), we obtain perfectly noncorrespondent patterns. If BRC concordant with and equal to the MFC component is added to the right-hand set, we obtain perfectly correspondent patterns. Another way to describe these patterns is as combinations of the two basic types of correspondence and noncorrespondence that occur in interdependent relations: (a) MBC patterns and (b) equal-ratio combinations of MFC and BRC.

The resulting patterns are shown in Figure 4.7. (The two columns of matrices on the right are characterized by the same degrees of correspondence, namely, perfect correspondence.) The most notable properties of the patterns are those we have noted before having to do with whether the MBC or the MFC plus BRC is the more important. Comparing the noncorrespondent or competitive relationships on the left, we observe that when MBC is predominant (in the upper patterns) each person is uncertain about what action to take. He prefers to see what the other person will do so that he can then make the best counteradjustment to that action. Of course, there is no reason for either person to act first or to agree on or settle on any joint action. Toward the bottom of the figure, with increasing MFC plus BRC, this property of the relationship decreases in importance. Thus in the lower patterns, in which the MFC plus BRC aspect is predominant, each has a preferred or dominant action (generated by his RC) and each can take that action because it is better for him, no matter what the partner does.

The correspondent or cooperative patterns at the right vary in a similar manner from the upper to the lower ones. With a relatively strong MBC component there tends to be more than one mutually desirable point of

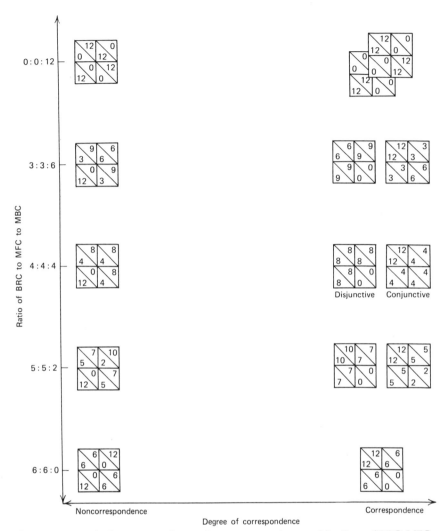

Figure 4.7 Perfectly correspondent and noncorrespondent combinations of BRC, MFC, and MBC.

coordination. With a relatively strong MFC plus BRC component there is only one mutually best point which is attained if each follows his RC. The patterns in which the MFC plus BRC complex is concordant with the MBC component (on the far right) are superior to the discordant in both respects. For even low values of MFC plus BRC the RC-maximizing actions take the pair to what is best for both.

The set of matrices in Figure 4.7 can be visualized in Figure 4.6 as lying along lines connecting matrices on the front surface with those corresponding at the rear of the solid. The noncorrespondent matrices extend from point M (the equal-ratio, discordant combination of MFC and BRC) to point N (noncorrespondent MBC); the correspondent ones extend from point O (the equal-ratio, concordant combination of MFC and BRC) to point P (correspondent MBC). The upward slope of these lines (which the reader is asked to imagine in Figure 4.6) carries an important implication, mentioned before but emphasized here. This is that conflict of interest (noncorrespondence) reaches its maximum in the MFC realm at *moderate* degrees of interdependence. The same can be said, of course, with respect to commonality of interest. Correspondence reaches its maximum in MFC relationships only at moderate degrees of interdependence. Both conflict and commonality of interest occur with *maximum* interdependence only for coordination (MBC) patterns.

We examined a sizable number of the three-component matrices to be found in the interior of the solid implied by Figure 4.6. Most different from the two-component patterns summarized in Figures 4.3 through 4.5 are the equal-ratio patterns in which the BRC:MFC:MBC ratio is 4:4:4. The remaining patterns are blends or intermediate cases having the properties of various matrices already familiar to us. We do *not* find patterns that are "better" versions of those we have already seen. We do not find, for example, a Prisoner's Dilemma game that represents the properties of the PDG to a greater degree or in a clearer manner than the two-component PDG identified in Figure 4.5. Indeed the three-component patterns most similar to any of the classic patterns (such as the PDG) seem to be versions of it that are less clear than the two-component patterns identified. This complex point is considered in Chapter 5.

The equal-ratio, three-component patterns constitute 10 of the 30 two-outcome-level matrices considered earlier. Three of the 10 are the perfectly correspondent and noncorrespondent patterns in the middle row of Figure 4.7. The two correspondent patterns reflect different "task requirements" (Thibaut and Kelley, 1959, Chapter 9). The left matrix incorporates a disjunctive task requirement: if either person makes the correct response, both receive the maximum reward. The second represents a conjunctive task requirement: only if both persons make the proper response do both receive the maximum reward. These patterns are of special interest when the two response alternatives for the two persons are the same. Assume that under this condition the two persons are uncertain which response is correct (eg., which path to take or which vacation to go on). If the pattern is known to be disjunctive, then it is desirable for each to make a different response; for example, in searching for their lost child (who is found, of course, if either parent finds him), the mother and father should take different paths of the two he might have followed. Under uncertainty, the conjunctive pattern might be called the blame game, inasmuch as it creates problems of credit and blame for the pair. The first person to commit himself to a given response requires the other to follow suit, unless failure is to be guaranteed. Thus the first actor becomes clearly responsible for the pair's success or failure; for example, the one who decides which road to take when the situation constrains the pair to travel together becomes subject to blame if it is the wrong one.

The two equal-ratio, three-component patterns shown in Figure 4.8 (which are also two-outcome-level matrices) have the same location in the domain of 2 × 2 matrices but they differ in important ways. Their differences derive from symmetry versus asymmetry in con-cordance–discordance. In both patterns person B is dependent on A's making a certain response that is contrary to A's RC. In the right matrix the same discordance holds for A's dependence on B, but in the left matrix B's RC preferences are concordant with what A prefers him to do. The left matrix is the prototype of the threat game described in Chapter 2 and earlier in this Chapter. The asymmetry of concordance–discordance cre-ates a situation in which B's preferences promote the conditions under which A is able to gain high outcomes but B is not. The threat of acting against his own preferences in order to punish A is the means available to B to induce A to act contrary to his preference in order to permit B (sometimes) to obtain high outcomes.

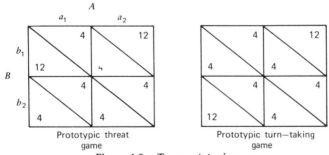

Figure 4.8   Two prototypic games.

In the same way that the left matrix is a prototype of the threat game the right matrix in Figure 4.8 is the most elementary version of a set of more complex, symmetrical, turn-taking games. Like Battle of the Sexes and

Hero, this pattern lends itself to coordinated alternation as a means of enabling each person occasionally to have his high outcome. A contrast is to be made with the noncorrespondent MBC pattern (upper left matrix in Figure 4.7) in which an alternation of high outcomes between the two persons is generated simply by one person alternating his choice while the other maintains his (much as in the Threat game except that *either* person may hold while the other alternates). In contrast, the turn-taking pattern requires *coordinated* shifting, both going simultaneously from a_1b_2 to a_2b_1 if mutually low outcomes are to be avoided.

SOCIAL PSYCHOLOGICAL SIGNIFICANCE

A basic fact of interdependence is that one person's dependence provides a basis for the other's power. In dependence relationships as we have described them, person B has power over the dependent one, A, to the extent that A is dependent. The nature of this power depends on the basis of A's dependence, the differences here being reflected, as explained in Chapter 1, in our terms for these two bases of dependence. With fate control B can affect A's level of outcome; with behavior control B can make it desirable for A to adjust his behavior to that of B. In either case the ease with which B can exercise the control depends on B's reflexive control. The greater B's RC, the more his behavioral preferences limit his flexibility in varying his behavior and therefore in exercising control over A. If B has fate control over A, then the probable consequences of B's power depend on the correspondence or noncorrespondence between their outcomes. With high correspondence B will tend to enact the behavior that satisfies A (B's RC is concordant with his FC over A). With high noncorrespondence B will tend to enact the behavior that yields low outcomes to A (B's RC is discordant with his FC over A). (These two cases are illustrated in the upper portion of Figure 4.10.)

In interdependent relationships the mutual dependence results in mutual power. Each person has power over his partner to the extent that the partner is dependent. Again the nature of this power depends on the basis of the partner's dependence, whether FC or BC. Also, the ease of using power depends on the RC of its possessor. This is appropriately illustrated by several versions of the threat game (Figure 4.9). In all three cases person B may need to threaten A with a drop in outcomes (achieved by the b_2 action) in order to induce A occasionally to give B high outcomes. In the two-outcome-level pattern in Figure 4.9 (Matrix F) B can produce the threatened drop at no loss in his own outcomes (assuming A is persisting with the a_2 action). In Matrix G, the RC + FC combination from

Figure 4.5, B produces the drop in A's outcomes only by suffering a similar loss in his own outcomes, and in Matrix H to carry out his threat B must incur a greater drop in outcomes than the one he produces in A's. These three cases represent increasing difficulty in B's carrying out the threat action. Social-psychologically, they represent decreasing degrees to which it will be credible to A that B will back up with action any verbal threat he makes.

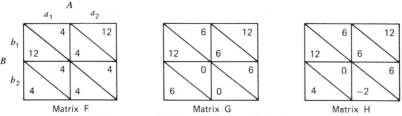

Figure 4.9   Different versions of the threat game.

A different social psychological perspective on the various patterns of interdependence is provided by considering the problems they pose to the dependent person or persons. In dependent relations the important significance of the FC versus BC distinction is that it determines the problem situation in which a dependent person finds himself. The fact that a person is dependent means that getting a high outcome is not wholly under his own control. Thus he is faced with a problem—a problem involving what if anything he himself must do, what action is required of his partner, the consequences of that action for the partner, and the means at his disposal of influencing the partner's action. The specifics of these matters are readily seen in the two-outcome-level patterns shown in Figure 4.10. All the matrices are arranged in this figure so that the dependent person is A, who makes the choice between columns. For simplicity high outcomes are indicated by plus signs and low outcomes, by blanks. When subject to FC, as in the upper part of the figure, A is helpless to do anything about his outcome directly. He can only plead with B to make the choice that will benefit him. The correspondence of outcomes is such on the right that he may be able to count on success, but in the left matrix the noncorrespondence makes his prospects seem rather bleak. When subject to BC, as in the lower pattern, A can obtain his high outcome by waiting for B's move (or anticipating it from B's RC) and then coordinating with it. On occasions on which he is subject to both FC and BC A's problem is a mixture of dependence on B's action and on his own coordinating choice.

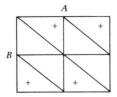

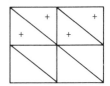

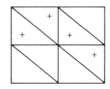

Figure 4.10   Some two-outcome-level patterns of dependence.

With mutual dependence *both* actors have problems. Again these are well illustrated by two-outcome-level patterns (Figure 4.11). The problems may be similar, as in the MBC patterns in which both have the problem of coordinating with each other or in the MFC pattern in which each has the problem of inducing his partner to perform the appropriate action. The latter can be described as exchanging the benevolent use of fate control. In general, patterns characterized primarily by MFC pose problems of *exchange*. In contrast, patterns characterized primarily by MBC pose problems of *coordination*. With the mixtures of FC and BC components in the middle of Figure 4.11 the two actor's problems may be similar (as in the turn-taking game) or different (as in the threat game and the FC, BC pattern), but in every example of these mixtures the problems are complex.

For any given matrix, as in Figure 4.11, it is not difficult to imagine the interaction process that is set into motion as the two persons try to solve their respective problems. (By writing descriptions of A's and B's problems for various patterns and then spelling out the probable resulting scenarios, the reader will see for himself the amazing array of subtle variations in interaction generated by the simple two-outcome-level matrices.) A major determinant of this interaction process will be the correspondence or noncorrespondence between the two person's outcomes because this determines the degree of compatibility of the solutions to their problems. When the solutions are compatible, as in cases of high correspondence, it is easy to imagine how a shared or common problem emerges with joint attention to fulfilling the intersecting requirements

MFC

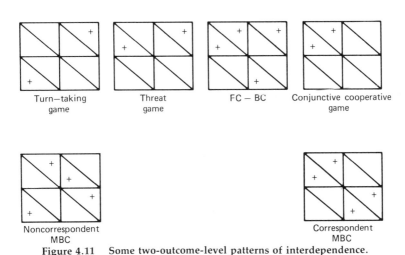

| Turn–taking game | Threat game | FC – BC | Conjunctive cooperative game |

Noncorrespondent MBC

Correspondent MBC

Figure 4.11   Some two-outcome-level patterns of interdependence.

expeditiously and without mistakes. Correspondent MBC in Figure 4.11 is probably more susceptible to incoordination than the conjunctive cooperative matrix because it does not profit from a convergence of the preferences on a single obvious solution. Accordingly, we should not be surprised to see the development of a crude role differentiation between the person who quickly takes the initiative and the one who acts more slowly and imitatively. When the solutions are not compatible, as in noncorrespondence, we can imagine what each person may attempt to ensure that his *own* requirements are met: outwaiting the partner, feint-ing or faking out the partner, making false promises, proposing self-advantageous rules, and so on. Circumstances permitting, we can expect pairs with incompatible solutions to devise ways of extending the interac-tion and making them partly compatible by turn taking over successive occasions. In this way, by taking turns in obtaining their respective high outcomes by coordinated shifting in the turn-taking game, the incom-patibilities are reduced and the interdependence is changed. Of course, the incompatible requirements may not always be reconciled and the ultimate adaptation of the dependent person may often be to accept the nonachievement of his best outcome. These matters are considered later in relation to sequential transformations and bargaining processes.

To summarize the present discussion, the distinctions we have used in organizing our map of the 2 × 2 domain reflect the basic ways in which interdependence structures differ. They obviously have implications for the process deriving from each structure. Mutuality and degree of dependence relate to power differences or, putting it otherwise, differences between the two persons in their vulnerability. The properties of the pattern undoubtedly relate to such things as asymmetries in orientation and attention to the interaction, amount and quality of communication, and allocation of outcomes. The degree of correspondence or noncorrespondence relates to the amount of conflict of interest in the relationship and to the rate of cooperation or competition in the emerging interaction process. The basis of interdependence, whether FC or BC, specifies important aspects of the problem the dependent person faces in trying to attain his high outcomes and the means, if any, at his disposal for solving that problem. In cases of mutual dependence and some degree of correspondence these distinctions define the problem the pair faces jointly, the MFC end of the continuum being the locus of exchange problems and the MBC end, the locus of coordination problems.

The present discussion has focused on the interaction process appropriate to each interdependence matrix. Without making it explicit, we have assumed for the most part that the pattern is the one that characterizes the *effective* matrix; that is, most of our comments have assumed that the matrix under consideration reflects the outcomes that each person is trying to maximize in the course of the interaction. In later chapters we consider patterns as they relate to the *given* matrix. In Chapter 7 we analyze a variety of patterns of *given* matrices as settings in which people learn social rules and values. In Chapter 8 we take up the related issues of self-expression and -presentation. *Given* matrices are viewed there as settings in which individuals can show themselves to be certain kinds of persons.

Prior Research

It is not our intention to make a thorough review of the research that relates to our theoretical analysis. Reference to several studies at this point, however, may serve to indicate the relevance of the distinctions to the empirical investigation of interpersonal relationships.

A study by Wish, Deutsch, and Kaplan (1976) suggests how some of the properties of interdependence patterns may be represented in perceptions of interpersonal relationships. Subjects were asked to rate a large number of relationships (e.g., siblings, parent and child, business partners, and political opponents) on a number of semantic differential scales (e.g., very cooperative versus very competitive, very active versus very inactive). The results were analyzed by a method of multidimensional scaling to reveal the distinctions the subjects make among the various relationships. If, as we have argued, the properties of interdependence patterns produce important variations in the interaction process, we should expect the properties to be reflected in the terms in which people differentiate relationships. This assumes, of course, that an entire relationship can be characterized by a single matrix or at least by a delimited set of matrices. It is obvious that any extensive relationship, as between a parent and child, encompasses many areas and many kinds of interdependence. Yet it is possible that a relationship may take its meaning from the one or two interdependence patterns that are most characteristic of its problems and situations.

Consistent with the last assumption, the perceived dimensions of interpersonal relations derived by Wish, Deutsch, and Kaplan correspond for the most part to the matrix properties. "Equal versus unequal," best defined by ratings on "exactly equal versus extremely unequal power," corresponds to mutuality (versus nonmutuality) of dependence. "Intense versus superficial," best defined by "intense versus superficial interaction with each other," seems to reflect the degree of interdependence (or dependence) in the relationship. "Cooperative and friendly versus competitive and hostile," best defined by "always harmonious versus always clashing," is clearly similar to the correspondence versus noncorrespondence in the relationship. Only our distinction between FC- and BC-based relationships is not clearly reflected in the Wish, Deutsch, and Kaplan dimensions. They describe their fourth dimension as "socioemotional and informal versus task-oriented and formal." It is best defined by a rating scale of "pleasure-oriented versus work-oriented." Although the matter is not perfectly clear, it may mirror certain aspects that will indicate whether a relationship primarily involves MBC (coordination) or MFC (exchange). The latter is presumably more typical of economic or business transactions, and indeed such relationships are located exclusively in the task-oriented half of the dimension. Relationships at the socioemotional end of the scale (close friends, siblings, husband and wife) may prominently involve MBC for one or both of two reasons: (a) in these relationships specific activities are often less important than whether they are done *together* (i.e., in coordination); (b) these relationships commonly involve the sharing of limited living space and facilities which poses problems of coordination.

Proceeding on the assumption that Wish, Deutsch, and Kaplan's intensity and cooperative-competitive dimensions correspond respectively to the matrix properties of degree of dependence and correspondence–noncorrespondence, we used their data to test one of the implications of the matrix analysis. This is that the variance in correspondence–noncorrespondence will be greater for high degrees of interdependence than for low. The basis of this expectation is seen in Figure 4.2. With increasing dependence, either toward interdependence or dependence, there is, in general, an increase in the differentiation of the patterns with regard to correspondence–noncorrespondence. When the data from the two figures in the Wish, Deutsch, and Kaplan article are replotted appropriately, they appear to be consistent with this analysis. The relationships on the intense side of the superficial–intense scale show greater variance on the cooperative–competitive scale than do those on the superficial side. This result is presented not as definitive but merely to illustrate how the implications of the configurations in Figure 4.3 might be tested with the sort of data gathered by Wish and his colleagues; for example, a clear basis for distinguishing MFC-based interdependence from MBC-based interdependence would permit testing the implication that the maximum dispersion of correspondence–noncorrespondence occurs in relationships of moderate interdependence in the first case but of extreme interdependence in the second.

The FC–BC distinction is not clear in the Wish, Deutsch, and Kaplan work, but it has a clear and important parallel in Steiner's (1972) analysis of group process. In analyzing the process losses incurred in groups, Steiner distinguishes between (a) losses from lack of interpersonal coordination, matching, and temporal programming and (b) losses from inadequate member motivation to make high-quality contributions to the group (p. 83). The first clearly refers to problems created by MBC. The second reflects the role of MFC in combination with discordant BRC, as in the PDG or the perfectly competitive MFC + BRC pattern. The person prefers not to enact the behaviors that are desired by other members, either for reasons of laziness or other cost-avoidance motives or because alternative behaviors are more rewarding. Steiner's concern is with the effects of group size and its relation to these two types of process loss. In the present context we are interested simply in noting that the two bases of interdependence provide a theoretical foundation for the two types of loss he distinguishes.

SALIENT MATRICES

One of our purposes in exploring the domain of 2 × 2 matrices was to identify the "salient" or landmark patterns which by virtue of their location in the domain typify certain classes of pattern. In some cases these patterns stand at a corner of the domain and therefore represent in the extreme a particular kind of pattern. In others one of these patterns best typifies a subgroup of patterns by virtue of its central location in that group.

We merely list these salient patterns and indicate the preceding figures in which they may be found. Other students of the 2 × 2 matrix will undoubtedly wish to add to the list, but we find 22 matrices worthy of note:

Independence

1. Bilateral reflexive control (BRC). Figure 4.4 or 4.5

Interdependence

1. Mutual fate control (MFC). Figure 4.3 or 4.5
2. Correspondent mutual behavior control (CR MBC); Figure 4.3 or 4.4
3. Noncorrespondent mutual behavior control (NCR MBC); Figure 4.3 or 4.4
4. Combinations of MFC and MBC (Figure 4.3)
   4.1 Chicken
   4.2 Battle of the Sexes
5. Combinations of BRC and MBC (Figure 4.4)
   5.1 Hero
   5.2 Martyr
6. Combinations of BRC and MFC (Figure 4.5)
   6.1 Prisoner's Dilemma game (PDG)
   6.2 Maximizing difference game (MDG)
   6.3 Threat game
   6.4 Correspondent (cooperative or constant-difference) game
   6.5 Noncorrespondent (competitive or constant-sum) game
7. Fate control-behavior control (FC, BC); Figure 4.11
8. Equal-ratio combinations of BRC, MFC, and MBC
   8.1 Prototypic threat game (Figure 4.8)
   8.2 Prototypic turn-taking game (Figure 4.8)
   8.3 Disjunctive cooperative game (Figure 4.7)
   8.4 Conjunctive cooperative game (Figure 4.7)
   8.5 Noncorrespondent (competitive) game (Figure 4.7)

Dependence (Figure 4.10)

1. FC, RC
   1.1 Correspondent
   1.2 Noncorrespondent
2. BC, RC

The reader who has an understanding of these landmark patterns and a sense of their locations in relation to one another can be assured of finding his or her way through the terrain of the 2 × 2 domain.

5

Properties and Indices of Interdependence Patterns

ABSTRACT

This chapter proposes indices for the major properties of interdependence patterns and describes how they are related to the components of interdependence. This provides a systematic analysis of what was done intuitively in Chapter 4; namely, a delineation of the links between the properties of the matrix, on the one hand, and the components and their interrelations that underlie it, on the other. The analysis is also propaedeutic to those in Chapters 6 and 7, which show how the properties of the given *matrix govern the necessity for transformations to be made and how the properties of the* effective *matrix depend jointly on the components of the* given *matrix and the particular transformations made.*

The analysis of the bases of correspondence–noncorrespondence reveals the factors underlying the two persons' control over their joint outcomes and over the differences between their respective outcomes, which have implications for the discussion of the bargaining process in Chapter 10. Last, we give systematic attention to questions raised in Chapter 4 concerning the particular combinations of components and their weights necessary for optimal versions of various matrix games.

We now consider how the important properties of interdependence matrices, described in Chapter 4, may be indexed. An important purpose is to indicate how these properties are determined by the' components and their intermeshing. This analysis serves to suggest, by reference to Chapter 3, the possible social-psychological bases of various aspects of interdependence.

It would be helpful first to remind the reader of the meaning and derivation of the component weights, their magnitudes and algebraic signs, first presented in Figure 2.5 and its associated text. Further illustrations of these concepts are provided in Figure 5.1. The matrix there has been analyzed into the three component matrices and beneath each are shown the component weights of the two persons. Nonzero components that yield high values in the upper left-hand cell are given positive signs; otherwise they are given negative signs. The relations among the signs indicate what is apparent in the patterning of the components: RC_A is discordant with FC_B because they have opposite signs; the same is true of RC_B and FC_A; BC_A and BC_B are noncorrespondent because they have opposite signs. Although less obvious the pattern of signs also summarizes the concordance–discordance relations between the MBC component and each of the other component matrices; for example, the positive BC_B is discordant with the MFC component because the high outcomes of both persons are found in the upper right-hand cell (indicated by FC_A, positive and FC_B, negative). In what follows we use symbols for the component weights (RC_A, FC_B, etc.) in our formulas to refer to values that are calculated according to the conventions indicated in Figure 5.1.

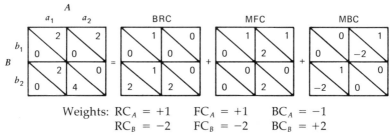

Weights: $RC_A = +1$ $FC_A = +1$ $BC_A = -1$
              $RC_B = -2$ $FC_B = -2$ $BC_B = +2$

Figure 5.1   Illustration of component weights.

DEPENDENCE AND INTERDEPENDENCE

In Chapter 4 we have seen that a relationship may be characterized by *interdependence*, both persons being dependent on what their partners do; *dependence*, A being dependent on B's actions but B not so on A's actions; or *independence*, neither person being affected by his partner's choice. These properties are readily ascertained by examining the relative magnitudes of the component weights of the interdependence matrix. The smaller RC_A is in relation to FC_A and BC_A, the more A's outcomes are under total or joint control by B.

In a 2×2 matrix the variance in A's outcomes under each of the three sources of control is proportional, respectively, to RC_A^2, FC_A^2, and BC_A^2. From this the proportion of the total variance in A's outcomes controlled wholly or partly by the partner can be calculated: $\text{Dep}_A = (FC_A^2 + BC_A^2)/(RC_A^2 + FC_A^2 + BC_A^2)$. This index of dependence, calculated separately for A and B, provides a generally appropriate characterization of the dependence properties of the relationship. For the matrix in Figure 5.1 $\text{Dep}_A = .67$ and $\text{Dep}_B = .67$. For pure BRC the two values are, respectively, .00 and .00, and for pure MFC or MBC they are 1.00 and 1.00. A case of unilateral dependence results in 1.00 for the dependent person and .00 for the independent.

Effect on Dependence of Certain Behavioral Assumptions

Here we encounter an example of a general problem that occurs in characterizing matrices. An index (of some particular property) appropriate for characterizing the *entire* matrix may not provide a good description of the particular *portion* that is most important in the persons' experience of their relationship. This becomes apparent when certain plausible assumptions about behavior imply that the interaction will encompass only parts of the matrix. (In Chapter 2 this problem was discussed in relation to the grand mean. It does not describe the average level of outcomes obtained in the matrix if the two persons manage to avoid the poorer ones. We also encounter this problem in the next section in connection with the "frontier" values in the matrix and their relevance for characterizing its degree of correspondence.) As noted in the preceding chapter (page 80), our primary purpose in the present analyses is to characterize the matrix per se, making no assumptions about the behavior of the two persons and attempting to avoid any confusion between structure and process. In this and several other instances, however, it seems useful to point out some of the ways in which their behavior and interaction process may affect the interdependent persons' experience with such phenomena as "dependence" and "conflict."

With regard to the experience of dependence, consider the three matrices in Figure 5.2. Intuitively, it is clear that the degree of mutual dependence is higher in Matrix II than in Matrix I. This difference is reflected in our labels for these two patterns (cf. Chapter 4), described, respectively, as disjunctive and conjunctive games. Similarly, it appears that B's

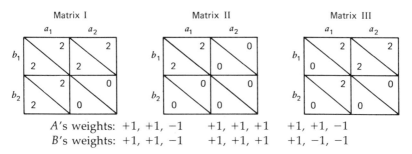

Figure 5.2 Matrices illustrating the problems of indexing dependence.

dependence is higher than A's in Matrix III. Yet an analysis of the matrices reveals that the absolute values of the components are the same for all three. As the weights listed below each one show, all three matrices are equal-ratio, three-component patterns. Thus the proportion of non-reflexively controlled variance for each person is the same in all three cases, and the index of dependence we have proposed does not differentiate them.

The examples in Figure 5.2 suggest the possibility that in determining a person's dependence within certain relationships we need not concern ourselves with the variance in his outcomes over the entire matrix. On the assumption that he is strongly oriented toward good outcomes and knows how to get them, we need only consider the variance in outcomes he can experience when he takes his most preferred action. If person A in Matrix III chooses a_1, the outcome variance controlled by his partner is zero; that is, A need not be dependent at all. Similarly, if both A and B choose their preferred responses in Matrix I, neither will be dependent on the other.

The circumstances under which the components generate patterns such as those in Figure 5.2 can be determined from the matrix analysis shown in Figure 5.1. Person A's outcomes from his preferred action (a_1) are not affected by B's action because two conditions are fulfilled: $|FC_A| = |BC_A|$ and the sign of BC_A is opposite the sign of the algebraic product of RC_A and FC_A. The second condition may be described alternatively in terms of a "discordance" between BC_A and the cell on which RC_A and FC_A converge. This condition is not met for person B; therefore, even though he has the same general pattern of weights as A, the outcome B derives from his preferred action depends greatly on A's action. Person B's situation is similar to those of both persons in Matrix II, Figure 5.2.

The psychological implication of this analysis is that in some 2×2 cases the FC and BC acting on a person cancel out one another's effect. When equal in magnitude, they produce an even distribution of good outcomes over one of the person's response alternatives. If this also happens to be the choice favored by his RC, the person can ensure himself good outcomes by following his RC; for example, in Case III of Figure 5.2 assume that A and B are husband and wife and parents of a small child. Assume further that the husband has three sets of overlapping preferences: (a) he wants his wife to go out (b_1), (b) he prefers himself to go out (a_1) and (c) he wants someone to stay home with the child (a_1b_2 and a_2b_1 are preferred to the other combinations). These preferences generate the Case III pattern in which, by going out (a_1) the husband gets good outcomes (has two preferences satisfied) no matter what his wife does. If she also goes out, she satisfies his first preference and if she stays home she satisfies his third preference; meanwhile he satisfies his second preference himself.

CORRESPONDENCE VERSUS NONCORRESPONDENCE OF OUTCOMES

The single most important property of any matrix characterized by dependence or interdependence is the degree of correspondence between the two persons' outcomes. This property specifies the extent to which their interests in the course of the relationship are the same or different and implies how smooth or conflictual their interaction will be. In this section we develop a definition of the concept, suggest an index of correspondence, and show how correspondence is affected by the components of control.

The Definition and Indexing of Correspondence

What is needed is an index of the distribution of values in the matrix that will reflect the degree of commonality versus conflict of interest. We can prescribe certain general properties for the index by reference to certain basic matrices: (a) The index must be +1.00 for a pure MBC matrix in which the two persons' outcomes covary in an identical manner and −1.00 for one in which they vary in an exact inverse manner. In the first the two will have commonality of interest in coordinating their actions, whereas in the second they will be in total conflict about which way to coordinate. (b) It must take intermediate values for intermediate patterns of MBC. We shall see what they are in a moment. (c) It must be .00 for pure MFC matrices, in which the two sets of outcomes bear no relation to each other; each person is able to raise or lower his partner's outcomes without any effect on himself. Thus there is no conflict of interest between taking the one action or the other, but at the same time there is no convergence of interest in what each one should do. (There is, of course, a common interest in *exchanging* the benevolent use of fate control, but that does not concern us here.) The same condition applies with respect to pure BRC matrices. (d) For mixtures of correspondent MBC and MFC, the index should move from +1.00 to .00 as the ratio of MFC moves from low to high. Similarly, for mixtures of noncorrespondent MBC and MFC, with an increase in the ratio of MFC to MBC, the index should move from −1.00 to .00. The same should also be true of mixtures of BRC and MBC. (These effects are shown in Figures 4.3 and 4.4.)

Intermediate Degrees of Correspondence for MBC.   The second condition (b) places an important constraint on our index, but before developing its implication for the index we must see what is meant by intermediate degrees of correspondence (or noncorrespondence) for MBC matrices. The answer is provided by Figure 5.3. Extreme correspondence means not only that the two persons have the same coordination preferences but that their preferences are equally strong. Intermediate degrees of correspondence reflect the fact that one person has more stake in the coordination of their behavior than the other. Thus in Figure 5.3 *B*'s interest in coordination is not so supportive of *A*'s preferences in the moderately correspondent as it is in the perfectly correspondent case. In this sense their interests are less convergent or less perfectly aligned in moderate correspondence. Similarly, extreme noncorrespondence reflects not only different coordination preferences but those that are equally strong. With a moderate degree of noncorrespondence, although *B* prefers a different coordination pattern than *A*, *B* is not so strongly opposed as he is with perfect noncorrespondence. Thus *B*'s interests are not so totally in conflict with *A*'s in moderate noncorrespondence. At the midpoint of the non-correspondence–correspondence continuum (not shown in Figure 5.3, although the center matrix is an approximation) *B* is totally indifferent to a coordination matter with respect to which *A* has strong preferences. Note that this is unilateral dependence, not interdependence! By comparing this intermediate degree of correspondence–noncorrespondence in MBC with that represented by MFC we seem to have two kinds of midpoint; at the first one party is totally indifferent to the other's actions and at the second each is concerned only with the partner's choices.

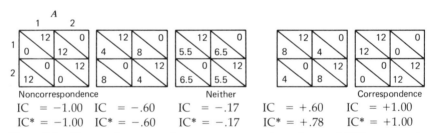

Figure 5.3   Degree of correspondence–noncorrespondence in pure MBC components.

Index of Correspondence.   It may have occurred to the reader that the Pearson product-moment correlation between the two persons' outcomes, calculated over the four cells, would provide a convenient index of correspondence. The treatment of intermediate degrees of correspondence for pure MBC matrices precludes adopting the correlation coefficient as our index. The reason is that it would yield only three values, $+1$, 0, and -1, for the various MBC matrices. Thus in Figure 5.3 $r = -1.00$ for the left three matrices and $r = +1.00$ for the two on the right.

An index that reflects more properly the continuous variation in correspondence shown in Figure 5.3 is the following:

$$IC = \frac{\sigma^2_{sums} - \sigma^2_{diffs}}{\sigma^2_{sums} + \sigma^2_{diffs}}$$

In this formula IC refers to the index of correspondence, σ^2_{sums} is the variance of the cell sums, and σ^2_{diffs} is the variance of the cell differences—the algebraic values when B's outcome is always subtracted from A's. (We use "variance" and σ^2 here to refer to the mean squared deviation from the mean; i.e., the computed "sample" variance and not an estimate of a "population" variance.) The index takes a value of $+1$ if $\sigma^2_{diffs} = 0$, -1 if $\sigma^2_{sums} = 0$, and 0 if $\sigma^2_{sums} = \sigma^2_{diffs}$. The five values of IC for the five matrices in Figure 5.3 are, from left to right, -1.00, $-.60$, $-.17$, $+.60$ and $+1.00$. For a matrix in the exact middle of the continuum, in which B has no coordination preference, $IC = .00$. Thus the index satisfies the first two criteria stated at the outset. The reader can determine for himself that it also satisfies the third criterion, being $.00$ for pure MFC (or BRC) matrices. It can also be shown that it moves from an extreme value toward zero as MFC (or BRC) is added in increasing ratio to MBC.

The more general meaning of the IC index can be shown graphically (Figure 5.4) in which we plot A's outcomes against B's and sketch in with arrows the sum and difference dimensions of the scatterplot; the lengths are proportional to the two variance terms. In our IC index the term σ^2_{sums} reflects the magnitude of the sum dimension of the plot and the term σ^2_{diffs} reflects the magnitude of the difference dimension. The conflict of interest is high when the difference dimension is the larger of the two and commonality of interest is high when the sum dimension is larger. This representation also suggests that the IC index is appropriate for describing the correspondence of a matrix of any size.

Presenting the IC index in terms of variance of sums and differences facilitates relating it to the components of interdependence and to different aspects of control over pair outcomes (cf. next section). Alternatively, the index can be understood according to the following formula, in terms of its relation to the product-moment correlation:

$$IC = r \left[\frac{2\sigma_A \sigma_B}{\sigma_A^2 + \sigma_B^2} \right]$$

Here the σs refer to the standard deviations of the outcomes of the two persons. The bracketed term of the equation is 1.00 when the two σs are equal; otherwise it is less than 1.00. In other words, the index reduces the product-moment correlation in proportion to the amount of difference between the dispersions of the two sets of outcomes.

Correspondence as a Function of the Components

For 2 × 2 matrices it can be shown that the two variance terms in the formula for the index of correspondence are related to the components:

$$\sigma^2_{sums} = \frac{1}{4} \left[(RC_A + FC_B)^2 + (RC_B + FC_A)^2 + (BC_A + BC_B)^2 \right]$$

and

$$\sigma^2_{diffs} = \frac{1}{4} \left[(RC_A - FC_B)^2 + (RC_B - FC_A)^2 + (BC_A - BC_B)^2 \right]$$

These equations indicate the conditions under which correspondence will be positive, negative, or near zero. The IC index will be +1.00; that is, there will be perfect correspondence when the appropriate pairs of RC and FC terms are equal and have the same sign (i.e., FC is concordant with RC) and when the two BC terms are equal and have the same sign (i.e., when there is correspondent MBC). The equations highlight the two sharply different cases of perfect correspondence already noted in Chapter 4, one in which the RC and FC terms are zero and the correspondence is entirely due to the correspondent MBC component and the other in which the BC terms are zero and the correspondence is entirely due to the equal and concordant RC and FC terms. Of course there are various mixtures of the two. In a similar manner the equations reveal that perfect noncorrespondence may reflect noncorrespondent MBC, equal and discordant RC and FC, or mixtures of the two. Unilateral control (e.g., in which RC_B and FC_A are equal and large but RC_A and FC_B are zero) also yields perfect correspondence or noncorrespondence, depending on the concordance or discordance between the first two terms. This can be seen in the lower left panel of Figure 4.2.

The value of IC approaches zero as the difference between the paired terms (i.e., RC_A and FC_B, RC_B and FC_A, and BC_A and BC_B) become large or, to put the same point differently, as one of the terms becomes small in relation to the other. This includes the case of the intermediate degrees of correspondence in the MBC component in which one person is indifferent to the BC exercised over him. It also includes cases approaching pure MFC (the BRC terms are small) and pure BRC (the MFC terms are small). The generalization to be drawn here is that neither the cooperative nor the competitive interests in the dyad can predominate unless the various "paired" component weights in the equations are equal in magnitude.

Computational Form.   The following formula for IC is more convenient than the one above for computing the value of the index:

$$IC = \frac{2(RC_A FC_B + RC_B FC_A + BC_A BC_B)}{RC_A{}^2 + FC_B{}^2 + RC_B{}^2 + FC_A{}^2 + BC_A{}^2 + BC_B{}^2}$$

Effect on Correspondence of Certain Behavioral Assumptions: The Frontier Values

Again we must take note of how the two persons' experience of a property of their relationship may be partly determined by how they act within the context of the matrix. If their actions result in their encountering only limited portions of the matrix, an index characterizing the entire matrix may not be an appropriate predictor of that experience.

The IC index takes account of the total set of pairs of outcomes available to the two persons. One might argue that only the higher values for each person should be considered. The assumption would be that conflict of interest ordinarily develops only with respect to most preferred outcomes. People do not quarrel over what to do about a set of options none of them wants or has to take. So perhaps the index of correspondence should be especially sensitive to the relations between the outcomes for the cells that are most (or more) preferred by each person. (Of course, under special circumstances, the two persons may "lock-in" on some set of options that are considerably inferior to the best, in which case their experience of conflict might be determined by the properties of the pairs of suboptimal outcomes. This observation highlights the fact that the adjustment in the index of correspondence proposed below is based on particular assumptions about behavior and process that may not be warranted in all cases.)

The problem at hand is illustrated by Matrices III and IV in Figure 5.4. Matrix IV has one cell most preferred by both A and B, whereas III shows a difference in their most preferred cells. Thus, even though the IC index is identical for the two ($+.59$), the conflict about what to do might be higher in III. In fact, it might be even greater than in Matrix II in which the difference dimension is larger in relation to the sum dimension

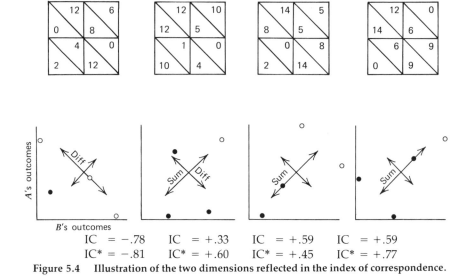

Figure 5.4   Illustration of the two dimensions reflected in the index of correspondence.

(IC = +.33); the reason is that the same cell is most preferred by both persons in Matrix II.

These considerations might suggest limiting our attention to only those cells that each person most prefers, perhaps computing an IC index only for them. A counterargument, however, suggests the wisdom of some middle course. In the plot for Matrix III the location of the two upper right pairs in relation to the lower left pairs (which enter into the IC index) is probably not totally irrelevant to the amount of conflict the matrix will create. The lower pairs provide a context within which *both* upper pairs are likely to appear pretty good to *both* persons and the difference between them may seem insignificant. Thus, although we might want our index to take special account of the upper right pairs, we would not want to disregard completely their location in the total distribution.

Following this reasoning, we suggest that IC might be corrected by taking account of the magnitude of σ^2_{diffs} computed only for the "frontier." This is the subset of pairs left over after all "dominated" pairs are excluded. A "dominated" pair is one for which there can be found at least one other pair that both persons prefer (or one person prefers another pair and the second person is indifferent between the two). The dominated pairs are shown in Figure 5.4 as filled circles and the frontier pairs, as open circles.

In addition to computing σ^2_{sums} and σ^2_{diffs} for the entire set of points

σ^2_{diffs} is also computed for the frontier subset. The two σ^2_{diffs} terms are then combined and the resulting value is used as the σ^2_{diffs} terms in computing the index. We refer to this corrected index as IC*.

The question exactly how the two σ^2_{diffs} terms should be combined, that is, what relative weights they should be given, is probably to be answered on empirical rather than logical grounds. What is desired is a characterization of the index that is maximally predictive of such phenomena as degree of perceived and experienced conflict in the relationship. For now we consider the consequences of a simple averaging in which the two terms are weighted equally.

In general, compared with the uncorrected IC values, the corrected IC* values for matrices near the center of the scale are shifted toward the closer extreme end. This can be seen by reference to Figures 5.3 and 5.4. The shifting is greater for matrices in the correspondent half of the scale, the reason being that the frontier values there generally constitute a smaller subset of the entire matrix. IC* for pure MFC is +.33 and IC* for the matrix at the very center of the MBC continuum is also +.33. An important consequence of the correction is seen in Figure 5.4 in which it will be observed that by the corrected index Matrix III is slightly less correspondent than Matrix II and markedly less correspondent than Matrix IV.

Effect of the Components on the Frontier. Let us consider now the effect of the interdependence components on the value of IC* by analyzing the manner in which they determine the shape of the frontier. We have already seen how correspondent MBC, indicated by both BC_A and BC_B as positive or both as negative, contributes to high overall correspondence. We have also seen how noncorrespondent MBC, indicated by a difference in signs between BC_A and BC_B, contributes to overall noncorrespondence. When we examine the degree of conflict existing at the frontier points, we find that there is an important difference between the two similar sign cases. It is the concordance or discordance of the MBC term with the BRC and MFC terms that affects correspondence by affecting the shape of the frontier. This effect can be shown for the 2×2 matrix, although we must admit uncertainty about its generalizability to larger matrices. Figure 5.5 employs a simple scheme to show the location in the resultant matrix of the various components. To simplify the illustration we treat the weights of all the components as equal in value and use $R = RC_A = RC_B$, $F = FC_A = FC_B$, $B = BC_A = BC_B$, and 0 to stand for zero. What we are interested in is whether the largest sum occurs in one cell along with a small difference between the outcomes of A and B (a correspondent frontier) or whether it occurs in two cells with a sizable

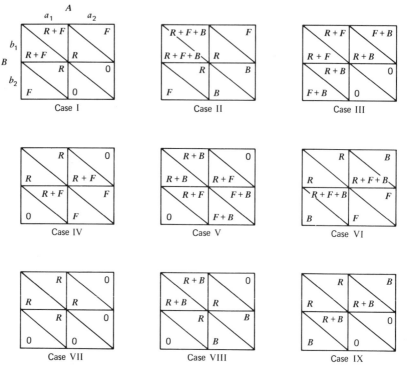

Figure 5.5 **Effect of positive versus negative correspondent MBC on differences at the frontier.**

difference favoring A in one instance and B in the other (a non-correspondent frontier). When both R and F are present and both are positive (Case I), they make the sum largest in the a_1b_1 cell and the difference there small; the frontier therefore consists of one point. Adding positive and correspondent MBC (Case II) only increases for both persons the advantage of the a_1b_1 cell in relation to the other cells. Adding negative and correspondent MBC (Case III) adds two points to the frontier set, but in neither case will the difference in outcomes be large. When R and F are both present and F is negative (Case IV), they yield a constant-sum game (R and F being equal). The addition of positive and correspondent MBC (Case V) leaves a_1b_1 and a_2b_2 as the cells with the largest sums and also with the smallest differences—a no-conflict frontier. In contrast, the addition of negative and correspondent MBC (Case VI) converts cells a_1b_2 and a_2b_1 into those with the largest sums, and these have large differences, one favoring A and the other favoring B. Thus negative and correspondent MBC creates a frontier characterized by conflict. The remaining cases in Figure 5.5 show that this same effect occurs when F is absent. Again, positive and correspondent MBC maintains a nonconflict frontier and negative and correspondent MBC creates a frontier characterized by conflict. The reader can readily demonstrate for himself that the same is true when only F is present.

The generalization suggested by these examples is that if the R and F factors are discordant or unequal in magnitude, the degree of conflict at the frontier will depend on whether the correspondent MBC term is concordant or discordant with them. When R = F and they are concordant, the orientation (sign) of the correspondent MBC term has little effect, but when F and R are discordant or greatly different in size, the orientation of the MBC term has a large effect on the frontier. This result may be compared with that in the section dealing with the index of dependence. In both cases the concordance–discordance of the MBC term plays no role in the index based on the total matrix. (Here IC depends wholly on the BRC–MFC concordance and the correspondence in the MBC component.) In both cases, however, the concordance–discordance of the MBC term has an important effect on that part of the matrix that, granting certain plausible assumptions about behavior and process, the persons are most likely to experience.

CONTROL OVER PAIR OUTCOMES

In the analysis of degree of correspondence we distinguish two *pair scores*, the sum and the difference. The proposed index of correspondence reflects the relative degree to which these scores vary as the two persons move over the domain of cells in the matrix. We now consider the degree of control exercised over them by the two persons. As we discuss later, this control figures prominently in the problem-solving and negotiation processes that occur in the dyad.

One of the important consequences of the location of a pattern on the MFC–MBC dimension (Figure 4.3) is the manner in which the two persons control the pair outcomes; for example, the FC and BC components determine whether the satisfaction of the common interest (represented by the sum score) depends solely on one person's actions, on the sum of their respective actions, or on their joint and coordinated action. The problem can be illustrated by Matrix I in Figure 5.6 which portrays a threat game. The sum and difference scores are indicated in separate derived matrices. It is clear in this case, which happens to be the most extreme, that person B totally controls the variance in the sums whereas A totally controls the variance in the differences. In less clear cases, as in Matrix II, it is possible to calculate the relative degree of control the two exercise over the two scores. An analysis can be made of the components of the sum and difference matrices in the same way that we have analyzed the components of the individual score matrices. It is apparent in Matrix II that the two persons jointly control the sum score but that each separately controls part of the difference score.

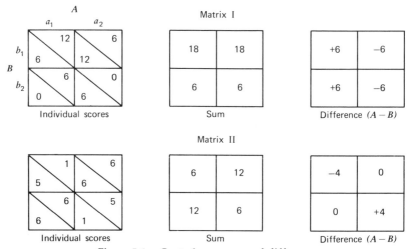

Figure 5.6   Control over sum and difference.

In 2×2 matrices the degree of control each person exercises over the sum and difference scores and the degree of control they jointly exercise can be readily calculated from the components of the matrix. This can be seen by referring again to the equations for the variance of the two pair scores:

$$\sigma^2_{\text{sums}} = \tfrac{1}{4} \left[(RC_A + FC_B)^2 + (RC_B + FC_A)^2 + (BC_A + BC_B)^2 \right]$$

and

$$\sigma^2_{\text{diffs}} = \tfrac{1}{4} \left[(RC_A - FC_B)^2 + (RC_B - FC_A)^2 + (BC_A - BC_B)^2 \right]$$

The first of the three terms in each equation specifies A's control over the sum and difference. Similarly, the second term specifies B's control and the third term specifies their joint control. Thus for Matrix I in Figure 5.6 $(RC_A + FC_B)^2 = 0$, $(RC_B + FC_A)^2 = 144$, and $(BC_A + BC_B)^2 = 0$, which reflect the fact that the sole contributor to variance in the sum is person B. Similarly $(RC_A - FC_B)^2 = 144$, $(RC_B - FC_A)^2 = 0$, and $(BC_A - BC_B)^2 = 0$, which reflect person A's total control over the difference score. In Matrix II $(BC_A + BC_B)^2 = 36$, where both $(RC_A + FC_B)^2$ and $(RC_B + FC_A)^2 = 0$, indicating that the sum score is entirely controlled by their joint moves (in a manner analogous to behavior control). The shared control (and absence of joint control) over the difference is indicated by $(RC_A - FC_B)^2 = (RC_B - FC_A)^2 = 16$ and $(BC_A - BC_B)^2 = 0$.

These examples make it clear that the pair outcomes may be controlled in quite different ways in different matrices. Four patterns can be distinguished:

1. *Differential Control*. One person controls the sum and the other controls the difference. This is epitomized by the threat game (Matrix I in Figure 5.6) in which B determines how much the pair gets and A determines the allocation of the total outcomes between the two. If B does not like A's division, his only recourse is a threat to modify the total score; hence the labels for the two positions as "allocator" and "threatener."
2. *Unilateral Control*. One person controls both scores as shown in Matrix I of Figure 5.7. This occurs with unilateral dependence; the partner is dependent on the person who controls the two pair scores.
3. *Joint Control*. The pair jointly controls both scores. As shown in Matrix II of Figure 5.7, this is an effect on the pair scores analogous to behavior control.
4. *Shared Control*. Each person independently controls part of each score (Matrix III of Figure 5.7). There may also be mixed cases, as in Matrix II (Figure 5.6), in which they exercise joint control over the sum but share control over the difference. By reference to the equations for the sums and differences the reader can determine the necessary conditions for the 2 × 2 case (in terms of the relative magnitudes and intermeshing of the components) for any of these patterns to exist.

The analysis of control relates to our earlier discussion (page 103) of the problems that each person faces because of his dependence. To the degree that there is variance in the sum (i.e., with high correspondence) there is a problem for the pair or group which concerns the common interest and can be described as one of obtaining high joint outcomes. Exactly how that problem must be solved depends on who controls the sum, whether one or both. If both have control, then whether it is joint or shared is important. If joint, coordination is the means to high joint outcomes; if shared, the exchange of their respective contributions is the means to the common end.

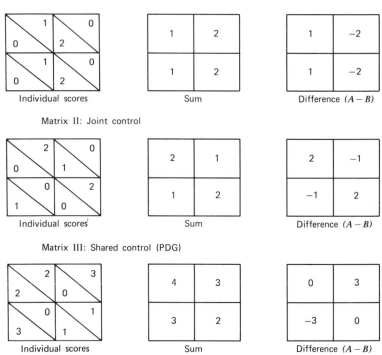

Figure 5.7   Some of the types of control over sum and difference.

Under high noncorrespondence, as epitomized by the constant-sum game, there is no group problem but only those of the individuals. This means that there is considerable variance in the difference score and each person's problem is to obtain an outcome advantageous to himself or, if that is not possible, one that is minimally disadvantageous. Again, the solution depends on who controls the difference score and how it is done. If the control is shared, each person can merely act in the way that yields the difference most favorable to himself and hope that his partner will not. If the control is joint, the problem is one of preventing the partner's coordination while somehow managing a coordination favorable to one's self. In both cases the person is faced with the necessity of getting as much as he can for himself and of protecting himself from his partner's actions.

In the case of intermediate correspondence there is a mixture of group and individual problems. It seems reasonable to assume that in general the group, by virtue of the common interest, will find it useful to help members jointly to achieve solutions to their respective problems; that is, the pair will probably take on the individual problems so that they will not interfere with the solution of the common problem. Thus both members of the dyad have an interest in obtaining maximum joint outcomes, but they are also likely to be concerned with allocation or justice which can be viewed as derivative of the individual problems present under high noncorrespondence. Just as in the zero-sum, perfectly competitive relationship, each person is concerned with (a) getting as much as he can and (b) protecting himself, so it is true in the mixed situation that the pair has an interest in protecting each person and at the same time keeping him contented or happy (helping him to feel that he is getting as much as he can). Systems of justice can be viewed as having to do with (a) providing each person with security against the lower end of his outcome scale and (b) providing him with a satisfactory or equitable level of gain.

These implications of control over sum and difference scores appear again in our considerations when, in Chapter 10, the negotiation process in dyads is analyzed. The manner in which the sum is controlled determines the process of selecting among the frontier values, i.e., those among which wise participants will attempt to negotiate an agreement. The control of the difference scores figures importantly in the positions from which this bargaining will be conducted and in the threats available to the negotiators.

OPTIMAL PATTERNS AND CHOICE DILEMMAS

At several points in Chapter 4 the question of the optimal versions of certain patterns such as the PDG was raised. This question brings up two interrelated issues, the first concerning the optimal number of components and the second the optimal ratio of weights for a given set of components. We consider the optimal number of components first.

In exploring the three-component matrices, we wondered whether any of the important patterns noted among the two-component matrices would be enhanced by the addition of the third component; for example, is there a better version of Prisoner's Dilemma or Chicken than those in Figures 4.5 and 4.3? This question concerns the effect of adding a third component to the two-component patterns; specifically, whether the effect is to sharpen or blur the properties of these patterns. If we explore the regions of the domain adjacent to these patterns, we will observe that each pattern is maintained only so long as the third component is small; for example, the Battle of the Sexes is described in Figure 4.3 with a BRC:MFC:MBC ratio of $0:4:8$. (This is a shorthand expression for the following: $|RC_A| = |RC_B| = 0$; $|FC_A| = |FC_B| = 4$; $|BC_A| = |BC_B| = 8$.)

The similar matrices with a ratio of 2:3:7 possess the basic properties of the Battle of the Sexes, but the matrices with a ratio of 3:3:6 do not, nor do matrices in which the proportion of BRC is even higher. This fact is illustrated in Figure 5.8 which shows the original matrix along with the three possible variations produced by adding BRC in the three possible concordant relations with the other two components. In the 0:4:8 matrix each person prefers doing *D* while his partner does *C* but his second choice is the opposite combination. Their least preferred outcomes occur when both play *D*. This set of preferences, hence the basic properties of the relationship, is maintained with the 2:3:7 ratio but is lost in one respect or another with the 3:3:6 ratio. Even with the 2:3:7 ratio one or another property becomes blurred as the gaps between scores at the successive preference levels are shortened and lengthened. Thus the addition of the third component, the BRC, first blurs the structure of the relationship (at low values) and then destroys it altogether (at higher values).

This point can be made by logical argument, as shown in Figure 5.9 for the PDG. The basic PDG pattern is described in the upper half of the

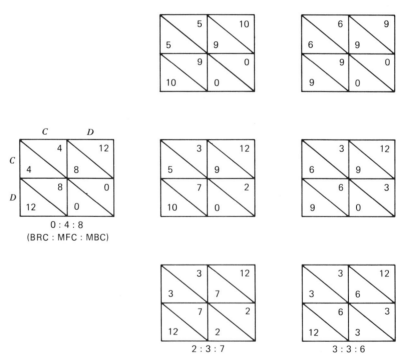

Figure 5.8   **Modifications in Battle of the Sexes with the addition of BRC.**

figure where BRC and MFC are combined in a discordant relationship. The magnitudes of the RC and FC components are portrayed by the letters R and F (where F is greater than R) and 0 stands for zero. In the resulting pattern the four values for each person are ordered in magnitude with $(F + R) > F > R > 0$. In the lower half of the figure MBC is added in a concordant orientation to the basic PDG pattern; the increments are indicated by B. We then consider how large these increments may be without destroying the original rank order of the four cell values for each person which defines the PDG; that is, what constraints must be placed on B if in the new pattern PDG′ it is still true that $(F + R) > (F + B) > (R + B) > 0$. The answer is clear from the first comparison: for $(F + R) > (F + B)$ it is necessary that $R > B$. Thus the MBC component must be smaller in magnitude than the BRC component if the PDG pattern is to be maintained. A similar conclusion is reached if we add correspondent MBC in a discordant orientation to the original pattern or if we add noncorrespondent MBC to the PDG. (A further constraint is placed on the magnitude of B by the usual criteria for the ordering of the cell *sums* in the PDG: $2F > (F + R + 0) > 2R$. For this to be true when correspondent BC is added concordantly or discordantly F must exceed $R + 2B$ which requires that B be less than $1/2(F - R)$.)

The above conclusion is reached for all the unequal ratio, two-component patterns mentioned earlier, that is, for the PDG (MFC + BRC), MDG (MFC + BRC), Chicken (MFC + MBC), Battle of

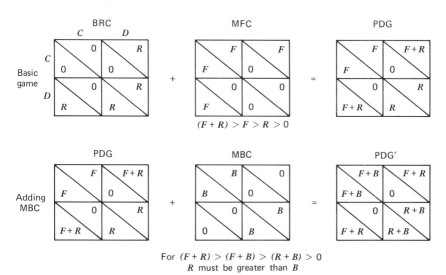

For $(F + R) > (F + B) > (R + B) > 0$
R must be greater than B

Figure 5.9   Analysis of the effects of adding MBC to the Prisoner's Dilemma game.

the Sexes (MFC + MBC), Hero (MBC + BRC), and Martyr (MBC + BRC). In all these cases the ordinal relations among the outcomes present in the two-component version are maintained with the addition of the third factor *only if that factor is smaller in magnitude than the lesser of the original factors*. Thus, for example, Figure 5.10 shows that BRC can be added to Chicken without changing the basic pattern if it is smaller in magnitude than the MBC component in the orginal version.

The preceding analysis suggests that the two-component versions of any one of the "classic" games lies at the center of the subdomain of patterns satisfying the rank-order requirements of that game. As we add the third component we move toward the boundary of the domain and beyond a certain magnitude the additional component shifts the pattern into a different subdomain altogether. Similarly, in considering the patterns generated by successive shifts in the ratios of the two components (see Figures 4.3 through 4.5), it seemed that a given game was best presented by an intermediate ratio (e.g., BRC and MFC in a ratio of 4:8 for the PDG). Can it be asserted, then, that the two-component patterns with certain ratios are optimal versions of the various games?

A first argument in support of this assertion can be made from the perspective of the confusability of various patterns. If a particular game is defined by a certain preference ordering among the person's four outcomes, then that game exists in its clearest form when the differences in outcomes between successive members of the preference order are equal; for example, in Figure 5.8 the 0:4:8 version of the Battle of the Sexes has each person's preferences equally spaced. This preference ordering of *first*, own D, other's C, *second*, own C, other's D, *third*, both C, and *fourth*, both D, is represented by the regular descending outcome sequence of 12, 8, 4, and 0. As we have noted the addition of BRC tends to destroy this ordering; for example, mapping it onto the irregular outcome sequence of 12, 7, 3, and 2 with a small amount of BRC and wholly eliminating certain aspects of the order with larger amounts (e.g., the sequences 12, 6, 3, and 3 or 9, 9, 6, and 0). A glance at Figure 4.3 will also make it clear that the 0:4:8 Battle of the Sexes is the particular two-component version that yields the regular, evenly spaced sequence of outcomes. (Compare the 4:8 Battle of the Sexes with the 2:10 pattern below it.)

The argument here is essentially a perceptual one. In terms of the clarity of the person's preference ordering, which version of a given game is least confusable with adjacent games? It seems reasonable to assume that if the outcome difference representing a given step in a person's preference order is small, he will occasionally overlook it or regard it as unimportant. If so, on these occasions he will be locating himself in a different interdependence pattern. The patterns least susceptible to such errors or confusions are the two-component patterns with two-to-one ratios, as indicated in Figures 4.3 through 4.5. (The threat game represents a different case and is not to be included in this generalization.) These "best" patterns are, of course, those identified in Rapoport and Guyer's analysis of matrices in which each person's preferences are described simply in terms of rank order. The implication of the present discussion is that the best patterns are those in which these ranks represent evenly spaced outcome values.

Acuteness of Choice Dilemmas

A second argument can be made for the optimality of the two-component, two-to-one patterns. This is based on a consideration of the nature of the choice dilemma that confronts an actor in a given game. The basic idea is that the number and magnitude of components affect the acuteness or sharpness of the dilemma a person faces. Again, the dilemmas seem to be most acute for the particular two-component patterns mentioned above.

Consider the PDG. Referring to the top portion of Figure 5.9, the difference $(F + R) - F$ is often referred to as the "temptation" to make the D response; $R - 0$, as the "risk" involved in making the C response; and $F - R$, as the "gain" to be achieved by cooperative exchange of C responses. In the simple two-component PDG "temptation" and "risk" are both equal to R and "gain" is equal to $F - R$. With $F = 2R$ (as in the 4:8 version) all three terms are equal. In other words, temptation = risk = gain when the four outcomes $(F + R, F, R,$ and $0)$ are equally spaced, and this is true only for the 1:2 versions of the PDG.

The dilemma in the PDG is that you have one action that is better no matter what your partner does (represented by the temptation and avoidance of the risk), but if you take that action and your partner does likewise, you do more poorly than if you both had done otherwise (represented by loss of the gain). It seems reasonable to assume that the dilemma is most acute when these two considerations exactly offset each other, that is, when the temptation (and risk avoidance) incentive favoring the D response is exactly as strong as the gain incentive favoring the C response. It will be clear by now that this is true for the 4:8 version of PDG.

It may be asked why it is necessary for the temptation $(F + R) - R$ to be equal to the risk $R - 0$. (This equality requires that MBC be zero.) The answer lies in the unbalancing of one side of the dilemma that their inequality introduces. The side of the dilemma favoring D is made up of both approach and avoidance motivation—to achieve the benefits represented by the temptation and to avoid the penalties represented by the risk. The optimal (4:8) version of the PDG has the two incentive properties represented equally in the set of considerations counterposed to the gain. Other versions accentuate one of these properties in relation to the other; for example, in the lower part of Figure 5.9, with the concordant addition of MBC, the temptation is reduced and the risk is increased. The reader can determine for himself that a discordant addition of MBC increases the temptation and decreases the risk. The addition of non-correspondent MBC increases temptation and decreases risk for one person but has the opposite effect for the other person. Thus, with the added MBC component, a person's choice becomes primarily defined by the temptation versus the gain *or* by the risk versus the gain *or* one way for one person and the other way for his partner.

A similar argument can be made for the game of Chicken—that the 0:8:4 ratio creates the most acute dilemma for each person. Here, however, there is the interesting special fact that the dilemma facing an actor depends in part on the acuteness of the conflict he can create, by his choice, for his partner. Chicken is shown, schematically and in several versions, in Figure 5.10. The basic game pattern is defined by the following preference order: *first*, own D and other's C; *second*, both C; *third*, own C and other's D; and *fourth*, both D. This order can be constructed by using only MFC + MBC, MFC being the larger term (Matrices I and II). In these cases, in which BRC is absent, if required to make a choice without knowing his partner's choice the person has no clear basis for deciding between C and D. If, however, he knows what his partner has chosen, the MBC term provides a basis for choice. Similarly, if he can choose first and make his choice known to his partner, he can provide him with a basis for choice. The latter is a particularly attractive possibility because by choosing D and letting his partner know it he can provide him with an incentive to choose C, which would result in his own highest outcome. It is because of this possibility that Chicken is described as a preemption game. Preempting the D action—taking it irrevocably and notifying the partner of this fact—is a means of attaining one's best outcomes.

Chicken is a special preemption game, however, (others are Battle of the Sexes and Hero). As suggested by the situation from which it takes its name it provides a setting in which a person may demonstrate his *courage*. This reflects the fact that the dilemma for the prospective preemptor is whether to play it (relatively) safe with C or to take a chance with D. For an early commitment to D to constitute a display of courage it is necessary that the payoff matrix have two properties: (a) There must be no basis for choice other than the differential riskiness of the two alternatives. This means that no other interpretation can be placed on the D choice than that

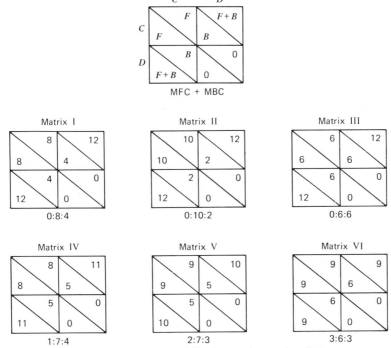

Figure 5.10   The game of Chicken and several variations.

of risk taking. This precludes an *RC* favoring the *D* choice because other people might simply infer that its choice represents what is on the average, the better bet. (b) There must be no clear basis for predicting the partner's response to the preemptive move. This means that the preemptor must be taking his action under maximal uncertainty. If made with assurance that the partner will reciprocate the *D*, we would describe the preemptive move as foolish, and if made with assurance the partner will respond with *C* we would simply describe it as obvious or "showboating."

The latter creates the interesting point in the analysis. *Uncertainty for the preemptor depends on the acuteness of the conflict in which his action places the other party.* Person *A*'s uncertainty about the outcome of his preemptive action will be maximal if the other person has no obvious response to make but rather is placed in sharp conflict between complying and resisting; for example, in Matrix I, Figure 5.10, if *A* preemptively chooses *D*, the partner can get either 4 or 0. His conflict about what to do would seem to depend on the magnitudes of these outcomes in relation to the 8 that might have been attained with mutual C choices. The 4 is considerably lower than 8 but also considerably better than 0. His conflict will be marked. In contrast, faced with the same situation in Matrix II, after comparing the 2 with the 10, he is likely to conclude that he might as well take the 0. In contrast, in Matrix III he is likely to conclude that because the 6 is what he might have obtained anyway it is clearly preferable to 0. In the last two cases his conflict is less than for Matrix I. This reasoning suggests that the partner's uncertainty about what to do is greatest when B falls exactly half way between F and 0. Thus it should be true that $F - B = B - 0$ or that $F = 2B$. If we impose the additional condition suggested by (a), that there be no RC for the preemptor, it must further be true that $(F + B) - F = F - B$. Thus, the two conditions are best satisfied when the four ordered outcomes are evenly spaced from highest to lowest. The lower matrices in Figure 5.10 shows that the addition of BRC concordant with the MFC disrupts the equal spacing.

6

Logical Analysis of the Transformation Processes

ABSTRACT

This chapter examines the shifts in matrix pattern generated by applying various mathematical operations and sequential rules to given *patterns. Only certain plausible transformations, corresponding to common values and temporal concepts, are investigated. These include cases in which the person (a) gives some direct weight to his partner's outcomes in his decision-making criteria (outcome transformations), (b) attempts to be the first or second to act on a given occasion out of regard for how the choices are changed for the second actor (transpositional transformations), and (c) adopts a policy governing his successive choices over a series of interactions in the* given *matrix (sequential transformations). The several transformations are analyzed for the effect they have on the patterns of interdependence and, therefore, such things as the components of the pattern, the correspondence or noncorrespondence of outcomes, and each person's basis for choice.*

We now consider how a particular 2 × 2 matrix can be transformed and the consequences of the various transformations for the pattern of interdependence that results. Transformations are made possible by the pattern of outcomes in the *given* matrix. Psychologically, they are the ways in which a person can reevaluate or reconceptualize the *given* matrix. In doing so, he no longer responds to his own outcomes in each cell. Instead, he views these outcomes in the contexts provided by his partner's outcomes and by past and future actions and interactions within the relationship.

When a person takes account of his partner's outcomes, he is able to adopt new criteria for making decisions and evaluating their consequences; for example, he can make it his goal to cause *both* sets of outcomes to be as high as possible. In effect, by adopting this criterion he is acting as if the matrix were something different than the *given* one. We refer to these new criteria as social or personal values and describe this type of transformation as an *outcome transformation*.

A second possible consequence of considering the total pattern of outcomes is that the person can recognize the importance of the timing of events in any interaction; for example, the pattern of outcomes may indicate that a person who "goes first" is more likely to get a high outcome than one who waits and lets the other go first. The person who recognizes the benefits of "preemption" and acts on this insight is effectively operating within a different matrix than the *given* one—a matrix within which the choices for the second actor are redefined and in which the values reflect a transposition of those in the *given* matrix. We refer to this modification of the *given* matrix as a *transpositional transformation*.

When a person takes account of past and future interchanges, he can adopt a policy of varying his choices over successive occasions; for example, when he and his partner obtain their respective highest outcomes from different combinations of actions, an alternation of his choices over successive times may make it possible for both equally, though only occasionally, to enjoy these high outcomes. In considering such policies, the person is in effect making choices within a new matrix, one in which the alternatives are various sequential rules and the outcomes are the long run (or average) consequences of their various combinations. This kind of modification of the *given* matrix is described as a *sequential transformation*.

Logically, transformations can be represented by three different operations on the *given* matrix, corresponding to the three transformational phenomena outlined: (a) mathematical operations on own and other's outcomes corresponding to various outcome transformations; (b) transpositions of cells in the matrix corresponding to the consequences of preemptive action; and (c) averaging values over portions of the *given* matrix representing the consequences of combinations of sequential rules. We now consider each of these in turn. We analyze the way in which each of these operations affects the properties of the *given* matrix; that is, how the *effective* (transformed) matrix relates to the *given* one. In Chapter 7 we consider the more specific consequences of these transformations and treat the actor as a policy setter, choosing among different transformations and evaluating their consequences. We also determine how, for various patterns, certain transformations induce easy and mutually satisfying decisions, whereas others either worsen or do not improve intrapersonal and interpersonal conflict.

OPERATIONS ON OWN AND OTHER'S OUTCOMES

The research of McClintock and his colleagues, discussed more fully in Chapter 7, suggests that people may have preferences not only with respect to their own outcomes but also to their partner's (other's) outcomes, the joint outcomes (own and other's), and the relative outcomes (one's advantage in relation to the other's outcome). The mathematical operations we consider here include these three criteria along with a fourth that relates to justice—a preference for minimal difference between own and other's outcomes.

Maximize Other's Outcomes

The simplest *social* criterion that a person may apply in his actions is the altruistic one of maximizing his partner's outcomes (*max other*). In the *effective* matrix his outcomes are those of his partner in the *given* matrix. It is apparent that he now becomes subject to the same sources of variation in his outcomes as his partner in the *given* matrix, except that their meaning is somewhat changed for him. Assuming that B adopts the *max other* criterion (using primes to indicate the component weights of the *effective* matrix), then $BC'_B = BC_A$, but $RC'_B = FC_A$ and $FC'_B = RC_A$. In short, what was fate control over A now is reflexive control for B and what was reflexive control for A now is fate control over B. This will be intuitively obvious to the reader: if I totally identify with my child and his outcomes become my own, then ways in which I exercised fate control over him become ways in which I affect my own outcomes, and ways in which he exercised reflexive control over himself now become ways in which he exercises fate control over me.

It will also be intuitively clear that if B unilaterally makes the *max other* transformation (while A maintains an interest exclusively in his own outcomes), the *effective* matrix becomes perfectly correspondent. As A's *given* outcomes are larger or smaller, so are B's *effective* ones. This follows from the fact that RC_A becomes FC'_B, FC_A becomes RC'_B, and BC_A becomes BC'_B. The reader will recall that the index of correspondence is +1 when $RC_A = FC_B$, $RC_B = FC_A$, and $BC_A = BC_B$.

If both persons adopt the *max other* criterion, the various components simply switch places as indicated by the arrows in Figure 6.1. There is no change in the degree of correspondence because the pairs of RC and FC terms and the two BC terms remain the same. The pattern, however, may change in degree of interdependence as the magnitude of RC relative to the other components increases or decreases. The consequences of these shifts can be seen most readily by referring to figures in Chapter 4. The interchange of the RC and FC terms means that matrices in Figure 4.5 reverse their position in relation to the horizontal medial axis of the array. Thus PDG and the matrix directly below it exchange positions as do MDG and the one directly below it. The three matrices on the horizontal axis (competitive, threat, and cooperative) remain unchanged. In Figures 4.3 and 4.4 the consequence of the RC–FC interchange is to exchange be-

Components

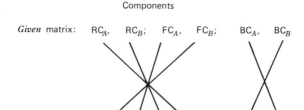

Given matrix: RC_A, RC_B; FC_A, FC_B; BC_A, BC_B

Transformed matrix: RC'_A, RC'_B; FC'_A, FC'_B; BC'_A, BC'_B

Figure 6.1   **Relation of transformed components to** *given* **components with mutual** *max other* **transformation.**

tween the two figures matrices located in similar positions. Thus Chicken becomes Martyr and vice versa; Battle of the Sexes becomes Hero and vice versa, and, of course, MFC becomes BRC and vice versa. In brief, mutual *max other* leaves the degree of correspondence unchanged, but if the initial balance of RC and FC is unequal it shifts the matrix up or down on the independence–interdependence scale. The latter effect is caricatured by the pair of persons who, on becoming closely identified with each other, find themselves being wholly affected (MFC) by what earlier had been independently controlled sources of satisfaction (BRC).

An important aspect of the *max other* transformation is that a person may have greater RC than before. This depends, of course, on his partner's FC and how it compares with his own *given* RC. In patterns such as the Battle of the Sexes the criterion provides a person with RC where he had none before.

Maximize Both Own and Other's Outcomes

A more complex but also more common criterion is that of maximizing both one's own and one's partner's outcomes, referred to as *max joint*. The person can give different weight to the two sets of outcomes by, for example, placing more emphasis on his own than his partner's. Considering the simplest case in which he weights them equally, the component weights for the transformed matrix become (for *B*):

$$RC'_B = RC_B + FC_A$$
$$FC'_B = FC_B + RC_A$$
and $$BC'_B = BC_B + BC_A$$

In other words, added to *B*'s own components are the appropriate ones of his partner. The same is true for *A*'s components.

In *mutual* use of the *max joint* criterion the following equalities prevail:

$$RC'_A = FC'_B = RC_A + FC_B$$
$$FC'_A = RC'_B = RC_B + FC_A$$
and
$$BC'_A = BC'_B = BC_A + BC_B$$

These are summarized in Figure 6.2, which shows the pair of *given* terms combined to form each transformed term. The equalities between pairs of terms in the transformed pattern show that the relationship is perfectly correspondent. This is intuitively obvious. If both persons take equal account of both sets of given outcomes, their respective transformed outcomes will be identical in each cell.

Components

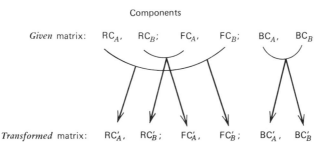

Figure 6.2   Relation of transformed components to *given* components with mutual *max joint* transformation.

Intuitively, it seems that *unilateral* adoption of the *max joint* criterion will increase the correspondence between the outcomes of the two persons. Thus, as he applies this criterion, B's outcomes vary to a greater extent than originally with the same factors (A's choices, B's choices, their joint choices) as do A's outcomes. In general, this is true. There are exceptions, however, that can be understood by referring to the case of perfect correspondence shown in Figure 6.3. Although in the original matrix IC = +1.00, the IC for the transformed matrix is +.80. The reason is that the variance in A's outcomes increases sharply. Because the IC is equal to the correlation reduced by any inequality between the dispersions of the two sets of outcomes, the increased variance in A's outcomes reduces the correspondence. The psychological meaning is that although A and B still share the same preference ordering for the four possible events, the correspondence between the preferences is reduced by the fact that A cares so much more than B that better outcomes be attained. A rough generalization about the unilateral use of the *max joint* criterion is that it increases the degree of correspondence if the correspondence is not too high in the *given* matrix.

Although the mutual *max joint* transformation always yields perfect correspondence, it has drastically different effects on the degree of interdependence, depending on the given matrix. As was true of the *max other* criterion, the use of *max joint* can produce RC where there was none originally. Illustrations are provided by MFC, Battle of the Sexes, and Chicken. The threat game becomes a pattern of unilateral dependence in which B is in control of both RC_B and FC_A; this simply reflects B's control over the sum score in the orginal matrix. Perfectly noncorrespondent games have no variance at all in their transformed versions, which is another way of noting that perfectly noncorrespondent games are constant-sum patterns.

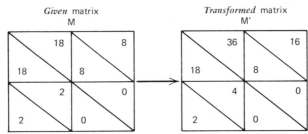

Figure 6.3   Matrix for which the *max joint* transformation reduces degree of correspondence.

Maximize Own Advantage

This competitive value transformation can be represented in its simplest form by the algebraic difference (own–other). We refer to it as the *max rel* criterion, remembering that the difference (meaning "own relative advantage") is positive if own outcome is larger than other's and is negative if other's outcome is larger than own.

The components of the transformed matrix are calculated by making proper subtractions among the terms for the *given* matrix:

$$RC'_A = RC_A - FC_B \qquad RC'_B = RC_B - FC_A$$
$$FC'_A = FC_A - RC_B \qquad FC'_B = FC_B - RC_A$$
$$BC'_A = BC_A - BC_B \qquad BC'_B = BC_B - BC_A$$

It will be seen that $RC'_A = -FC'_B$, $FC'_A = -RC'_B$, and $BC'_A = -BC'_B$.

Thus the matrix resulting from a mutual *max rel* transformation always has a perfectly noncorrespondent pattern.

This transformation is, of course, a mirror image of the *max joint* transformation. Not only does its mutual use lead to noncorrespondence (where *max joint* leads to correspondence) but its unilateral use generally leads to increased noncorrespondence (just as unilateral *max joint* generally results in increased correspondence). The exceptions to this generalization are similar to those applying to *max joint* usage. Unilateral *max rel* use increases the noncorrespondence only if the initial degree is not too extreme.

The effects of the *max rel* criterion on interdependence also provide a mirror image of those for *max joint*. Perfectly correspondent *given* patterns have no variance in their transformed versions, reflecting their constant-difference property. Thus the correspondent MBC terms drop out for such patterns as Chicken and Hero. For *given* patterns with non-correspondent MBC the transformation enhances the term. The threat game again has unilateral dependence, but this time A controls both terms, reflecting his control over the difference scores in the *given* matrix. Like the other criteria considered so far, *max rel* can generate RC for a person who has none in the *given* matrix.

Minimize Difference

Persons interested in justice might place a negative value on any difference between the outcomes of the two persons. Thus they would attempt to minimize the absolute difference, own–other's. The larger the difference, the larger the *negative* transformed value.

The relations between the *given* components and those of the pattern resulting from the *min diff* transformation are exceedingly complicated: let

$$A = RC_A - FC_B$$
$$B = FC_A - RC_B$$
$$C = BC_A - BC_B$$
and
$$D = GM_A - GM_B$$

Then
$$RC'_A = FC'_B = 1/4(|A + B + C + 2D| + |A - B - C + 2D| - |B - A - C + 2D| - |C - A - B + 2D|),$$
$$FC'_A = RC'_B = 1/4 (|A + B + C + 2D| - |A - B - C + 2D| + |B - A - C + 2D| - |C - A - B + 2D|),$$
and
$$BC'_A = BC'_B = -1/4 (|A + B + C + 2D| - |A - B - C + 2D| - |B - A - C + 2D| + |C - A - B + 2D|).$$

Several aspects of the *min diff* transformation may be noted. The first is that the mutual use of the *min diff* criterion results in a perfectly correspondent pattern, revealed by the paired equalities among the terms of the transformed pattern.

Second, the grand means of the two sets of *given* outcomes affect the components of the transformed matrix. This, of course, reflects one of the sources of differences between the scores of the two persons. The greater the degree to which one person is generally more favored in the *given* outcomes of their interaction, the larger the negative outcomes for whomever applies the *min diff* criterion.

Third, a difference between the two persons in their total variance in outcomes contributes to all three components of the transformed pattern. This is apparent from the fact that the first term $A + B + C + 2D$ increases the value of all three transformed components. This term is partly a function of the difference between the sums of the original components of the two persons. The effect of this difference in variance may be offset by the difference between the means, but if the mean difference is close to zero the difference in variance acts to increase all three derived components. The psychological significance is that minimal differences between the two sets of outcomes are possible only if the two persons are affected to about the same degree by the different combinations of their behavior. On the one hand, a person who is greatly pleased by all events in the interaction will inevitably have different *given* outcomes from his partner who is rather indifferent to all the events (the effect of a mean difference). On the other hand, a person who is highly responsive, with both pleasure and displeasure, to the different events will have different outcomes from a partner who is only mildly responsive (the effect of a variance difference).

Fourth, independently of the similarity or dissimilarity between the means and variances of the two persons' outcomes, the degree of correspondence or noncorrespondence between them affects the components of the transformed pattern. (This is readily determined by comparing noncorrespondent and correspondent ranked-outcome patterns because all such patterns have the same mean and variance.) In Chapter 5 we saw that correspondence is maximal when the pairs of components in the *given* matrix (RC_A and FC_B, RC_B and FC_A, BC_A and BC_B) are equal and have the same signs. *Non*correspondence is maximal when the pairs are equal and opposite in sign. Referring to the first equations (page 145), the reader will see that in the first case each of the A, B and C terms is zero; in the second case they have values, respectively, of $\pm 2RC_A$, $\pm 2FC_A$, and $\pm 2BC_A$. Substituting these values in the equations for the transformed components and, for simplicity, assuming that $GM_A = GM_B$, we find that the transformed components are zero for the first case (correspondent *given* matrix) and nonzero for the second (noncorrespondent *given* matrix). The first is merely another manifestation of the fact that a perfectly correspondent matrix is also a constant-difference game and there can be no variability from one cell to another in the magnitude of the difference. In contrast, for any degree of difference between GM_A and GM_B perfectly noncorrespondent matrices have maximal variability among the cells in the magnitude of the difference.

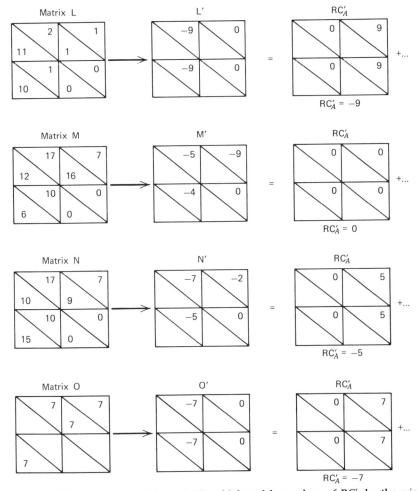

Figure 6.4   Illustrations of matrices yielding high and low values of RC'_A by the *min diff* transformation.

The equations may be examined with respect to the conditions under which a person will have RC in the transformed matrix. If RC $_A$ is large and the other terms are small, RC' $_A$ will, of course, be large. Also, as shown in matrix L of Figure 6.4, RC' $_A$ will also be high if person A exercises high FC $_B$. In both cases the A term in the formulas is large. There is also a difference between the grand means. For the case in which GM $_A$ = GM $_B$, it can be seen that RC' $_A$ is large if the A term is small and B and C are large and equal both in sign and magnitude. This is illustrated in Figure 6.4 by matrix M which yields no RC' $_A$ and matrix N which yields a sizable one. The essential components of matrix N, reflecting the B and C terms, are shown in matrix O, which shows that the simple FC and BC combination generates RC' $_A$ despite the absence of RC $_A$ in the original matrix.

For the case in which RC $_A$ = RC $_B$, FC $_A$ = FC $_B$, and BC $_A$ = BC $_B$ the components in the *min diff* transformed pattern are easy to determine. Under conditions in which GM $_A$ = GM $_B$, the transformed RC' and FC' terms are zero and BC' $_A$ = BC' $_B$ = (RC $_A$ − FC $_A$). An illustration is provided by the PDG in Figure 6.5. All such matrices, in which the outcomes are symmetric around a diagonal, yield transformed patterns characterized wholly by correspondent MBC.

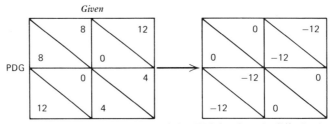

Figure 6.5   Transformation of the PDG by the *min diff* criterion.

Nonlinear Transformations Involving the Comparison Level

The preceding transformations bear linear relations to own and/or other's *given* outcomes. The functions relating the *given* and the *effective* outcomes, however, may sometimes be nonlinear; for example, in comparing his own outcomes with those of his partner the person may not find that his resultant satisfaction increases linearly with the (own–other) algebraic difference. Instead, he may experience a great gain in satisfaction as he moves from being just below the partner to being just above him. In the extreme case there is a stepwise or discontinuous transformation, all outcomes below those of the partner being equally negative and all outcomes above, equally positive. As shown in Figure 6.6, if this discontinuous *max rel* transformation is made by both persons, a given matrix of moderately high correspondence will be transformed into a two-outcome-level matrix of perfect noncorrespondence. This transformation is probably encouraged by experience in win–lose reward systems in which "winner takes all" and second best gets nothing, no matter how close he comes to winning.

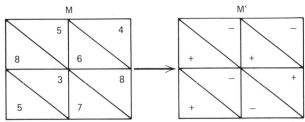

Figure 6.6   Consequences of a discontinuous *max rel* transformation.

More generally, the person's comparison level (CL) not only defines a zero point for his outcomes—the dividing line between satisfaction and dissatisfaction—but may also introduce a stretching out of the values in that particular region of the scale. Indeed, psychologically, this seems to be the implication of the distinction between satisfactory and unsatisfactory outcomes—that there is a region of discontinuity in the outcome scale. This view of the nonlinear transforming effects of the CL is consistent with Sidney Siegel's proposal that the level of aspiration be defined as the upper boundary of that region of the objective utility scale in which there is the sharpest rate of change in subjective utility (see Siegel 1957, for references to the evidence in support of this proposal).

The nonlinear effect of the CL would be reflected in the *given* matrix insofar as the CL exists before the present interaction. Thus the experimenter may set outcome goals for one or both players in a game, thereby defining success and producing a stretching of the outcome scale between those values below a goal and those above it. The nonlinear effect would constitute part of the transformation process generating the *effective* matrix to the extent that the CL is modified in the present relationship by information about the partner's outcomes. Thus the partner's generally higher level of outcomes (his higher GM) may raise the person's outcome aspirations. In the extreme case illustrated in Figure 6.6 each person's CL is totally defined by the partner's outcomes. As these examples show, there is a close similarity between the processes underlying CL and the *max rel* outcome transformation.

Whether the CL is externally or internally anchored, the effect of its nonlinear transformation depends on (a) the preceding pattern of inter-dependence and (b) the levels of CL for the two persons. This is shown in Figure 6.7 in which the given PDG and MDG matrices have been trans-formed by low, medium, and high CLs. For each transformation the scale has been stretched six points at the CL. The transformed values are deviations from the CL with three points added for the positive and three points subtracted for the negative. The indices of correspondence show that the medium CL decreases noncorrespondence and the low and high CLs increase noncorrespondence (slightly) for the PDG. In contrast, for the MDG pattern the medium CL decreases correspondence, whereas the low and high CLs increase it. Of course, the transformation tends to change the type of pattern as well; for example, the transformed version of the PDG resulting from the high CL no longer satisfies the condition of the original pattern that the joint outcome be highest in the upper left cell. The examples in Figure 6.7 show that the effects of a nonlinear trans-formation associated with a CL depends on the level of that CL in relation to the values in the matrix and the pattern of the *given* matrix. These effects occur only for values of the CL that are within the range of values in the matrix. If the CL is outside that range, its "stretching" effect does not modify the pattern of the matrix.

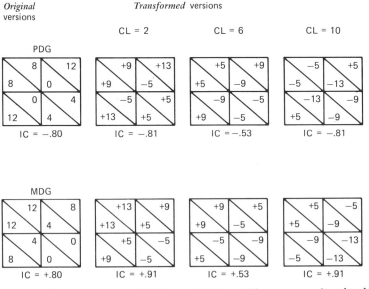

Figure 6.7   Transformations of PDG and MDG by different comparison levels.

TRANSPOSITIONS OF CELLS IN THE GIVEN MATRIX

This and the next section deal with certain temporal aspects of the interaction. In the present case we consider only the single interaction, defined by the time interval during which both persons enact or become committed to enact items from their respective behavioral repertories. Various possibilities relate to the sequence of their separate actions or decisions as well as to the intercommunication of their actions or decisions. In one extreme case they make their decisions simultaneously and independently, without communication or knowledge of each other's decisions. In a different case, of special interest here, one person acts and makes that action known to the partner before the latter makes a decision.

If, on a given occasion of interaction, one person acts first, the partner is permitted to take account of that action in deciding on his own. In effect, the first action provides the partner with a decision different from the one he would have faced otherwise. This can be described in terms of *match* or *not match*, match meaning that he makes the same choice as the first actor and not match meaning that he makes the opposite choice. (By *same choice* we mean the action with the same subscript as that taken by the partner. Thus a_1 is the same choice with respect to b_1 but the opposite with respect to b_2. Some of the examples that follow may be easier to understand if A and B are assumed to have identical sets of behavioral options, but the logic of the analysis does not require this.)

This set of events generates a transformed matrix that is simply the *given* matrix with two cells transposed. We refer to this process as a *transpositional* transformation. It is illustrated for Chicken in Figure 6.8. Person B's first action, by providing the "match versus not match" alternative to A, transforms the matrix in the manner shown.

It is this transpositional transformation that often motivates interdependent persons, depending on the *given* matrix, to try to act first (preempt) or to have the partner act first (wait). In Chicken B's interest in acting first is clear. He provides A with RC'_A in favor of not matching. If B's first action has been b_2, this RC'_A works to B's advantage. The various preemption games derive their name from this fact. An example of a matrix in which a person is motivated to wait and let the partner go first is provided by MFC. As shown in Figure 6.8, by matching B's first response A can reward B for b_1 and withhold reward for b_2. Thus the successful "waiter" is able to convert his FC to BC.

Noncorrespondent MBC in Figure 6.9 provides another case of a person's gaining from successful waiting. Person B's first action provides A with RC'_A which ensures A a good outcome; B's reluctance to transform the matrix in this manner is predictable because he becomes unilaterally

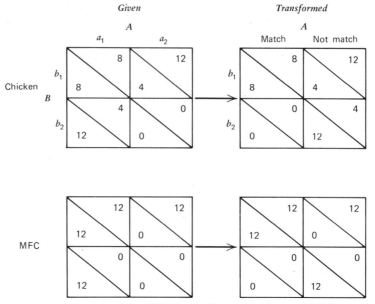

Figure 6.8   Effect of *B's* first action on Chicken and MFC.

dependent on *A* in a situation in which FC'_B is discordant with RC'_A. Transposition has this consequence for all the patterns with dominant noncorrespondent MBC.

Correspondent MBC (Figure 6.9) provides each person with an interest in both preemption and waiting. Thus *B's* preemption eliminates the common coordination problem, and although it makes him unilaterally dependent on *A* this may be acceptable because of the concordance between FC'_B and RC'_A.

We shall not go into the question of exactly how a person manages successfully to preempt or wait. The transformed matrices are presented here merely to show the logical consequences of preemption. It is important to note that the transpositional transformation occurs *only if the partner of the person who acts first knows that the action has actually occurred*.

The relation of the components in the transformed matrix to those in the *given* matrix is shown in Figure 6.10. This is for the case in which *B* has acted first. (By interchanging subscripts Figure 6.10 also describes the relations when *A* acts first.) It is apparent that transposing cells in a given row will have no effect on the between-row sources of variance (RC_B and FC_A). The other terms are interchanged. The transformation of the BC terms into RC'_A and FC'_B is illustrated by the MBC matrices in Figure 6.9.

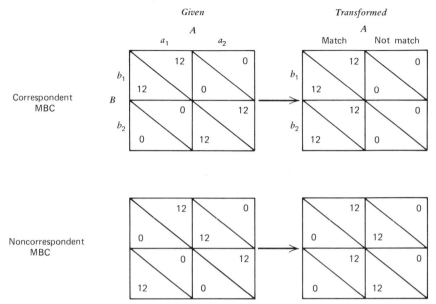

Figure 6.9 Effect of *B*'s first action on correspondent MBC and noncorrespondent MBC.

The transformation of FC$_B$ into BC$'_B$ is illustrated by MFC in Figure 6.8. In the latter, it may seem strange to consider *A* as having BC over *B* (BC$'_B$) when *B* has already acted. BC, however, has the same significance in this transformed matrix as it has in any other matrix. In selecting his (first) action, *B* must realize that his outcome depends on what *A* does — whether he matches or not. Furthermore, if *A* has already made a choice in the transformed matrix, in this case, between match and not match,

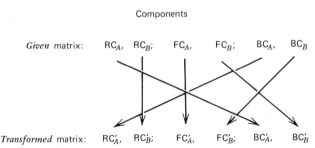

Figure 6.10 Relation between components of *given* matrix and those of the matrix resulting from *B*'s first action.

then B will make his choice according to the BC pattern. We return to this point when considering double transpositions.

The transpositional transformation has no effect on the degree of correspondence. It can be seen that any discordant relations between RC–FC pairs are carried forward or translated into noncorrespondent MBC and that noncorrespondent MBC is translated into a discordant relation between RC'_A and FC'_B. More intuitively, it will be realized that because the pairings of outcome values do not change with transposition the degree of correspondence can undergo no change.

Double Transpositions

If person A can commit himself to a certain choice in the transformed match versus not match matrix *before* B acts, then *that* matrix itself is transformed. This is shown for the PDG in Figure 6.11. The meanings of "match" and "not match" in PDG' have been spelled out so that we may be clear about the meaning of B's new alternatives in PDG". A's match is equivalent to "I will do a_1 if you do b_1 and a_2 if you do b_2." His not match means that his actions will be the opposite under these two circumstances. Following A's preemption of match or not match, B's choice (assuming that he is willing to act first) now becomes one between "I will do b_1 if you match and b_2, otherwise" and "I will do b_2 if you match and b_1, otherwise."

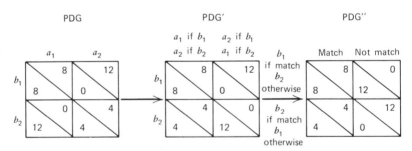

Figure 6.11   Double transposition of the PDG.

The consequences of this double preemption are apparent. In the original PDG each person's following his RC resulted in both getting less than they might have. PDG' (as generated by B's simple preemption) does not improve the situation. B would be unlikely to preempt with b_1 and his b_2 first choice generates a matching response because of BC'_A in PDG'. Matters are different in PDG", however. Person A can commit himself to match with confidence that B's response will be b_1, by virtue of RC"$_B$. (For the same reason A will not commit himself at the outset to not match.) The result will be the attainment of the set of outcomes that is as beneficial as possible to both parties.

This analysis is essentially that of Nigel Howard in his metagame theory (1971). It should be viewed as a logical possibility in relation to any pattern of interdependence but not as one that is necessarily to be expected. Like all these transformations, it requires considerable understanding of logical implications and consequences. This is especially true for the person (A in our example) who first states a matching rule. More importantly, that person must have (a) a means of making a convincing commitment (to match, in our example) and (b) the ability to wait until the partner takes his action in the original matrix. Finally, because both persons can play either role, there may be a problem of coordinating role assignments. The analysis is thwarted if both become committed to matching at the same time. Among these several problems the one of commitment seems the most central. The analysis states that the two come to the point at which B can say "I am proceeding with b_1 because I understand you are then required, by your prior commitment, to match it," and A can only say (or think), "According to my commitment, which I am now unable to overturn, if you are doing b_1, I must do a_1."

AVERAGING OVER SUCCESSIVE OCCASIONS

Most relationships involve repeated interaction about the same or similar things; that is, there are a number of separate occasions on which both persons enact items from their respective behavioral repertoires. This makes it possible for the persons to think about the pattern of their individual and joint actions on a series of occasions. Perhaps the most common example is the mutual patterning of choices involved in turn taking. "You have what you want this time, and the next time I will have what I want." As this example suggests, sequential rules for choice often evolve in noncorrespondent relations to provide a mutually acceptable equalization of the two persons' outcomes. Other rules serve the interests of the individual, as in protecting him from exploitation by his partner. In either case the effect of these rules, which we refer to as *sequential* transformations, is to transform the *given* matrix. (It will undoubtedly be clear to the reader that we are dealing here with a temporal pattern of events over *successive instances* of mutual action. This is to be contrasted with the preceding section in which we considered the implications of the temporal sequence of events during a single *instance* of mutual action.)

The Consequences of Sequential Transformations

Following a systematic sequence of choices in a *given* matrix is a means of limiting the outcomes to certain portions of the matrix or, in some cases, of spreading the outcomes systematically over the entire matrix. This is most readily illustrated when A always chooses a_1 and B alternates between b_1 and b_2. Obviously the result will be an alternation of outcomes between those in the a_1b_1 cell and those in the a_1b_2 cell. Some of the many possibilities are shown in Figure 6.12 in which we present six simple rules (e.g., for B): (a) repeatedly play b_1, (b) repeatedly play b_2, (c) play b_1 and then alternate (i.e., alternate between b_1 and b_2, beginning with b_1), (d) play b_2 and then alternate, (e) randomly choose b_1 or b_2 each time (in ratio of $50:50$), and (f) "tit-for-tat," which means "play what the partner played last time." Figure 6.12 shows the consequences of the two persons' adopting various pairs of these rules. The part of each small matrix drawn in heavy outline is sampled by the given pair of sequential rules. The outcomes gained by each member of the pair would yield an average equal to his average outcome in the indicated portion of the matrix. (The consequences of tit-for-tat are only approximately as shown because the person will have to make a first choice before being able to match what his partner did before and the partner will have a final "unanswered" choice. The consequences of mutual tit-for-tat are equivocal, depending on the initial choices the pair happens to make.) Although some of the rule combinations in Figure 6.12 focus on one cell, of greater interest here are those that average over two cells or all four cells. (More complex rules may average over three of the four cells, e.g., $b_1b_1b_2b_1b_1b_2 \ldots$ paired with $a_2a_1a_1a_2a_1a_1 \ldots$).

The specific consequences of any of these combinations of rules will depend, of course, on the distribution of outcomes in the *given* matrix. A convenient way to represent the possibilities is by a plot of the four pairs of A's and B's outcomes in the *given* matrix. This is shown in Figure 6.13 for the PDG, the threat game, and symmetric and asymmetric games from Figure 4.4. Each pair of outcomes in the *given* matrix is plotted as an x. It is a fact that the average of *any combination* of cells in a given matrix falls within the convex polygon formed by connecting its four pairs of values (the four x's). This is shown for each of the four patterns by the crosshatched area. Thus any set of sequential rules must yield, as an average outcome, some point within that area. The consequences of seven of the pairs of rules, corresponding to the numbered pairs in Figure 6.12, are plotted in the areas of Figure 6.13. The particular rules we have chosen yield outcomes located midway between pairs of outcomes in the given matrix and at the center of gravity of the crosshatched area. Other

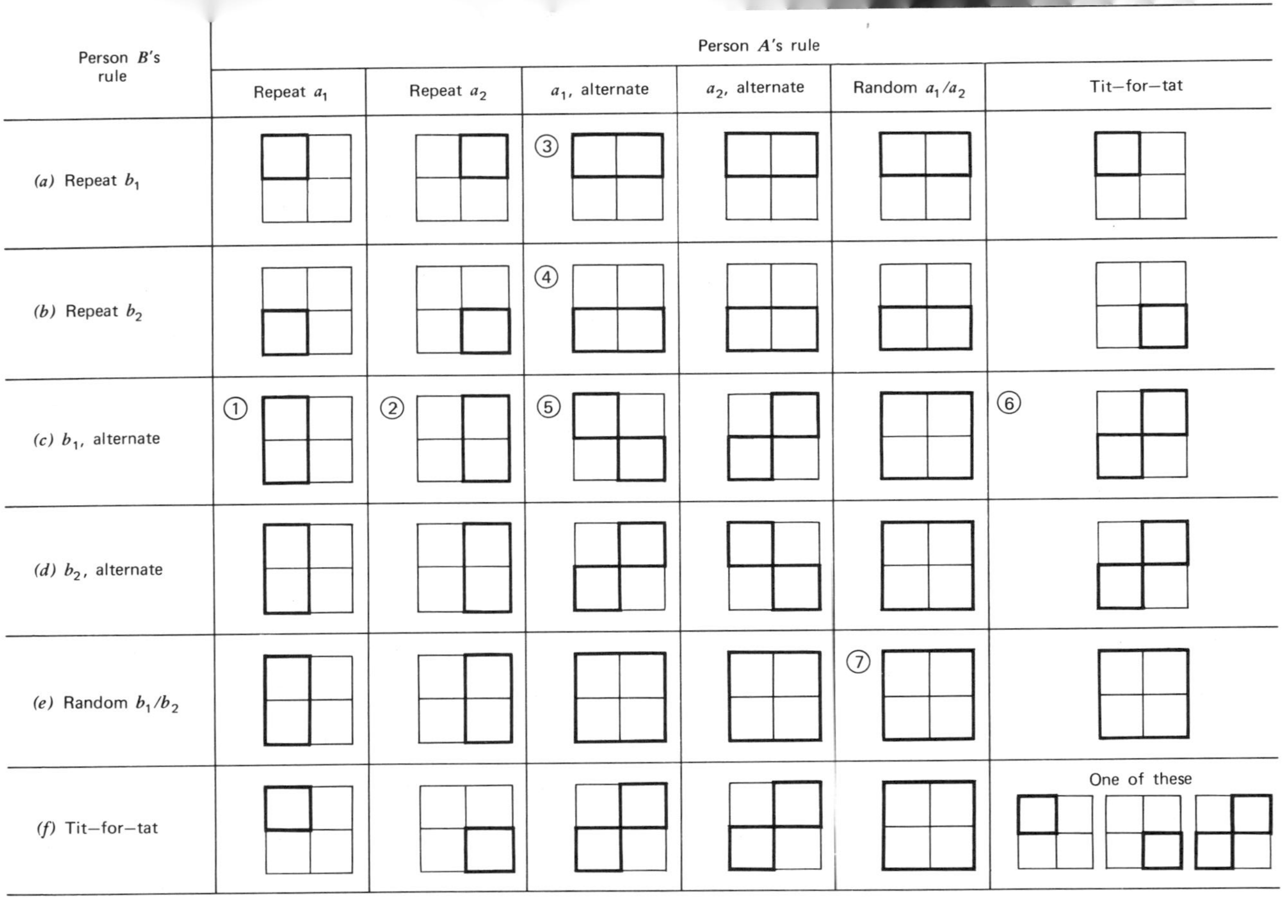

Figure 6.12 Portions of the *given* matrix sampled by various combinations of sequential rules.

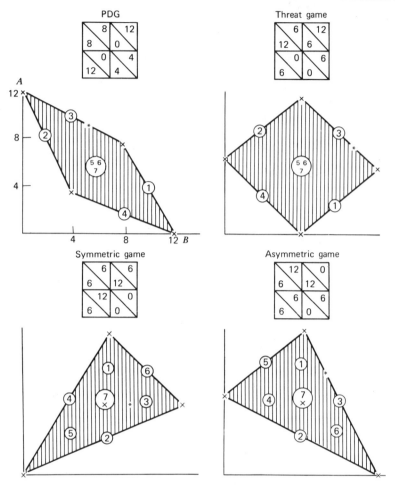

Figure 6.13   Consequences of different combinations of sequential rules for four different patterns.

rules, representing various weightings of the combinations of cells, would yield outcome pairs in other parts of the area; for example, rules producing a_1b_1 and a_2b_1 in a ratio of 2:1 would yield the outcomes indicated by asterisks. (This results in equal outcomes for A and B in the asymmetric game.)

These examples serve to make two points: (a) Sequential transformations can yield new sets of outcomes on the frontier of the relationship. (Cf. the discussion of frontier in Chapter 5.) Thus, in effect, they make it possible to increase the degree of correspondence in the relationship. The particular sequence required to accomplish this depends, of course, on the *given* pattern; for example, pair 3 (or any pair sampling the upper row) yields new frontier points for PDG and the threat game, pair 6 (or any pair sampling the a_1b_2 and a_2b_1 cells) does so for the symmetric game, and pair 3 (or any pair sampling the upper row) does so for the asymmetric game. More generally, the consequence of most pairs of sequential rules depends greatly on the *given* matrix, as shown in Figure 6.13. (b) Sequential transformations do not add pairs of outcomes outside the limits of the set defined by the *given* pairs. The domain of pairs, indicated by the crosshatched polygon, is not changed in shape. It *is* changed by various outcome transformations, which fact, as discussed in Chapter 7, creates the basis for the *joint* use of sequential rules and outcome transformations. At present it is important to note that the various pairs of rules differ in the degree to which they satisfy various value criteria. Pair 3 satisfies both the criteria of *max joint* and *min diff* in the threat game, and pair 6 has the same effect on the symmetric game. The special pair indicated by the asterisk satisfies *min diff* but not *max joint* for the asymmetric game. (See discussion in Chapter 4 of irreconcilability between MJP and equality of outcomes in such patterns.)

The Choice Among Sequential Transformations

When a person adopts a particular sequential policy, he is, in effect, acting within an interdependence matrix in which the alternatives are different policies. An example is the 6 × 6 matrix that can be derived for any game by entering A's and B's respective average outcomes in the 36 cells of Figure 6.12. A transformed matrix of this sort obviously has some relation to the *given* matrix on which it is based, its components depending in a systematic way on the components of the *given* matrix. We shall not attempt to determine the relations between these two sets of components but instead merely point out some of the major consequences of adopting certain policies.

The pattern of sampling the cells of the *given* matrix, described in Figure 6.12, reveals that in most cases the consequences of B's following a given sequential rule depend to a great extent on the rule A adopts. Those that are least affected by what the partner does, "repeat b_1" or "repeat b_2," simply sample one row or the other. These clearly do not benefit B unless he already has a considerable degree of RC in the *given* matrix.

Tit-for-tat has the interesting property that it samples cells located symmetrically with respect to the major axis (upper left to lower right) of the *given* matrix, regardless of the rule the partner follows. This has the important consequence that in symmetrical games the difference between own and other's average score is minimized. Thus a person solely concerned about the *min diff* criterion and interacting in a symmetrical pattern can fulfill this criterion merely by the tit-for-tat sequential rule. (This is not exactly true, for the reason, mentioned earlier, that in any finite interaction sequence the person must make an initial choice without following the rule—before his partner has established a "prior choice," and then on any last play the partner makes a choice to which the tit-for-tat sequence has no opportunity to reply.)

It seems clear that for most *given* matrices the consequences of a given *alternation* rule depend a great deal on what rule the partner adopts. Against a similar alternation rule it samples the major diagonal of the matrix. Against the opposite alternation rule or against tit-for-tat it samples the minor diagonal. (Against a tit-for-tat with a one-step lag—"do what the partner did time before last"—the alternation rule would also sample the major diagonal.)

Random choice of the two responses (in a 50:50 ratio) produces a sampling of the entire matrix against all the other variable sequential rules (i.e., except against repeat a_1 or repeat a_2). Under these circumstances it yields the person his grand average GM_B and the average difference between his and his partner's score is $(GM_B - GM_A)$. Just why a person might wish to sample the whole matrix requires some explaining. Superficially, this policy seems contrary to the central theme of the interdependence analysis, which is that the person takes account of the controls involved and attempts *through selective action* to use them to his own benefit. However, in games of very high conflict of interest (the constant-sum game is the best example) there are certain instances in which the best way a person can protect his own interests is by random response. Three constant-sum games (zero-sum games) are illustrated in Figure 6.14. In all such games, because of the strict conflict of interest, there is no basis for agreement between the two persons. Each must assume that the other, in the pursuit of his own interest, will consistently work against one's own interest. In Case I, characterized mainly by BRC, each will follow his RC, and the interaction, however often repeated, will result in $a_1 b_1$—A making one point and B losing one. (We might doubt that B would stay in the game unless for reasons not specified in the matrix he is required to.) Case II, characterized largely by RC and BC, also has a consistent outcome but for a slightly different reason. B's RC leads him to enact b_1 and, anticipating this, the BC impinging on A leads him to enact a_1.

Case III, characterized primarily by MBC, poses an entirely different problem. The preferred action of each depends on what the other does.

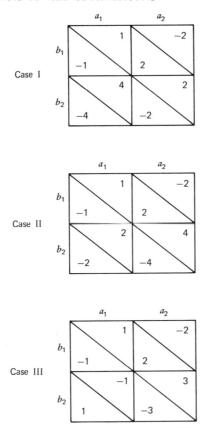

Figure 6.14   Three constant-sum games that require different means for protecting the individual's interests.

Accordingly, of course, each would prefer to wait to see what the other will do before deciding. Precluding this possibility (assuming that the movement of events requires both to act and prevents either from "waiting"), a random sequential rule has an advantage. Turning over the decision to the toss of a coin prevents one's partner from anticipating one's choice in any way. This is true for each single trial, but also over a series of trials it prevents his detecting any explicit or implicit patterning in one's successive choices. Furthermore, a particular random rule (referred to as a *mixed* or *randomized strategy*, and not necessarily selecting the two choices in a 50:50 ratio) has the special consequence that no matter what sequential rule the partner follows it yields one the same average value. In other words, if we imagine placing this particular rule in the matrix derived from Figure 6.12, *its outcome is the same regardless of the partner's sequential rule*.

A mixed strategy with this property is calculated, for example, for person A in the third matrix of Figure 6.14, by determining an allocation of choices between a_1 and a_2 such that A's average outcome will be the same when B chooses b_1 as when he chooses b_2. The proportion p of the time for A (randomly) to select a_1 is determined by solving the following equation which is simply a mathematical translation of the preceding sentence:

$$p(1) + (1 - p)(-2) = p(-1) + (1 - p)(3)$$

The numbers in the equation are A's outcomes in the matrix. The value of p is 5/7; therefore a_1 is chosen on five-sevenths of the occasions and a_2, on two-sevenths. A random sequence with these proportions will yield A an average outcome of +1/7 no matter what B does.

A similar argument and calculation could be made for person B. His best mixed strategy is to choose b_1 four-sevenths of the time and b_2, three-sevenths. This rule will yield him an average outcome of −1/7. It is the minimax theorem of game theory (Luce and Raiffa, 1957) that these two sequential rules are in equilibrium—that they represent the best each person can do in the face of the other's conflicting efforts. B minimizes the maximum loss A can impose on him and A maximizes the minimum gain B can restrict him to. It may be appropriate to remind the reader that the randomized sequential strategy, calculated as described above, is appropriate only for patterns in which the dominant component is MBC, as in Case III in Figure 6.14. The interested reader is referred to Appendix 3 of Luce and Raiffa (1957) for a summary of the three cases and other related ones.

The Modifiability of Sequential Transformations.   It is difficult to believe that a person would adopt a sequential rule for some purpose, for example, to sample the minor diagonal in the symmetric game in Figure 6.13 and then stick with it even though he found that his partner's sequential rule was yielding a sampling of the major diagonal. Ordinarily such policies are highly modifiable in the light of their early consequences. Clearly, the sequential rule has no intrinsic property that requires its persistent pursuit, once adopted, regardless of the results. (In this respect the alternatives in the 6 × 6 matrix probably differ from ordinary behavioral alternatives. The latter ordinarily acquire some irreversibility or commitment during their enactment.) In view of this modifiability of sequential rules it is reasonable to assume that they are adjusted in successive interactions and that these adjustments are made on the basis of the rule(s) the partner seems to be following. Similarly, once a person has learned what the various consequences are and can assume that his partner has similar sophistication, these adjustments can be made in advance by a "vicarious trial and error" process. In this, the person reasons somewhat as follows: "If I follow rule 1, my partner will find it advantageous to follow rule 6. In that case I'll find it desirable to shift to 3 and he'll shift to 4 and that will be O.K. with me. So I might as well start out with 3 and he'll either start with 4 or shift to it when he sees what I'm doing." Indeed, because of their modifiability, the adoption of sequential rules is essentially a matter of agreement between the two persons. This is obvious for rules that serve their common interest such as alternation which permits turn taking. However, it is even true, although in a slightly different sense, for the rules that protect each person's interests in a constant-sum game. The adoption of simple or mixed strategies that are in equilibrium at least indicates that the two persons see the relationship in the same way. It also suggests a kind of convergent conversation of the type above.

Sequential Transformations in the Service of Outcome Transformations

We noted earlier that sequential transformations do not change the shape of the plot of points (Figure 6.13), but they do make it possible for the distortions produced by outcome transformations to yield different *effective* matrices than they would otherwise. This results from the fact that sequential rules yield new points within the domain of the *given* plot that better satisfy various criteria, such as *min diff* or *max joint*. Therefore it seems reasonable to assume that sequential transformations are often used with various outcome transformations. This is described in Chapter 7.

THE CONSEQUENCES OF REPEATED PLAY

In most experimental research on interdependence matrices the subjects are required to make choices among their alternatives simultaneously and independently (without communication) and to do this repeatedly for a number of trials. Does this procedure affect the nature of the interdependence between the two persons? The answer has already been implied in the foregoing discussions, but because of the widespread use of this procedure it must be made explicit and given some emphasis. This is necessary to counteract the unfortunate tendency for investigators to analyze a game theoretically in terms of "one-shot play" and then to be surprised when repeated play does not conform empirically to their analysis. Our point is, of course, that the procedure of repeated play transforms the pattern of interdependence. As a result the choices facing a person in simple, single-trial play in a *given* matrix may be quite different from those he faces in the transformed matrix generated by repeated play.

The course of interaction over repeated trials can be exceedingly complex. Even for a simple interdependence pattern (e.g., MFC), what the two persons manage to communicate, how they succeed in influencing each other, and how their motivations and intentions wax and wane can be very different from one pair to another. Therefore it is impossible to analyze in simple terms the exact transformational effects of repeated play. We can, however, illustrate some of the possible components of this transformational process and explain some of the ways in which the interdependence may be modified.

One aspect of repeated play is that it makes possible a detection of the outcome transformation the partner is making and a corresponding adjustment in one's own transformation. As shown in Chapter 7, the outcome transformation that a person should make (in terms of achieving high *given* outcomes) is contingent in part on the transformation the partner adopts. With one-shot play one can only make assumptions about the partner and act accordingly. With repeated play, one is faced with what is effectively a coordination problem of adapting one's choice criterion to the one the partner seems to be following.

Perhaps the most obvious aspect of repeated play is that it affords a person the opportunity to decide in advance on a specific policy for his successive choices. The *effective* interdependence matrix for him at that point is the one constituted by the various rules available to him, those available to his partner, and the consequences of various pairs of rules. Figure 6.12 is illustrative of this effective matrix. As we have noted, the outcome pattern in this "rule matrix" depends on the *given* matrix in which the repeated play occurs. When the *given* matrix is characterized by considerable interdependence (i.e., when the BRC component is relatively small), the matrix of sequential rules is characterized by considerable MBC. Thus in Figure 6.12 the consequences of the nonrepetitive rules depend to a great degree on the rule the partner adopts. (The repetitive rules are appropriate only when one or both persons have dominant RC. An exception among the nonrepetitive rules is randomization, but this is a defensive way to avoid the implications of the interdependence that is appropriate only for a subset of the constant-sum matrices.) In brief—and this general idea will be intuitively clear to the player—the sequence one must follow for good outcomes depends on the sequence one's partner follows. This is true even for MFC in which your outcomes are totally under your partner's control. With repeated play your problem is not simply whether to use your FC to the partner's benefit or detriment (as it is in one-shot play) but rather it is how to use your FC to induce your partner to use his FC to your benefit. For this conversion of FC to BC, it is necessary to make sure that the partner experiences only (or mainly) outcomes from the main diagonal of the MFC matrix (see Figure 6.8), that is, that he be rewarded only when he rewards you and not otherwise. How to do this obviously depends on what he does; for example, for the limited set of rules specified in Figure 6.12 only certain combinations yield the main diagonal. The point is that even though the *given* matrix is an MFC pattern the person's problem is one of coordinating with the partner in a sequential pattern of choices. Effectively, the person is in an MBC situation.

Another aspect of repeated play (and one related to the sequential effects above) is that it makes possible something akin to a transpositional transformation of the given matrix. In the course of repeated play a person often has some opportunity to indicate his intention to match or not match his partner's choice. If he succeeds in doing so, a double transposition of the given matrix is made possible. Using MFC as one example, we can see in Figure 6.15 that, when person A makes a ,commitment to match, B has RC in the effective matrix. B ensures himself a reward by helping A because A automatically returns the favor. In repeated play, if A can manage to make his choice each time after first seeing B's, he will find it fairly easy to communicate his commitment. The same is true for repeated play in which the two persons alternate in making their separate choices (as is easily done with decomposed versions of the PDG). Person A shows his intention to match B simply by always choosing the action previously chosen by B. Problems develop only if B is trying to communicate a similar intention, in which case they may become locked-in on an exchange of nonrewarding choices. In repeated play involving *simultaneous* and independent choices (a common experimental procedure) the matching commitment is more difficult to convey because

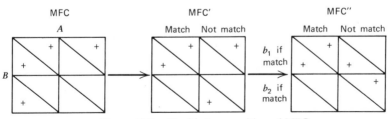

Figure 6.15   Double transposition of MFC.

on trial N person A can only match B's choice on trial $N - 1$. Thus paired with B's *current* response is an action that matches his *prior* response, a fact that he is likely to overlook. Thus the communication of commitment that is necessary to accomplish the double transposition involves a good deal of noise and ambiguity.

In general, these illustrations suggest that repeated play tends to transform the *given* matrix. The transformation is not simple in form and many ambiguities are involved. A person will have difficulty in determining the policy his partner is following and in communicating his own policy. A major source of confusion will be in sorting out the portion of his partner's behavior that reflects his policy and the portion that reflects his reactions to one's own actions. We might expect more efficient achievement of understanding if one person is more strongly guided by a policy intention and the other is more reactive and open to influence. Some of the communication and attribution problems alluded to here are considered in Chapter 8.

The effect of repeated play on game behavior has been impressively documented by Shure and Meeker (1968). Subjects playing repeated trials of the PDG yielded about 50% competitive choices, which is close to the typical rate of such behavior in experiments using this procedure. In contrast, subjects playing under the same conditions but believing they were paired up with a new partner on each trial (the series thus constituting a succession of one-shot games) yielded a competitive choice rate of more than 80%. As the authors note, the latter is more in conformity with the one-play logic of the game which is to take the dominant (RC-favored) choice. At the other extreme are results presented by Deutsch (1958) for a procedure involving reversibility of choices. The PD game used was one that yielded a competitive choice rate of about 65% under standard simultaneous choice conditions. The reversibility procedure permitted each person to make tentative choices which could then be changed until both persons, knowing both choices, were satisfied. Under standard "individualistic" motivational conditions this procedure yielded a competitive choice rate of only 23%. We may suggest that the reversibility procedure permitted a player to communicate his intention to match the partner which then produced the *effective* matrix of the doubly transposed PDG (Figure 6.11).

7

Origin and
Evocation of
Transformations

ABSTRACT

This chapter considers the factors that are broadly responsible for the occurrence of transformations. At the outset an analysis is made of the functional value of the transformations described in Chapter 6 as applied to the salient patterns of interdependence identified in Chapter 4. This analysis identifies the functional bases for learning to make, under certain conditions, particular transformations for particular patterns of the given *matrix. A subsequent section briefly considers the conceptual problems associated with interpreting behavior as providing evidence of transformations. We then discuss the evidence bearing on situational factors that evoke or elicit various types of transformation. A brief review is made of evidence pertaining to the existence of individual differences in transformational tendencies. A final section points to the general theory of self-regulation of motivation that is implied by the present special theory of transformations in contexts of social interdependence.*

In Chapter 6 we have analyzed the ways in which certain simple transformations modify the *given* matrix and create different interdependence problems for the dyad. We described a range of possible effects of transformations—possibilities that depend on the transformation or combination of transformations that each person makes and on their *given* relationship. In the present chapter we move from possibilities to actualities. We first continue the theoretical analysis by examining the potential benefits the two persons may gain from making certain transformations. This analysis of the functions served by transformations provides the basis for speculations about how interdependent persons learn to make them.

FUNCTIONS OF TRANSFORMATIONS

Why would interdependent people not behave according to the outcomes in the *given* matrix but instead transform it in some manner by treating it as if it were some other matrix? In our approach to this question we consider the functional values various transformations have for the individual. The benefits a person can derive from making a given transformation provide a basis for that transformation to be learned as a value, enacted under appropriate conditions, and maintained without sermons or examples. Also, of course, the experience of these benefits may heighten the person's imitativeness of others who manifest similar transformations and may lend credibility to moral lectures.

The strategy of our analysis is to examine a diverse sample of patterns of interdependence and to consider the advantages there might be for a person or pair of persons to adopt a given transformation. On the assumption that our sample of patterns adequately represents the learning situations in which, *in general* (across different cultures, social strata, and family and personal circumstances), such values might be acquired, the results of the analysis suggest the transformations that generally exist in human social life. In a later section, we raise the possibility of identifying different patterns of experience in interdependent relationships that generate individual differences in favored transformations.

It is possible to distinguish two major functions that transformations may serve for the individual. First, they may *provide a basis for action* where none exists in the *given* matrix. The transformed matrix may have RC' or BC' along with the partner's RC' where the *given* matrix has neither (neither RC nor BC with partner's RC). (As in Chapter 6, RC' refers to reflexive control in the transformed matrix and RC, to reflexive control in the *given* matrix.) Second, they may enable the person more certainly to *attain better given outcomes* than he would otherwise. By following his RC' or BC' the person may obtain better outcomes *in the given matrix* than he would have if he had acted merely according to the RC or BC terms in the *given* matrix.

An example provided by MFC is shown in Figure 7.1. If each person makes a *max joint* transformation, he has RC' (favoring his first behavior) where in the orginal matrix he had none. If both persons act according to

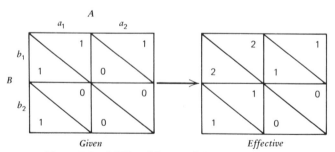

Figure 7.1   MFC and its *max joint* transformation.

their RC' values, each is assured of getting his best *given* outcome (+1), whereas in the absence of transformation his outcome is uncertain and may be 0.

In the manner illustrated by this example we examined the consequences of a variety of transformations, specifically *max joint, max other, max rel, min diff, min other,* transpositions in which self or other goes first, and sequential transformations. This was done for the 22 matrices identified in Chapter 4 as salient, representing diverse regions and landmarks within the domain of 2 × 2 matrices. (The reader is referred to p. 109 for a list of these matrices and for references to the figures in which they appear.) We focused this analysis on matrices in which RC is absent and/or in which mutual following of RC results in poor *given* outcomes for one or both persons. In each case we determined what the consequences were for the individual who made a particular transformation when his partner made the same transformation or a different one (or none).

The Functional Value of Prosocial Transformations

The analysis reveals first that it is *mutually desirable* for the pair of persons to make certain transformations under certain conditions of interdependence. With mutual fate control, as shown above, and with fate control and behavior control (one person subject to FC, the other to BC), if both persons make the *max joint* or *max other* transformation, each has RC' or BC' coupled with partner's RC'. If followed by both, this yields them their best *given* outcomes. In Chicken these same two transformations provide RC' when none is present in the given matrix, and in PDG they shift the reflexive control from the D to the C action. If the resulting RC' values are followed, in the case of PDG both persons receive more than they would have by following RC and in the case of Chicken, they avoid the lowest outcomes in the matrix and receive the next to the highest. Because these transformations do not yield the best outcomes in these latter cases, perceiving their benefits might be somewhat more difficult than in the preceding cases. Thus for PDG a person might require some experience with the low outcomes generated by mutual adherence to RC before he could fully appreciate the gains to be had in, say, a *max joint* transformation.

With regard to the transpositional transformations, the correspondent mutual behavior control pattern makes it mutually desirable that *someone* (either A or B) act first and the FC–BC pattern makes it mutually desirable that a particular one (the one exercising the BC) do the same. In both cases the effect of the proper first action is to provide the second person with

RC' which, if followed, will be to their mutual benefit. It is true for both patterns that in the absence of transposition each person's outcomes are uncertain. Thus there is a basis in these patterns for persons to learn that if they have BC over their partner it is beneficial to take the initiative in the interaction. Of course, counterinstances are provided by non-correspondent mutual behavior control, and the rule should be learned as being adaptive only in the case of correspondence.

A transformation involving coordinated sequencing is found to be functional for the turn-taking game shown in the upper part of Figure 7.2. Without some transformation A and B both get nothing at a_2b_2 by following their RC values. A sequential transformation in which they shift between a_1b_2 and a_2b_1 permits them to divide up 12 units in various proportions, depending on the ratio of a_1b_2 to a_2b_1 occurrences. When *max joint* and *min diff* transformations are also introduced, the pair of persons has a basis for agreeing to coordinate on a_1b_2 and a_2b_1 in *some way* (to *max joint*) and, specifically, to coordinate with a strict alternation or turn-taking pattern (to *min diff*). Once the sequential transformation is made the problem is implicitly a bargaining one, and the further *max joint* plus *min diff* transformation provides the equivalent of a "prominent" solution (in Schelling's sense, 1960) to that problem.

This transformation "package," of sequential shifting guided by *max joint* and *min diff*, is mutually beneficial for a number of patterns similar to the turn-taking game, including Battle of the Sexes and Hero (also shown in Figure 7.2). The common component in these cases is correspondent MBC but the turn-taking configuration stems from the discordant MFC and/or BRC components.

Another setting in which the *min diff* transformation has functional value, though in a different way, is the threat game. This situation has been described by Thibaut and Faucheux (1965) as requiring an agreement between the allocator and the threatener in which the former agrees to be just if the latter is loyal. This, of course, amounts to the one making a *min diff* transformation and the other, a *max joint* transformation. As in the turn-taking game, fulfilling the *min diff* criterion requires a sequential shifting, though with the difference that only the allocator must shift, and there is no need for coordination to attain the sequential transformation. The basic similarity between the turn-taking and the threat games is shown by the transposition of the latter in Figure 7.3. By insisting that the allocator (A) always makes his choice first before he himself decides what to do, the threatener (B) can transpose the threat game into the turn-taking game. It is to B's advantage to make the transposition because it then creates the configuration in which there are mutual benefits to be derived from the sequential and *max joint* plus *min diff* transformations.

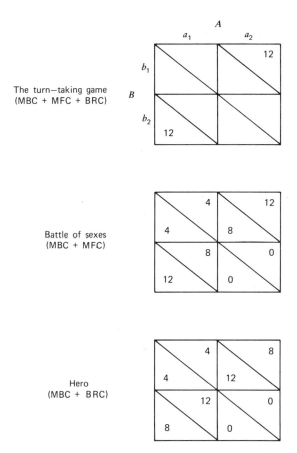

Figure 7.2   Some patterns in which a sequential transformation and *max joint* plus *min diff* are mutually desirable.

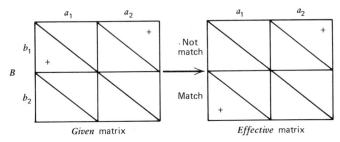

Figure 7.3   By transposition the threat game becomes the turn-taking game.

The preceding analysis has focused on the positive benefits to be gained from making certain transformations of the *given* matrix. By implication this analysis reveals the function of transformations in avoiding costly conflict and the aggressive retaliatory sequences that follow from unfair exchanges. A more complex analysis would deal with the cost–avoidance functions more directly but would require more differentiated matrices, both in behavior alternatives and outcome levels, and more consistent distinctions between the rewards and costs of interaction. An analysis of this sort would highlight the anxiety–avoidance motives that often are involved in learning to make prosocial transformations.

It may be important to note here that in our analysis the *max other* criterion is never found to have greater functional value than the *max joint* criterion. In other words, these patterns of social interdependence do not suggest that there is any unique basis for learning pure altruism as contrasted with a "general welfare" outlook in which the "general welfare" includes one's own interests.

The Learning of Prosocial Transformations

From the preceding illustrations we see that for some patterns of interdependence there is mutual benefit from *max joint* and *max other* transformations, for other patterns there is mutual benefit from transpositional transformations, and for still other patterns, from a sequential *max joint–min diff* package of transformations. In each case the mutual interest provides a basis for possible discussion and agreement about making the particular transformations and subsequently for experiencing their benefits. These situations seem ideally suited to concept and value learning, for the discussion is likely to make explicit the conceptual aspects of the transformations and, by raising the specter of the poor consequences of action in the untransformed matrix, to instill a positive evaluation of the transformations.

The foregoing scenario suggests that the learning of mutually desirable transformations occurs in explicit discussion. This would, of course, include the tutelage of a naïve or imperceptive interactor by one more sophisticated or sensible. The question naturally arises whether a person who has insight into the mutual desirability of transformations can induce a partner to make them without explicit communication, wholly by actions within the relationship. It must be noted first that, in a number of matrices with a mutual interest in prosocial transformations, if one person acts according to such a transformation, the other is better off by acting according to his own *given* outcomes than by adopting a similar transformation. This important phenomenon is discussed when we consider the functionality of egoistic transformations. The problem is epitomized by the PDG in which the person who acts according to a *max joint* or *max other* criterion is exploited by the person who acts according to *max own* (no transformation) or *max rel*. It is also apparent that making the first move necessary for a sequential transformation need not clearly convey to the partner the desirability of entering into a turn-taking sequence. The outcomes he gains from having a first turn may encourage him to expect more without having to reciprocate. (One wonders here about the *unlearning* that may sometimes be necessary in relation to the belief that other persons will *max other* while oneself can continue to *max own*, a belief based on the child's early experiences with benevolent parents.)

The conclusion to be drawn from these considerations seems to be that prosocial transformations can probably not be taught (or, at least, not effectively) by pure interaction without the benefit of explicit communication. This seems true for *max joint* and *max other* in certain mixed motive games and for the sequential transformation in other mixed-motive (turn-taking) games. The single exception seems to be the "going first" transposition in the highly correspondent MBC and FC–BC patterns. Here there is a common interest in the proper exercise of initiative and no possibility of exploiting its occurrence.

That certain prosocial transformations cannot be taught effectively by interaction without communication does not, of course, preclude the possibility that such transformations can be learned by observation and modeling (Bandura, 1969). The example of dyads who obtain good *given* outcomes by taking into account their effect on each other may provide the observer with much the same basis for valuing such "taking into account" as does his own experience in dyads. Furthermore, once learned, a transformation may be evoked by the example of the partner's behavior. The person well inculcated with the norm of reciprocity will find the partner's beneficent first move to be a clear signal to initiate sequential turn taking.

Domain of Functional Value of Prosocial Transformations

As we have seen, the *max joint* and *max other* transformations are useful for games with prominent MFC components (MFC, PDG, Chicken); that is, for the "exchange" games. The sequential *max joint–min diff* package of transformations is useful for games with a prominent MBC component and discordant additional components (turn-taking, Battle of the Sexes, and Hero), which may be described as the "bargaining" games. Transpositions are functional for simple coordination games, best exemplified by correspondent MBC. What has been implicit should now be made explicit, that the highly noncorrespondent patterns and the other correspondent ones (based on BRC + MFC) involve no mutual interest in prosocial transformations. In the perfectly correspondent combination of BRC and MFC and in the disjunctive and conjunctive cooperative games, without the conflict of interest and without a need for coordination (both persons have RC), there is nothing to be gained from transformations. The same is true of the maximizing difference game and Martyr. In the high conflict of interest patterns (noncorrespondent MBC, noncorrespondent BRC + MFC) and the several patterns of unilateral dependence there is no *mutual* interest in making any of these transformations and therefore, no basis for a negotiation of transformations. The settings, then, in which prosocial transformations may be learned are primarily the relationships characterized by interdependence and intermediate degrees of correspondence—the mixed motive relationships in which individual interests neither fully coincide nor are in complete conflict with each other. These patterns of interdependence are probably common in human social life.

The Functional Value of Egoistic Transformations

Under certain conditions a person finds it beneficial to make no transformation or an egoistic one. Depending on the pattern and the criterion the partner is following, the person may find that his own *given* outcomes are higher if he follows a *max own* criterion (no transformation) than if he adopts a prosocial criterion, and he may find similar profit in a *max rel* transformation or a preemptive transposition.

In Chicken and the Battle of the Sexes, if person B is simply maximizing his own outcome and A makes a *max rel* transformation which he *makes known to B*, A will get a better *given* outcome than otherwise. The shift in relationship is shown in Figure 7.4 for Chicken. The *max rel* transformation gives A a clear basis for action (RC'), and knowing that, B will presumably follow his BC'. These same two patterns also permit one person to get his *best given* value, if circumstances permitting, he is able to make a preemptive transposition. Thus these patterns in which correspondent MBC is combined with discordant MFC may provide experience that will encourage the display of a tough and competitive stance in which outdoing the other is valued and there is a commitment to the means of doing so. In Chapter 10 we discuss a related fact—that the person may benefit from conveying a firm intention to follow the *max rel* criterion on a contingent basis, that is, unless the partner meets certain conditions. This occurs in connection with the use of threat in bargaining.

By and large, the most effective threat action is one that gives the threatener the greatest advantage over the other person. In his experience in identifying such actions and communicating a contingent commitment to them the person may learn the wisdom of scanning bargaining problems in terms of the *max rel* criterion.

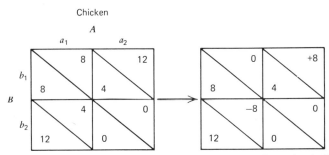

Chicken

Figure 7.4   Change in pattern when *A* alone adopts a *max rel* transformation in Chicken.

Chicken and PDG have the property that if *B* makes a *max joint* or *max other* transformation and *A* merely follows *max own* he gets his best *given* outcome. (Battle of the Sexes has the same consequence if *B* makes a *max other* transformation. The same is true for the threatener in the threat game and for either person in the turn-taking game. In neither of the last two, however, is there any reason for the partner to make a *max other* transformation.) What is particularly significant in Chicken and PDG is that these patterns create (a) a mutual desirability for a prosocial *max joint* or *max other* transformation and (b) a unilateral advantage for the person whose partner makes such a transformation but who himself continues to use the egoistic *max own* criterion. There is, in these patterns, the opportunity to learn to discriminate what value transformation the partner is making and to act accordingly. If he is acting egoistically, there is mutual benefit in encouraging a bilateral *max joint* transformation, but if he is already acting according to the prosocial criterion there is personal benefit in focusing exclusively on own outcomes.

The other side of the coin is that the person who makes the prosocial transformation in the face of the partner's egoistic action suffers low outcomes in the *given* matrix. They are low in the absolute range of outcomes and, of course, low in relation to what might be attained by interaction with another person who also makes a prosocial transformation. Rather similar are the examples mentioned earlier (Chicken and Battle of the Sexes) in which a person benefits from *max rel* when the partner simply persists in *max own*. The latter receives a smaller outcome than he might find reasonable to expect from the relationship.

The Tension Between Prosocial and Egoistic Transformations

The foregoing analysis shows that interdependence relationships provide settings in which, by virtue of the rewards they yield the individual, both prosocial and egoistic transformations may be learned. In two respects the learning must involve discrimination: (a) learning to make a transformation appropriate to the *given* interdependence pattern and (b) learning to make a transformation appropriate to the partner's current or potential transformation. The latter is of particular importance because, as we have seen, in certain situations there are losses to be sustained by being more prosocial (or less competitive) in one's transformations than is one's partner. At the same time potential gains may go unrealized by failure to perceive the partner's readiness for a joint move to prosocial transformations. The counterposed aspects of the situation are complex. Both persons may gain by such a joint move, but one may gain even more if he can meet the partner's prosocial transformation with an egoistic one. However, that may be only a short-run advantage if its effect is to discourage the partner from continuing the transformation, in which case the possibilities of mutual gain in a joint prosocial orientation may be delayed or even made impossible. Aware of these opposing considerations, the socially sophisticated individual will experience a tension between prosocial and egoistic transformations. As we describe in Chapter 8, in his attempt to resolve this tension wisely, he will be deeply concerned with the attributional problems of inferring the partner's actual and potential transformations and the presentational problems of creating a proper image of his own actual and potential transformations.

The Functional Approach

The preceding analysis provides a scenario both for the collective experience of interdependent people and for the individual experience of each person. In the course of social history mankind will have developed beliefs about the value of various behavioral rules and choice criteria, beliefs that reflect the benefits of these rules and criteria in reducing, under certain conditions, intrapersonal uncertainty and interpersonal conflict. These beliefs will be reflected in the moral and practical teachings of each human group and society. In the course of his own life history, as he moves through a variety of interpersonal relationships, the individual will experience the same benefits of these rules and criteria. Because of their availability in the common beliefs, he need not discover them anew. If well formulated and communicated, the rules reflected in the shared beliefs will afford him convenient guides for working out conflict-avoidant and outcome-optimizing agreements with his counterparts. Thus, being considerate of other persons' needs and helping them attain their goals will often be found necessary in order to obtain the cooperation from them that the individual desires. Furthermore, the elders and authorities in his group will urge the beliefs on him, reward his adherence to them, and even, on occasion, insist that he follow them. The elders have a direct interest in his adoption of the beliefs, not only as they affect his interaction with them but also as they affect his interaction with his peers (as when the mother invokes turn taking between her children in order to reduce conflict that is costly to herself as well as to them). If the social teachings are appropriate for the types of interdependence relationship and the other persons that the individual encounters, he will find that the social beliefs are confirmed by his experience. The social principles his parents recommend will prove to be useful in practice. From their beneficial consequences and the social incentives provided for their adoption the individual is likely to internalize the rules and criteria, gaining some satisfaction or dissatisfaction from his adherence or nonadherence to them that is independent of their instrumental efficacy in any particular interaction.

Our argument here is a functional one—that the patterns of interdependence make possible and, indeed, even require the learning of value transformations. Because of their good consequences for him, in terms of his basic *given* outcomes, the individual learns to deal with the *given* pattern of interdependence as if it were a different pattern. This learning is reflected in his tendencies to apply action criteria that take account of the partner's outcomes and to follow certain rules of timing and sequencing in interaction.

Our approach is "functional" in the sense stated by Ralph Turner in an unpublished manuscript:

> Ideas, concepts, and imagery develop, persist, and seem vitally real because in some fashion they help to facilitate action. Concepts arise because using them makes a difference to those who employ them. This is an application of the fairly commonplace functional approach employed by such students as Dewey . . . and Malinowsky . . .

Our conclusion from this functional analysis is to be contrasted with views that emphasize exclusively the prosocial or egoistic nature of man. In our examination of the interdependence conditions for the acquisition of social concepts and motives we find no basis for concluding that altruistic or cooperative orientations are learned to a greater degree than selfish and competitive ones. Ashley Montague asserts that

> . . . the reproductive process is a cooperative one, and, in addition, development as one of a litter or group of siblings represents another early experience in the development of co-operation; development within a family represents a still further experience in the learning and practice of co-operation (1951, p. 46).

If our matrices can be taken as representing the patterns of inter-dependence within heterosexual relationships, between siblings, and within families, we are required to disagree with Montague. If these relationships include the dilemmas, conflicts, mixed interests, and types of control reflected in the matrices (and we believe they do), it seems more reasonable to conclude that they *also* provide experiences in the learning and practice of distrust, competitiveness, and exploitation. At their best the fruits of such learning are represented by an individual flexibly and appropriately capable of both cooperative and competitive behavior.

Our analysis has focused on interdependence patterns as sites for acquiring socially relevant values and behavioral tendencies, including an "altruistic" concern for the outcomes of others. The analysis assumes that initially the person has an interest only in his own outcomes. It is possible, as certain evolutionary theorists have argued (e.g., Hamilton, 1964; Trivers, 1974), that some of the prosocial transformational tendencies are innate and therefore present without the kind of learning we have envisioned. We are in no position at present to specify the links between these two approaches to the origins of prosocial behavior. A basic similarity may be noted, however. The Trivers argument begins with the "mixed-motive" relation that exists between parent and offspring because they share some genes but not others. Whereas each organism has an interest, so to speak, in perpetuating all of its own genes (this being true from the viewpoint of natural selection processes), the partial overlap of genes creates a selection pressure for behavioral tendencies that are partly prosocial and partly egoistic. Thus there is a selection for some parental behavior that is altruistic toward the offspring (e.g., initiating nurturant behavior during its vulnerable early life) but also for some self-interested behavior (e.g., rejecting the offspring during weaning which serves to preserve the mother's health so that she may pass on her genes to further progeny). The rough parallels to our analysis, which points to the mixed-motive relationship as the crucial learning site and implies the desirability of learning conditional behavior rules, will be apparent to the reader. It is not inconceivable that the parallels are closer. Thus the demands of interdependent social life that "select" for certain behavior tendencies in the course of the individual's life may also have selected genetically for humans with those tendencies or, at least, with the aptitude for readily learning them.

EVIDENCE OF TRANSFORMATIONS

As noted briefly in Chapter 1, the necessity for developing a theory of the *effective* matrix and of the transformation processes that link it to the *given* matrix is created by evidence that people commonly act in ways that are inconsistent with their own immediate outcomes as specified in the externally defined payoff structure of their relationship. As one of his propositions about social motivation, McClintock (1972b) states that ". . . the attractiveness of outcomes for one actor may be influenced not only by the outcomes he receives, but also the outcomes which he judges the other(s) will receive" (p. 444). As exemplary evidence for this proposition McClintock refers to consistent observations from the maximizing difference game that subjects choose the (counter-RC) alternative that, from the point of view of the given values, is irrational. They do so because they ". . . define the value of outcomes to themselves not in terms of the absolute number of points each receives, but in terms of how many points more or less than the other player they attain" (p. 444); that is, they use the *max rel* criterion. Given this definition of value, their choices in the game represent a rational strategy. McClintock's description of what we call the transformation process is that ". . . an individual actor establishes the final attractiveness of an outcome by considering and comparing both own and other's outcomes" (p. 445). He notes that four outcome orientations have been suggested by empirical studies: maximization of own gain, *max joint*, *max rel*, and *max other*.

In his important paper McClintock observes that choice behavior in a situation of interdependence may reveal what the person intrinsically values, his social motivation, *or* may be "a strategic response designed to affect the other's subsequent choices. . . ." McClintock proposes that a distinction be made between "choices that are means versus those that are ends," that is, between strategies and goals. In drawing this distinction, he implicitly raises the question: when can behavior inconsistent with the *given* matrix be taken as evidence of a transformation?

In considering this question, we must first make clear that the payoffs officially specified, as by a salary schedule or the experimenter's game rules, may not define the *given* matrix. It is obvious that two persons may attach different subjective values to the same objective outcomes; for example, because of different states of satiation and need, different general comparison levels, or different degrees of boredom or fatigue with the behaviors on which the rewards are contingent. The official schedule only partly defines the *given* matrix because it is also a function of various general psychological factors not related to the specific relationship. Thus differences in reactions to a given official schedule are not to be equated entirely with differences in transformations.

Setting aside that problem and assuming that we know the *given* matrix (at least, locally), the problem that McClintock raises is that behavior may depart from what is indicated by the *given* matrix either for strategic reasons or because of the person's social motivation. This is most clearly a problem if behavior is part of a continuing relationship in which there will be future interaction (the evidence bearing on this factor is presented in the next section). For example, a person who benefits from an initial allocation of rewards that favors him over his partner may be observed to modify the allocation toward a more equal one (as by a side payment to the partner). This action, however, may be profitable to the person in terms of his own interest, permitting him to establish and/or maintain good relations with his partner and thereby later to attain the goals involved in that relationship; it may also enable the person to gain a positive evaluation from some third person observing his actions and thereby promote a relationship with that person that will serve important purposes. The outcome-equalizing behavior is, according to this view, a strategy to promote own gains and not attributable to the intrinsic satisfactions derived from equal outcomes (i.e., to an internalized value corresponding to a *min diff* transformation).

In this analysis McClintock points to an important problem, although we are not comfortable with the terms in which he casts it. We believe the domain of social motivation should be expanded to include rules of turn taking and preemption as well as of giving weight to the partner's outcomes, that is, to include sequential and transpositional transformations as well as outcome transformations. This expansion of the domain would incorporate with it certain acts that McClintock would view as strategic; for example, when one person gives the other a first turn with the expectation of having the second turn. We grant that the first turn may be merely strategic, but it may also reflect the fact that turn taking is valued in and of itself, just as maximizing the joint welfare may be.

Most important in our analysis of the functional value of transformations is the suggestion that the means-end distinction will generally be blurred. From the *actor's* point of view and in terms of the dynamics of the choice situation there is usually no question whether a transformational rule is followed for strategic ends or because it is valued in and of itself. Both consequences are typically involved because the rules (as the central concept we prefer rule to goal or motive) define modes of behavior that are both effective and good. The strategy–goal dichotomy reflects the common dilemma of the *partner* when, uncertain about the future of the relationship, he wonders whether to attribute behavior to the situation (available means for satisfying personal interests) or to the person (stable motives). The partner's question does not necessarily provide the most fruitful distinction for the scientist, although perhaps because he shares the observer perspective with the partner he is likely to adopt it.

With regard to the operational problem of what constitutes evidence of a transformation we find more useful the question of the *total given matrix* within which behavior is to be interpreted. What is the real game—the bigger game, if any—that the person is playing? Is cooperative behavior in the PDG to be taken as reflecting a *max joint* transformation, elicited strictly by the local structure of the PDG? (If so, the actor is likely to say that it is the good and moral way to deal with the interdependence problem *and* that it is the effective way for him to realize a good return from the game. To repeat, the ends versus means aspect of the rule will not be important to him.) Is the behavior to be taken as part of a larger game in which positive appraisal from the experimenter is thought to be attainable by cooperation (the 2 × 2 is imbedded in a larger N-person game) or in which future good relations with the partner are thereby ensured (the experimental series of interactions is imbedded in a more extended time frame)? In the latter case if we know enough about the larger *given* matrix we may be able to identify prosocial (and also egoistic) transformational tendencies in the behavior; that is to say, simply because a person treats the local game as part of a larger one does not mean that he is necessarily pursuing only his self-interest (making no transformation) in the larger context. Rules of *max joint*, turn taking, and so on, are just as appropriate in a subject's relations to the experimenter or in his extended relationship with the partner as they are within the local confines of the experimental game itself.

In general, then, we suggest that the appropriate question is whether the person is acting (and possibly making a transformation) with respect to the outcomes in the locally defined matrix or whether he is acting (and possibly making a transformation) with respect to outcomes in a more extensive game, that is, a game involving relations with other partners and/or future interactions with the present partner. By the nature of social life this question is difficult to answer. It involves those whom the person believes to be the witnesses to his present behavior and what he suspects may be the lasting evidence of that behavior. So little social life occurs outside a larger social context (and, indeed, it may be none) that the experimenter's attempts to establish a context-free game situation run counter to the subjects' strong expectations and create puzzlement and incredulity. Perhaps our greatest interpretive error will be to assume that the narrow context usually encompassed by the investigator's analysis constitutes the total context governing the experimental subject's behavior.

EVOCATION OF TRANSFORMATIONS

In this section we consider the conditions under which transformations are evoked. These include the range of circumstances under which people are induced to behave in ways different from those indicated by the immediate *given* matrix. As indicated by the preceding discussion, it will not always be clear from the circumstances whether the divergent behavior reflects a transformation of that matrix or is oriented toward (and possibly involves a transformation of) the relationship as more extensively defined.

Information About Other's Outcomes

The transformation process is set in motion by information about the total pattern of interdependence, including both own and other's outcomes. As McClintock notes ". . . to the extent that an individual is unaware that he is in an interdependent relationship though he may be, he will assume an own gain orientation . . ." (1972b, p. 451). Beyond simple awareness of the interdependence, the person must have some conception of the relation between his own and his partner's outcomes. This conception may be based on direct evidence or on his expectations and beliefs about their respective outcomes for the given situation (see Chapter 8 on perceiving the *given* matrix).

A number of studies appear to demonstrate the arousal of a *max rel* transformation when each person has knowledge of his own and the other's outcomes. This seems to be clearly shown in the MDG, in which the cooperative choice promises to maximize both own and joint outcomes, whereas the competitive choice promises to maximize the difference between own and other's outcomes (*max rel*). Thus competitive choices are made at the expense of some loss of own absolute outcomes and reflect uniquely a motivation to gain an advantage over the other.

Increasing the salience of the difference between the two persons' scores also seems to evoke *max rel* more strongly. McClintock and McNeel (1966*b*) studied the effects in the MDG of displaying to each subject the cumulative scores of both self and other as compared with the cumulative scores for self only. The results are strong. Display of own and other's cumulative scores markedly increases the competitive response of choosing the *max rel* alternative. Here we must raise the issue discussed in the preceding section. The effect of the cumulative score feedback may reflect a process of imbedding the given game matrix in a broader one involving outcomes from the experimenter. This would be the proper interpretation of McClintock and McNeel's results (and would throw in question what transformation, if any, were being made) if it could be shown that the cumulative display constitutes an implicit message to the subjects that the experimenter is evaluating them in terms of who gets the higher score.

In considering further the tendency to choose the *max rel* alternative, it is not clear whether the aim of this choice is to move ahead or simply to catch up or avoid falling behind. If it is primarily the latter, then the motive might be better described in relation to *min diff*. Messick and Thorngate (1967) have developed an ingenious method for attempting to answer this question. A two-choice game that permits the subjects to opt for a relative gain was again used, and outcomes of both self and other were displayed after each trial of the game. In this experiment, however, the outcomes displayed to each of the two players were derived from different payoff matrices. In this way it was possible in one treatment (approach difference) to convey to each player that although he could never receive less than the other for any joint choice he could occasionally do better than the other. A subject's choice of the alternative affording this possibility is interpreted as reflecting a motivational orientation to surpass the other. In another treatment (avoid difference) each player perceived that although he could not surpass the other, one alternative gave him the possibility of falling behind. His avoidance of this move (i.e., his playing of the other move) then may be taken to reflect the strength of his motivation to stay even. The results show that the motivation to avoid falling behind is significantly greater than that of surpassing the other. Furthermore, the former increases over time and the latter remains constant at a relatively low level. Messick and Thorngate's results can be interpreted in terms of the combined effects of a strong *max rel* and a weak *min diff* tendency. These augment each other in the avoidance of falling behind and work against each other in the approach to gaining an advantage. Alternatively, the results may imply that the *max rel* transformation is nonlinear, similar to the nonlinear effects associated with the comparison level (Chapter 6).

One could pose the similar question: is there greater motivation to catch up if one finds himself behind or to stay ahead if one has the lead? In one approach to answering this question McClintock and McNeel (1966b) examined rates of making competitive (maximizing–difference) choices in the MDG when the display of the cumulative choices of both players showed the person to be behind the other one, ahead of him, or even. These proportions which reflected a competitive orientation were .40 for those behind, .44 for those ahead, and .12 for those who were even. American college-student subjects made .50 competitive responses when ahead and .35 when behind, whereas Belgian students made only .38 competitive responses when ahead and .45 when behind. The authors tentatively interpret these rates as indicating that the Americans were more strongly motivated to stay ahead than the Belgians, who were relatively more concerned about being behind. As the authors acknowledge, these data must be interpreted with caution. Factors responsible for being ahead or behind are confounded with the situation of being ahead or behind. It would seem preferable to make these comparisons for each person to assess the degree to which his rate of competitive choices changes as he moves from being ahead to being behind and vice versa. Even better would be to arrange experimentally for some subjects to be ahead and others to be behind. The latter approach has been taken by Marwell, Ratcliff, and Schmitt (1969).

Marwell et al. conducted an experiment in two stages. In the first stage two-thirds of the dyads (inequity condition) played a matrix game that systematically and inevitably gave higher monetary outcomes to one of the players; the remaining third of the dyads (equity condition) played a form of the same game that gave equal outcomes to the two players. In the second stage all dyads played the same MDG and everyone kept his first-stage partner. Cumulative scores (including first-stage scores) of both parties were presented on video. The dependent variable was frequency of competitive play in the MDG during the second stage.

In the inequity dyads those who found themselves behind were more likely than those ahead to take the action that gave them an advantage (i.e., enabling them to catch up). Those ahead did not, on the average, play less competitively than subjects in the equity condition. The former, however, were somewhat more tolerant of their partners' competitive moves, which is suggestive of a weak *min diff* orientation.

Using a similar method, Pepitone et al. (1970) obtained similar results in the PDG. American and Italian students made more competitive choices when they were arbitrarily caused to be behind than when they were caused to be ahead. Those ahead played somewhat less competitively (though not significantly so) than subjects in undifferentiated, control dyads. Transitional probability data, which might reflect tolerance of the disadvantaged person's attempts to catch up, are not available.

These studies provide some evidence, though not so strong as we might wish, of *min diff* transformation that leads the disadvantaged partner to initiate competitive behavior which tends to be unreciprocated by the advantaged member. *Max rel* in general seems to be a much stronger tendency in these experimental game settings, and the circumstances may not be the most favorable ones for observing the effects of *min diff*.

Salience of Destructive Aspects of Conflict

Earlier we saw that prosocial transformations have functional value only for patterns of intermediate correspondence. They are superfluous for patterns of high correspondence and nonfuctional (even detrimental to individual interest) for patterns of high noncorrespondence. On the assumption that their use is learned with this discrimination, transformations should be evoked most dependably for the intermediate, mixed-motive patterns. For more noncorrespondent patterns in which the possibilities of destructive conflict are more salient they cannot be counted on and explicit social processes will be necessary.

Typically, in gaming research no communication between the players is permitted either before play has begun or during the intervals between trials. When communication is not only permitted but encouraged, the subjects have the opportunity to negotiate plans that vicariously and imaginatively anticipate the consequences of alternative courses of action. From the argument above this negotiation should reflect the degree of conflict and be oriented toward ensuring the operation of prosocial transformations or rendering them unnecessary.

Bonacich (1972) has conducted an experiment in which such discussions were encouraged. A series of five-person groups played an extended version of the PDG for five trials under monetary incentives. On the first trial all of the groups played exactly the same game. On succeeding trials, however, half the groups ("high dilemma") were presented PDGs that increased sharply from trial to trial in outcome noncorrespondence, whereas in the remaining half ("low dilemma") the increase in noncorrespondence was slight. Thus the high dilemma groups experienced a sharp rise over time in the temptation to make the competitive (defecting, exploitative) move.

How did the high dilemma groups react to this potentially disruptive temptation? As Bonacich predicted, their reaction was to invoke strong normative forces to discourage self-aggrandizing and competitive behavior. In the discussion preceding each trial the high dilemma groups adjured one another not to acquiesce to temptation, characterizing competitive behavior in evaluative terms such as "cheat," "screw," "greed," and "fink." The frequency of use of such terms by these high dilemma groups remained high throughout the five trials, whereas in the low dilemma groups their use declined dramatically. Moreover, the high dilemma groups did in fact succeed in mobilizing a strong resistance to temptation. After each trial subjects were given this problem: "Assume that everyone in the group has agreed to cooperate. What is the minimum additional amount you would have to be offered before you would agree to make a . . . noncooperative choice? Assume that you cannot share this additional reward with the other members." After the first trial a relatively constant percentage of low dilemma group members, never more than 30%, said that they would have to be offered $20 or more to break the agreement to cooperate. Among the high dilemma members, however, this percentage increased steadily until by the last trial 82% would have to be offered $20 or more to break the agreement.

This experiment by Bonacich provides evidence that when planning and negotiation are possible the anticipation of the destructive consequences of conflict encourages the group to invoke moral norms that entail *max joint* transformations. Whether these transformations will be honored in the behavior of the group member depends on the degree of noncorrespondence of their outcomes: plainly the conflict of interest may become too intense to permit cooperative behavior. However, the process in the high dilemma groups may serve another purpose which is to imbed the PDG in a larger relationship (one that extends beyond the laboratory) in which correspondence is high enough that cooperative game behavior can be expected even in the absence of prosocial transformations. Thus labeling the competitive behavior in strongly negative terms may imply that a person had better not act in that manner if he values the positive regard of his associates outside the laboratory. In general, one way that social systems deal with local conflict is by imbedding it in larger patterns of interdependence in which there is greater overall correspondence of outcomes.

An effect similar to that of Bonacich appears in the earlier research of Thibaut and Faucheux (1965) and its subsequent variations (Thibaut, 1968), conducted in the setting of an asymmetrical relationship that is basically the threat game. Here, too, the negotiation and supplementation of transformations occurred mainly when the conflict of interest was critically high. When one member of the dyad was strongly tempted to be exploitative and self-aggrandizing and the other, disruptively disloyal, to defect, contractual agreements enforcing cooperation were negotiated by most of the dyads. These contracts involved a trade off between the first person's *min diff* and the second person's *max joint*. It was in this condition also—of high conflict of interest—that the parties agreed to impose the severest penalties for any contract violations. This is a clear case of imbedding the conflict situation in an extended one of greater common interest.

Future of the Relationship

Does anticipation of future interaction with a partner evoke a value transformation? Marlowe, Gergen, and Doob (1966) report two studies which suggest that it does. In their first study subjects played the PDG against a predominantly cooperative partner. Half the subjects anticipated that they would subsequently meet with their partners to ". . . discuss why you behaved as you did;" half had no expectation of a later meeting. Those who anticipated future interaction played more cooperatively in the PDG than those not anticipating further interaction. This finding suggests a straightforward effect of anticipated interaction in eliciting a *max joint* transformation. Of course, it may also be interpreted in terms of imbedding. The postgame discussion session enlarges the matrix within which the game choices are made.

The second study revealed a complexity. When personal characteristics of the opponent are revealed, this information may reverse the effects of anticipated interaction. When the partner is perceived to be humble and self-effacing, anticipated interaction works as it did in the first study to increase cooperation. When the partner is perceived to be egotistical and self-centered, however, one is less likely to cooperate with him when future interaction is anticipated than when it is not.

Results similar to those in the second study of Marlowe et al. are reported by Gruder (1971) in a bargaining study. When the opponent was perceived to be fair and reasonable, subjects bargained more cooperatively with him (made more concessions) if future interaction was anticipated than if it was not, but when the opponent was perceived to be exploitative and self-aggrandizing anticipation of future interaction had the opposite effect; there was less cooperation when interaction was anticipated than when it was not.

Hence from the last two studies it seems evident that anticipated interaction does not simply and generally elicit a *max joint* transformation. The transformation is contingent on perceived properties of the other person. Descriptively, the results of the two studies suggest that subjects take into account the properties of opponents whom they expect to meet and that this appraisal causes them to make the transformations in their experimental behavior that are appropriate to the larger relationship in which the game is imbedded. If they expect to meet another who is cooperative (humble, reasonable) this anticipation instigates a rehearsal of cooperative behavior entailing a *max joint* transformation. If they expect to meet another who is competitive (self-centered, exploitative), they begin to rehearse competitive behavior that entails a *max rel* transformation. In other words, they adapt to the transformation the partner is expected to make in the extended relationship just as subjects adapt to their partner's apparent transformations during game play (cf. below).

A different consequence of the extended game made possible by a future relationship is suggested by the Morgan and Sawyer (1967) experiment. Subjects were 10-to-12-year-old boys, all classmates. Pairs of friends and pairs of nonfriends bargained for monetary outcomes on a "bargaining board," which systematically favored one member of each pair. Generally, the pairs adhered to a norm of strict equality of outcomes (*min diff*). This was uniformly true for nonfriends, but it was true among friends only when the disadvantaged boy could inform his partner of his wish for equality. When information about the most desired settlement could not be transmitted, agreements between friends moved toward maximizing joint outcomes, with the advantaged boy gaining a larger share of the total outcome. A plausible interpretation is that friends (having a future of turn taking and exchange that works like a present side payment) are able to tolerate a momentary inequality, especially when it is created by an artificial advantage to one member that produces a larger joint outcome. The disadvantaged member is confident of being reimbursed later and the advantaged member feels no awkwardness about his future obligations; that is, about being forced to be nice later on. In brief, *max joint* can be given priority within the local game because the pair can assume that *min diff* will also, over subsequent interaction, be satisfied.

Evaluation Apprehension

Just as the context provided by anticipations of later encounters with the partner may evoke value transformations, so may that provided by the wider community, especially the community of peers, with whom relationships have both a future and a history and within which a "reputation" matters. When its presence is salient, physically or symbolically, and it communicates an evaluative message either explicitly or tacitly, dyadic members can be expected to respond with appropriate value transformations.

Some of these effects are shown in an experiment by Brown (1968). In a first phase male adolescents played the Deutsch and Krauss trucking game against a competitively programmed confederate. In the conditions relevant to the present discussion all subjects believed that they were being observed through a one-way mirror by a group of their classmates. At the conclusion of the first phase subjects received handwritten comments from the fictitious audience which described the subject as appearing either foolish ("weak," "a sucker") or not foolish ("fair," "played it straight").

In the second phase all subjects had an opportunity to retaliate: they now controlled the gate to the shorter one-way road and could charge tolls for passage through the gate. The charging of tolls, however, was costly to the subject himself, and the higher the toll, the greater the cost to self. Finally, half the subjects were led to believe that their opponent knew their costs for toll charging and half believed their opponents to be innocent of this knowledge.

The results show that when a person is made to look weak and foolish in full view of an audience of his peers he will retaliate strongly against the source of his humiliation. He will retaliate with heightened intensity when he believes his opponent is ignorant of his costs. If he knows that his opponent knows how badly the retaliation is hurting both of them, the zeal for it cools. When the audience reaction to him has been favorable (when he is viewed as fair), his retaliation is much reduced, although his opponent treated him just as badly as the humiliated subject.

It is tempting to conclude that public humiliation evokes a *min other* transformation because retaliation is made in the face of high cost to self; but since retaliation is suppressed when the opponent is aware of this high cost it may be more likely that the transformation aroused is *max rel*. When the audience evaluation is favorable, competitive transformations appear to be inhibited and a *max own* transformation is maintained, tinged (perhaps) with *max joint*.

Research by Madsen and his colleagues also suggests the effects of the peer culture on game behavior. Two examples of this research will suffice to illustrate the point. Madsen and Shapira (1970) studied groups of children of both sexes, 7 to 9 years old, from a rural Mexican village and from three urban Los Angeles samples: Mexican-American, Afro-American, and Anglo-American. Four children of the same sex and ethnic group were seated at the four corners of the Madsen Cooperation Board. A circle was located on the board near each child and a child won a prize each time a movable stylus crossed into his circle. Attached to the stylus were four strings each held by one of the children; therefore the stylus could be moved only if one or two of the children pulled his string while the others released theirs; any subset of the group could prevent the others from obtaining prizes. Hence only by coordinated action could prizes be won. The differences in the play of this game were dramatic. Groups from the three urban samples exhibited so much competitiveness that hardly any prizes were won. Groups from the rural village, however, showed a steadily increasing, systematic cooperation that yielded many prizes.

Using the same Cooperation Board, Shapira and Madsen (1969) studied 6-to-10-year-old Israeli children of both sexes, some from three different kibbutzim and some from a middle-class urban community. With a procedure similar to that used in the American study, the results again were clear cut. As in the Los Angeles samples, the urban children had great difficulty in coordinating, but the kibbutz children, like the rural Mexican children, quickly developed a systematic scheme for coordinating their actions. They also showed a great concern about equality in winning the prizes ("Everyone should get the same").

It seems reasonable to interpret the results of these two studies as reflecting normative pressures from preexisting and enduring relationships in the peer group (and possibly beyond). In the closely knit collective life of the kibbutz and the rural village norms that protect the welfare of the total group and that strongly discourage self-aggrandizing or exploitative behavior are likely to develop. In the city life is much less likely to be lived in an all-encompassing and monolithic enclave, and partners in an experimental session are likely to belong to only partly overlapping groups. Moreover, the norms that do develop will reflect the (putative) requirements for surviving in a city—the strength to compete in a succession of disparate encounters.

Hence it may be concluded that the extraexperimental context provided by urban life generally aroused a *max rel* transformation among the urban children. The rural and kibbutz children appear to be strongly under the control of a *max joint* transformation and also, particularly among the kibbutz children, a constraint toward *min diff*. Once again, however, the effects may reflect an imbedding of the experimental game in the larger game of life. The reputation one makes through game behavior, especially in the village, is likely to have implications for one's outcomes in extragame domains of interdependence.

A discussion of evaluation apprehension would be incomplete without raising the question of the effects of the subjects' perceptions of the experimenter's expectations. The experimenter is an omnipresent audience to game behavior and he can be assumed to be evaluating that behavior in terms of certain explicit criteria. Little is known about subjects' perceptions of these matters. Their interdependent relationship with the experimenter (whether his evaluation matters to them, whether he has any extragame power over them, what they sense to be his dependence on them) is particularly uncertain. Almost every dyadic experiment lends itself to interpretation in terms of the larger sub-ject–experimenter context within which the intersubject relationship exists. This problem has been perceptively discussed by Alexander and Weil (1969).

The Partner's Apparent Transformation

The theoretical analysis shows that the value of most transformations depends not only on the pattern of interdependence but also on the transformation the partner makes. Consistent with this is a great deal of experimental work on subjects' reactions to different programmed partners. The general result for the PDG (Oskamp, 1971) is that subjects respond somewhat competitively to consistently cooperative partners and strongly competitively to consistently competitive ones. The former probably reflects the joint effects of (a) the benefits in the *given* PDG matrix to be gained from using a *max own* or *max rel* criterion when the partner is using one that is *max joint* and (b) a tendency among some subjects to reciprocate a *max joint* transformation. The response to the consistently competitive partner is ambiguous regarding what trans-formation, if any, is involved. In the absence of alternative responses even the person who is interested in cooperation (*max joint*) may find it unacceptable to continue to attempt to cooperate in the face of the partner's persistent refusal to do so. The subject tends to be most coopera-tive when the programmed partner is cooperative but contingently so, depending on the subject's own cooperativeness. Thus, as would be expected from the mutual benefits to be gained from a bilateral *max joint* transformation, many subjects will shift toward cooperative behavior if the partner (a) refuses to be exploited and (b) shows willingness to be cooperative too.

One of the few studies in which transformations have been directly assessed during the course of interaction is that of Pruitt (1970). He found that subjects' description of their objectives as "helping the other person make as much money as possible," a *max other* criterion, increased over trials with cooperative input from the other and decreased over trials with competitive input. We may infer that the partner's behavior indicates his transformation (cf. Chapter 8) and, accordingly, that Pruitt's data show the process of adjusting one's own transformation to that of the partner.

Transformations Made by Social Models

Actors are influenced in their transformations not only by their partners but also by the transformations they observe social models to make. This is undoubtedly an important part of the process by which transformational tendencies are learned. The learning, as well as the subsequent evocation, is probably most effective when the model is in an interdependence situation similar to that subsequently facing the person himself. An illustration of the modeling process (and it is not clear whether it involves the *learning* of a transformation—as the investigators believe—or the *evocation* of one) is provided by an experiment by Aronfreed and Paskal, reported in Aronfreed (1968). These authors designed a "prototype" sequence of three phases that produced sympathetic behavior in 7-to-8-year-old girls. The girls individually performed a task requiring the pushing of one of three levers mounted on a choice-box to make a classification of various stimulus objects (toy replicas of real objects) according to whether they were most appropriate for a house (left lever), a dog (middle lever), or a school (right lever). The middle lever was in fact almost always inappropriate because the stimulus objects included almost no dog-relevant items.

Several experimental conditions were created, each consisting of three phases of activity. In the prototype condition designed to produce sympathetic behavior (and successful in doing so) the first phase was intended to link the child's own direct experience of pain with observed cues of another person's experience of the same distress. Child and experimenter sat opposite one another. Both wore earphones that were attached to the choice-box on the pretext of monitoring noise from within the box. The child was instructed that any noises that might occur would be louder in the experimenter's earphones than in her own. During some of the intertrial intervals following the child's classification decisions the child heard a highly aversive loud noise. The occurrence of this noise was unpredictable and not contingent on which lever was pushed. Just before the noise began the experimenter lowered her head in her hands as a distress cue (as though she could already hear the noise), continuing to show this cue until the noise heard by the child was terminated.

In the second phase of the prototype condition the child continued to wear the earphones. The experimenter, now without earphones, sat beside the child and used a second choice-box to make her own classifications after the child had made hers. She told the child that she might be able to use her box to turn off the noise that the child might continue to hear. Each time the child had made her classification of a toy replica the experimenter poised her hand over her own choice-box as though pondering her decision. The two outside levers were clearly the correct ones for almost all the toys and on half the classification trials the experimenter did choose an outside lever. On the other half the child again began to hear the unpredictable noise. On these trials the experimenter quickly pushed the middle lever, turning off the noise in the child's earphones and announcing that as her intention. Thus the experimenter's middle-lever response entails some small cost to her while relieving the child's considerable pain, as in Phase II of Figure 7.5.

The third phase of the prototype condition tested the child's tendency to reproduce the sympathetic response. Another girl, a trained confederate, now wore earphones. The subject, earphones removed, was assigned the role of using the second choice-box to classify each toy, following its classification by the confederate. For half the trials, just before the subject made her choice, the confederate placed her head in her hands, terminating this distress cue if the true subject made the task-inappropriate sympathetic choice of the middle lever. Choice of the middle lever during this third phase was thus the dependent measure of altruistic behavior. The subject's own middle-lever response entailed some small cost to her, while relieving the confederate's considerable pain, as in Phase III of Figure 7.5. The use of the middle response thus reflects a tendency to given consideration to the other person's outcomes, as in a *max other* transformation. Its use by the children experiencing the prototype series of events shows the influence of the model provided by

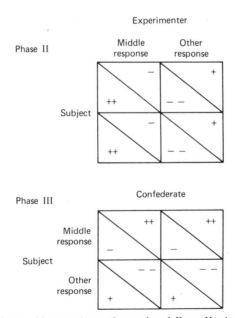

Figure 7.5   Two phases of the experimental procedure followed by Aronfreed and Paskal.

the experimenter's behavior in relation to the interdependence position in which the child later found itself.

Type and Amount of Incentive

In commenting on the research by Madsen and his associates, it was noted that different implicit meanings seemed to be attached to competition and cooperation at the two different kinds of site—urban and rural. Among the rural and kibbutz children there were likely to have been strong normative pressures that defined cooperation as the good and moral behavior and competition as bad and immoral. Among the urban children the predominantly aggressive behavior may have reflected a conception of social life in which the competitive response is the strong response necessary for survival and the *max rel* transformation is regarded as acceptable for a wide range of interpersonal situations.

These two orientations correspond to the two dimensions or factors that differentiated sites in a transnational study of negotiation conducted in three laboratories in Europe and five in the United States (Kelley, Shure, et al., 1970). The same experimental procedure was followed at all eight sites. Pairs of subjects were fully instructed in the rules and procedures of a bargaining game in which it was possible for each member to insure himself modest outcomes by direct unilateral action, but to attain large outcomes a cooperative strategy entailing a lengthened time perspective was necessary. Half the pairs at each site played for points and half played for rather substantial amounts of money. After the rules and procedures were clearly understood the subjects indicated privately on a series of bipolar scales how they expected the typical player would behave in the game and how they themselves expected to behave. These pregame ratings were factor analyzed to identify the main dimensions of "connotative" meaning (Osgood, Suci, and Tannenbaum, 1957). Two clear factors emerged: *evaluative* (E) and *dynamism* (D). Further analysis of these factors showed that cooperation versus competition had different connotative meanings at the different sites, reflected in the factor that the cooperative-competitive scale was associated with at a particular site. When associated with the E-factor, cooperation meant good, moral, and honest, whereas competition meant bad, immoral, and dishonest. When associated with the D-factor, cooperation meant weak and passive, whereas competition meant strong and active.

At all sites subjects cooperated more effectively under the money incentive than under points. They also cooperated more at sites characterized by dominance of the D-factor than at those dominated by the E-factor. Furthermore, it was observed that

... money tends to make the situation one in which cooperation-competition means *Dynamism* . . . rather than *Evaluation*. . . . This more subtle effect seems to be that the situation becomes a more instrumental or task-like one with *money* and more interpersonal or moral in its implications when the incentive is merely *points* (p. 434).

The moral orientation of the *E*-factor causes the person to construe a competitive response as being motivated by bad and immoral designs and such responses should be punished with indignation and self-righteousness. In the more instrumental orientation of the *D*-factor such responses mean that the other is making a strong and active attempt to deal with a difficult task and the counterresponse is likely to carry the same motivation. Similarly, under a point incentive the competitive response encodes the meaning that the other intends to beat you and perhaps even to humiliate you, whereas an opponent who makes a competitive response to gain money is more likely to be perceived to be under the control of a legitimate external pressure that carries no personal overtones.

It seems plausible that the types of relationship for which money* facilitates cooperation by giving an instrumental character to interpersonal strategies are those in which cooperative behavior dependably improves outcomes. When the cooperative alternative is the risky or vulnerable one, instrumental considerations will dictate the adoption of other, for example, competitive lines of action. This suggests two related hypotheses concerning the kinds of relationship in which the type of incentive and its magnitude will affect tendencies to cooperate by evoking transformations.

1. Money evokes a *max joint* transformation for matrix patterns in which *max joint* is a viable transformation and money evokes a *max rel* transformation for patterns in which *max rel* is an advantageous transformation, given that the other person has made (or may be thought to make) a prosocial (e.g., a *max joint*) transformation.
2. The greater the magnitude of money, the stronger the arousal of the *max joint* transformation for all matrix patterns in which *max joint* is a viable transformation.

From the data presently available it does not appear possible to evaluate these two hypotheses but there seems to be no disconfirming evi-

---

* More generally, by money we mean any item of value that can be accumulated and transported (without losing its value) outside the interactive situation—hence prizes of candy and the like would be included in this conception. Points per se, on the other hand, cannot be transported and have no value apart from what they symbolize in the situation.

dence. The evidence for hypothesis 2 seems straightforward within the range of situations that are relevant to test it. McClintock and McNeel (1966a, 1966b, 1967) report a series of experiments with the MDG in which monetary incentives were varied from relatively trivial to substantial amounts. The MDG is a game that structurally provides sufficient outcome correspondence to make unnecessary a *max joint* transformation. However, *max joint* serves to reinforce *max own* as a means to good *given* outcomes. Furthermore, *max rel* yields no advantage (in terms of *given* outcomes); therefore, if money heightens the importance of the *given* outcomes, it should suppress the *max rel* tendency. The results clearly indicate that subjects make significantly more cooperative responses under high monetary incentives than under low ones. Furthermore, the difference in cooperative responding was mainly attributable (McClintock and McNeel, 1966a) to the high incidence of cooperation among high incentive subjects after *both* members had made a cooperative response on the preceding trial. This "state-conditioned propensity" to increase the incidence of cooperation after both had exhibited cooperation suggests the importance of being reassured that the partner is also responsive to the *given* outcomes and is not making a *max rel* transformation.

Most of the research on incentives has varied money versus points (or imaginary money), hence is potentially relevant to hypothesis 1. The bulk of the research is concerned with the PDG. Although, as we have seen, joint outcomes are maximized by cooperative play, individual outcomes are not; the cooperative alternative is the joint solution but it entails a risk of exploitation. Therefore it would not be surprising if a monetary incentive did not consistently improve cooperation. The results are in fact uneven. Radlow, Weidner, and Hurst (1968) report heightened cooperation under a monetary incentive, whereas Gumpert, Deutsch, and Epstein (1969) report the opposite effect. Evans (1964) and Wrightsman (1966) report no differences, although their subjects played the game for only six and two trials respectively.

Other bits of evidence appear to be consistent with the hypothesis. Although it represents a complex situation, the trucking game of Deutsch and Krauss (1965) would seem to be one in which a cooperative arrangement could be negotiated with reasonable dependability and Gallo (1966) has found a substantial monetary incentive to improve cooperation over the rates obtained with imaginary money. Finally an experiment by Daniels (1967) provides a reasonable test of both parts of hypothesis 1 —that money will arouse a *max joint* transformation for patterns in which *max joint* is viable but that it will arouse a *max rel* transformation when that is advantageous, given the other person might make a prosocial transformation. In a simple exchange relationship in which the cooperative alternative was a dependable way of increasing outcomes, subjects under a monetary incentive cooperated more than those under a point incentive. When, however, the nature of the exchange relationship was modified to permit the exploitation of cooperative overtures, the monetary incentive impaired cooperation.

Decomposition

The logic and method of decomposing the PDG (Pruitt, 1967, 1970) and other matrices were outlined in Chapter 2. There it was shown that there is an indefinitely large number of ways of specifying and presenting to subjects the BRC component (your gains) and the MFC component (other's gains) in the PDG. A PDG matrix and three decomposed versions of it were presented in Figure 2.8.

Is there any evidence that these different ways of presenting the same matrix elicit different value transformations? The answer, provided by Pruitt's (1967) results, is a resounding "yes." The rate of the C choice (the "cooperative" choice) was about 50% for the matrix version of the game, consistent with other studies of this matrix. In contrast, Game II began at 50% but declined over trials to 10 to 20%, Game III was consistently at the 70 to 90% level, and Game IV moved over trials from the 50% level to 70 to 80%. Clearly, the particular way in which the given relationship was analyzed for the subjects had a great effect on their behavior within it.

Pruitt's second study (1970) draws on questions about goals, strategy, and satisfaction with partner's choices to determine what the basis for the different results might be. Game II, in which the choice is between (C) 6 points each for self and other and (D) 12 for self but −6 for other, was found to elicit an interest in the high (12 point) outcome along with, for some subjects, an interest in the fair division (via C). The latter *min diff* transformation is fragile and disappears when the partner chooses D. Game III, with a choice between (C) 12 points for the other and (D) 6 points for self, elicits the goal of achieving cooperation from the partner so that the large outcome (12) can be obtained. This interest persists in the face of some D choices by the partner. Game IV, with a choice between (C) 18 for other but −6 for self and (D) 6 for other, similarly creates an interest in the high outcome. This is initially offset by fear of the negative outcome but this fear disappears as the partner occasionally plays C.

Overall, these results suggest that subjects respond selectively to the highest component outcome delineated by decomposition. It must be questioned, then, whether they recompose the game, that is, whether they add up the components and respond to the total interdependence pattern. In addition, the results may reflect a transformational tendency not yet considered in our scheme. This is a tendency to "go for" one's own highest outcomes. This tendency can be described as a special non-linear transformation of the *max own* criterion and might suggest that especially great weight is given to the highest outcomes in the matrix in setting one's comparison level for that matrix.

DISPOSITIONAL SOURCES OF TRANSFORMATIONS

McClintock gives as one of his propositions about social motivation that "Individuals vary in terms of their likelihood to adopt one of the four motivational orientations across settings in which there is outcome inter-dependence" (1972b, p. 453). The different sorts of people we consider here are a selected set of those for whom some evidence exists about the kinds of transformation they are likely to make. We commence with sex differences.

Terhune (1970) has reviewed the sex differences found in gaming and bargaining research and his major conclusions can be paraphrased as follows: when women are confronted with a conflict between their own interests and those of another, they search for an accommodative solu-tion. If possible, they will seek to compromise and to avoid open com-petition. Their initial orientation is to cooperate and they will do so if from the beginning the other is cooperative, but if they are crossed they will respond to the exploitation with greater retaliation and apparent vin-dictiveness than will men. In contrast, when men encounter a partner who is highly cooperative from the beginning, they tend to exploit him. Men are more likely to adopt a tit-for-tat strategy and are more co-operative in response to such a strategy.

These differing orientations have a familiar ring: they sound very much like the differences between the E-factor and D-factor orientations of Kelley, Shure, et al. (1970) reviewed in the preceding section (p. 196). Women appear to adopt a moral-evaluative (E-factor) orientation and men, an instrumental, task-oriented (D-factor) orientation. Before elaborating on this interpretation we need to make note of another variable that has been shown to be related to value transformation.

In their research on Machiavellianism Christie and Geis (1970) have found that subjects differing in scores on the Mach scale show contrasting behaviors in a variety of bargaining and gaming situations. In one study triads composed of one subject scoring high on the Mach scale (high Mach), one in the middle range, and one low Mach played a modification of the coalition game of Vinacke and Arkoff (1957). High Machs out-bargained low Machs and won more points. High Machs were even more successful when the ambiguity of the game was heightened (i.e., when the relative weights given each player were kept secret, as in a poker hand). High Machs appeared to depersonalize the situation, approaching it as a problem to be solved by cognitive-probabilistic strategies. Low Machs, on the other hand, invested the interaction with a strongly personal tone and responded in a more emotional and moralistic way.

Under other conditions, however, the high Machs are more cooperative than the low Machs. Consider another experiment reported in the same book. The game was Chicken. On the first 10 trials all subjects played for points; on the next 10 trials half the subjects played for pennies and half for dollars (enabling them to win as much as 4 dollars per trial). All subjects played against a programmed other who always followed the same predominantly cooperative noncontingent strategy. On the first 10 trials the high and low Machs played about the same way—competitively on roughly 55% of the occasions. When money was introduced, the low Machs continued to play competitively, whereas the high Machs shifted significantly to a more cooperative strategy, particularly when they were playing for dollars.

From the results of these two experiments it seems clear that the high Machs compete aggressively when it is to their immediate advantage (as in the K-sum coalition game), but they also cooperate when that appears to be advantageous (in Chicken with a monetary incentive). Low Machs appear to have little tactical or strategic orientation. In a further study, reported in the same book, there is evidence that low Machs do understand bargaining situations intellectually, but in games having emotional issues they become distracted by their ego-involvement (e.g., they lost most on issues they most strongly endorsed). High Machs remained detached from such issues and concentrated on winning.

Again there is an apparent parallel between these orientations and those discussed earlier. The orientation of high Machs resembles that of male subjects and the orientation of low Machs resembles that of females (and women do score significantly lower than men on the Mach scales, according to Christie and Geis). Furthermore, these orientations appear to be similar to those induced by money versus points and by the D-factor versus the E-factor. Indeed, it is tempting to conclude that money versus points, men versus women, and high Mach versus low Mach all act in the same way to produce a D-factor or an E-factor orientation. This would have the further consequence that the former creates basically a *max own* transformation which then stimulates a *max joint* transformation when *max joint* improves own outcomes (as in patterns with relatively high outcome-correspondence) and a *max rel* transformation when (in less correspondent patterns) the other person can be induced to make a prosocial overture. However, the conditions that would be hypothesized to produce the *E*-factor orientation (points, women, low Mach) are heterogeneous in at least some of their effects. Points are not like femaleness and low Mach in creating an initial tendency toward cooperation, but points, women, and low Mach are alike in investing the relationship with a personal and moralistic meaning that leads to vindictive responding (a *max rel* or *min other* transformation) to the other's competition.

We have not speculated here about the possible origins of these differences in transformational dispositions, but we do note the approach to this problem that is afforded by our theoretical analysis. The basic assumption is that transformational tendencies are acquired by experience in situations of social interdependence. This experience may be direct or vicarious (provided by social models) and is supplemented (and, perhaps to some degree, supplanted) by explicit teachings of social rules and behavior. The learning experience will depend on the patterns of interdependence within which one interacts and the transformational tendencies of the partners with whom one interacts. Thus we would seek to explain sex differences in transformation tendencies by reference to differences between male and female children in the distribution of interdependence patterns in which they have their social interaction (including the literal games they play) and in the transformational tendencies their partners most commonly manifest. It would be necessary, of course, to take account also of different normative teachings to which the sexes are exposed. Yet we would expect these teachings to be effective only within some limits set by the youngster's experience in social interdependence.

THE GENERAL THEORY OF TRANSFORMATIONS:
THE SELF-REGULATION OF MOTIVATION

The notion of transformational tendencies that are learned through interdependence experience is not original with us. McClintock observes that

> . . . because of this interdependence, which begins very early in life, the child learns to define, compare, and evaluate his behavioral alternatives not only in terms of their implications for achieving his own preferred ends, but also in terms of their implication for the outcomes that will be afforded others (1972b, p. 438).

He refers to "the final attractiveness of an outcome" and two investigators influenced by McClintock refer to "the effective structure" a game has for subjects (Kuhlman and Marshello, 1975). Similar concepts and suggestions can be found in other writings in the literature on experimental games.

As much as we owe our transformational viewpoint to McClintock's research and writings, it differs from his "social motivation" approach in a number of respects. Perhaps most important is that our analysis points to a diversity of transformations not encompassed by the social motivation view. In addition to outcome transformations (which correspond to the "social motives"), there are others that are transpositional and sequential. Our analysis gives the same status to, say, turn taking as to *max joint*. Once the notion of sequential transformations is introduced, the distinction between means and ends (McClintock's goal versus strategy) becomes blurred. As we noted earlier, the benefit that A provides B as the first step in a turn-taking sequence might be viewed as a mere strategic move, done out of consideration of A's long-term personal interests. Yet it can be done with a sense that "turn-taking is something good we ought to do" and with no more sense that "it's the only way I'll ever get what I want" than using a *max joint* criterion in the PDG. In other words, turn taking is no different as a rule for social behavior than *max joint*. Both may (and, we would emphasize, do) involve mixtures of means and ends properties.

More generally our view regarding prosocial transformation is that (a) all such transformations are of instrumental value in some situations; (b) all have social norms associated with them [the norm of reciprocity (Gouldner, 1960) associated with turn taking is a prime example]; (c) all provide a basis for conflict avoiding or conflict settling persuasive appeals and explicit agreements (cf. Chapter 10); and (d) by virtue of their functional value all are represented to some degree as internalized tendencies. They are learned as "rules" rather than as "goals." As rules, they have a high degree of contingent, situation-specific applicability. They are not (as implied by the terms goal or motive) stable sources of behavioral causality with high generalizability across situations. They do not cease to have functional value or strategic benefits for the actor simply because they become internalized. Consequently, they define modes of behavior that, subjectively, have both practical and moral worth.

Our discussion of transformations does not begin to exhaust the list of behavioral tendencies that people learn in situations of interdependence. In our earlier work (Thibaut and Kelley, 1959) we summarized evidence that suggested that some people are overresponsive to the reward aspects of interpersonal relations and others, to the cost aspects. This can be described in terms of transformational tendencies that operate selectively with regard to different components of own outcomes, *max own* being

differentiated into *max rew* versus *min cost* components. In the earlier book
we speculated that these different tendencies derive from the person's
experience in social situations of uncertain outcomes and may reflect his
competency and success. These tendencies would affect the values in the
given matrix, hence might be distinguished from the transformations
emphasized here. Like the present transformations, however, the reward
versus cost orientation might also be evoked by the pattern of the *given*
matrix; for example, when a person focuses more on his rewards when
outcome correspondence is seen to be high but more on his costs when
outcomes are noncorrespondent.

Another transformation of own outcomes that may have high functional value for persons in certain relationships is the suppression of
interest in own outcomes. If a person can learn to "do without," to forgo
many common rewards, he reduces his dependence on others. This can
also be viewed as a means of placing a limitation on the power of other
people. Viewed in this way, it constitutes the transformational route to
what Homans describes as "the display of indifference" (1974, p. 88)
which makes a person appear powerful. As we have emphasized
throughout this chapter, a rule that has practical effectiveness (e.g., as a
power strategy) may also be internalized, in this case serving truly to
increase the ·person's independence of socially mediated rewards. In
terms of the component analysis described in earlier chapters the suppression of responsiveness to rewards might operate primarily with
respect to the FC and BC to which the person is vulnerable, this being
possible to the degree to which·the kinds of rewards involved are different from those in the RC component.

The phenomenon of commitment may also be conceptualized in transformational terms. It is central to a number of processes of concern in this
book, often being essential to the transpositional process (preemption)
described in Chapter 6 and playing an important role in the development
of stable relations (Chapter 8). Commitment involves a promise never (or
during some specified time period) to look at or consider certain alternatives (either certain behavioral alternatives, as in the preemptive
strategy, or certain alternative partners, as in committing oneself to a
particular relationship). The promise is psychologically viable if the person can manage to put these alternatives out of attention or consideration
so that the rewards associated with them are no longer effective.

The concept of commitment is closely related to that of decision. As
noted in Chapter 11, Lewin conceptualized a decision in terms of an
increase in the potency of one of the several overlapping situations
corresponding to the various conflicting goals. The increase in potency of
one of the situations can be considered a type of transformation. At the

decision point the person makes up his mind and puts the rejected alternatives out of consideration. The functional value of this transformation derives from its promoting more effective action than would be possible if the person persisted in thinking about the total set of alternatives. The reader will recognize the affinity of these ideas to the concept of a postdecisional dissonance reduction process (Festinger, 1957) and to the notion of unequivocal behavioral orientation or UBO (Jones and Gerard, 1967). In general, we believe a fruitful line of theoretical work would be to consider such concepts as these from the point of view of the types of behavioral situation for which they have functional value. A taxonomy of such situations and a functional analysis of the various relevant motivational concepts (tension system, dissonance, decision, commitment, UBO, and reactance) might suggest a coherent framework within which apparently diverse phenomena can be located and synthesized. This would constitute a theoretical investigation of the processes and tendencies involved in relation to the impersonal environment, an investigation analogous to the present analysis of the rules and procedures involved in relating to other people. For more on this point see Chapter 11.

Finally (although, again, we do not pretend to exhaust the domain of transformational phenomena), the ability to forego immediate rewards in favor of later ones—to delay gratification—is important in interdependent relationships. It is obviously essential to the process of turn taking during which the person must occasionally put off satisfying his own needs in order to permit the partner to satisfy his. Through its facilitation of the turn-taking sequence, the ability to delay gratification enables both persons to attain higher eventual outcomes in patterns of noncorrespondence (e.g., the turn-taking game) than they would if both maintained short time perspectives.

In his summary of the evidence regarding the antecedents of delay of gratification Mischel (1974) includes social interdependence learning settings of the sort the present perspective would emphasize (e.g., relationships in which other persons have kept their promises of future rewards). In the present discussion Mischel's writings are more important in providing the general theoretical context within which our analysis of transformations is located. He observes that "the meaning and impact of a stimulus can be modified dramatically by *cognitive transformations*" (1973, p. 260). The transformations determine how long a child will be able to wait for a preferred but delayed outcome. Thus the child confronted with actual pretzel sticks or marshmallows can wait longer (in order to obtain more of them) if he "cognitively transforms the stimulus, for example, by thinking about the pretzel sticks as little brown logs or by thinking about the marshmallows as round white clouds or as cotton balls . . ." (p. 260). In contrast, his ability to wait is less if he focuses cognitively on the consummatory properties of the objects (e.g., how they taste). From the present perspective these observations are highly suggestive of the kinds of perceptual and cognitive mechanism that make possible outcome transformations.

At a more general level Mischel's characterization of cognitive transformations has many parallels to our assumptions about the process. Cognitive transformations involve selective attention to and interpretation of certain aspects of the objective stimulus. In our examples the person focuses on certain aspects of the interdependence pattern and interprets his behavioral alternatives in a temporal or sequential framework. Cognitive transformations ". . . substantially alter the impact the stimulus exerts on behavior . . ." (p. 267). In our analysis transformations loosen the linkage between immediate stimuli and behavior by enabling the person to respond to a given interdependence matrix as if it were a different one. In this attenuating and modulating role cognitive transformations are part of the self-regulatory system. "The essence of self-regulatory systems is the subject's adoption of *contingency rules* that guide his behavior in the absence of, and sometimes in spite of, immediate external situational pressures" (p. 274). In his summary Mischel writes that

> . . . individual's self-regulatory systems include: the rules that specify goal or performance standards in particular situations; the consequences of achieving or failing to achieve those criteria; self-instructions and cognitive stimulus transformations to achieve the self control necessary for goal attainment; and organizing rules (plans) for the sequencing and termination of complex behavioral patterns in the absence of external supports and, indeed, in the face of external hindrances (p. 275).

It is unnecessary to note the specific parallels this list finds in our concepts of comparison level and the several varieties of transformation. Mischel's statement makes clear what has been only implicit in our analysis, namely, the self-regulatory role of the transformations. They free the person from the control of the given matrix of immediate outcomes and enable him, at least in part, to control his motivation and thereby to regulate his behavior. This self-regulation permits action that takes account of a broader range of factors (the future, one's partner, and so on) and is therefore more effective. Our assumption in this chapter has been that self-regulation is learned because of this very effectiveness.

8

Processes of Attribution and Self-Presentation

ABSTRACT

This chapter analyzes the processes by which the dyadic members learn the nature of the given *matrix and the transformations that are being applied to it. In discussing these processes, account is taken of the cues presented by each member and the resulting attributions made about the nature of the relationship. In a concluding section the analysis is extended to show how self-presentational and attributional processes operate in the development of trust and intimacy and in the escalation of conflict.*

Interdependent persons have strong interests in explaining one another's behavior. Each wants to know what the other person is really like in order to know what can be expected of him in the future and under what conditions his behavior will change. Predictability of the other person matters because most important social interaction occurs in relationships that extend into the future. Entering the relationship, committing oneself to it, implies using up scarce resources (time and energy investments that are irrecoverable), foregoing alternative relationships which then become unavailable, and so on. At other transition points (e.g., during periods of high conflict) the "terms" of the relationship may be questioned, and if the relationship is to continue a renewed commitment must be made. This commitment is made in the face of considerable uncertainty. The future issues, problems, and course of any temporally extended relationship cannot be entirely predictable. Therefore to make a decision to enter or continue the relationship the person must extract as much meaning as possible from the present behavior. This is equivalent to saying that he must attempt to understand (a) the pattern of the *given* matrix for the relationship and (b) the transformations that the other person is disposed to make. He must learn to make valid *attributions* about his partner and the relationship.

Interdependent persons also have strong interests in their respective self-presentations. Each person finds it important to convey the reasons for his own behavior clearly to his partner. In terms of the present analysis, these reasons include both the person's outcomes in the *given* matrix and the transformations he is willing to make in the particular relationship—his orientation to it; for example, expecting high rewards from the interaction, the person will wish to indicate to his partner that he values the early outcomes it yields. Similarly, valuing the relationship, he will wish to show his own commitment in order to reassure his partner and elicit a reciprocal commitment. With respect to transformations, the person will try to show that he is a considerate and fair person, again to reassure his prospective partner. In some instances, once sure of his partner's commitment, the person may wish to establish his own superiority in providing rewards in order to set the stage for gaining advantages in the relationship (e.g., establishing high CL_{alt} in bargaining).

Given the strong interests of interdependent persons in both attribution and self-presentation and, further, given that each person is usually (from moment to moment) both a self-presenter and an attributer, it seems probable that the same rules are used for both aspects of the process. In other words, there is a "language" relating to action in interdependent relationshps that is defined by a set of rules used for encoding (self-presentation) and decoding (attribution). In this chapter we discuss some of these rules and, in particular, how the interdependence and interaction context of an action determines what its actor can hope to convey and what the partner is likely to make of it.

Although there may be a common language of self-presentation and attribution, its use does not necessarily ensure agreement or common understanding. From Jones and Nisbett (1971) it seems clear that an actor and his observing partner may form quite different interpretations of the actor's behavior even though both may be applying the same coding rules to the behavior. Information that is salient for the actor may not be salient for the partner. In interpreting his own behavior, the actor tends to focus his attention on features of the situation that elicited and constrained him to a particular subset of responses. The observer, on the other hand, tends to interpret the behavior as a manifestation of stable dispositions—personality traits—of the actor.

Actors and observers are not only likely to find different kinds of information most salient but, indeed, when they never exchange roles (contrary to what we have assumed), they may apply quite different rules to the processes of encoding and decoding. Thus observers may make attributions that seriously misinterpret the meanings intended by the actor's self-presentations. Judges in relation to criminals, children in relation to their parents, and the public in relation to movie stars, animals in the zoo, and other "inmates"—in none of these instances does the observer have suffcient acquaintance with the actor's role to ensure valid attributions about the significance intended by the actor's self-presentation. Similar confusions are made by persons from different cultures. Triandis, Vassiliou, and Nassiakou (1968) have investigated some of these misunderstandings as they might arise between Americans and Greeks. For one example a Greek who *flatters*, *informs*, or *discusses matters with* another perceives that he is giving status to the other.* That is the self-presentational meaning of his behavior. The receipt of this kind of behavior is not interpreted by the American as status enhancing.

> Thus, a Greek may expect appropriate behavior by the American in exchange for the extra status the Greek has conferred on him. If the American fails to perceive the Greek's behavior as giving status, the Greek is likely to perceive him as ungrateful (p. 38).

Although a common language requires the use of the same rules for the encoding and decoding communications about the relationship, a kind of communication may occur that entails no deliberate encoding or self-presentation. Unselfconsciously expressive or involuntary behavior may provide cues (indicators, symptoms) that the actor never intended but can be accurately decoded by the other person. This kind of behavior includes paralanguage (voice qualities such as pitch and speech variations such as tempo and loudness), kinesics (body language), facial expressions, and eye contact. (For an integrative summary of research on these topics see Mehrabian, 1972.) These expressive, nonvoluntary communications may permit each participant to form reasonably good attributions about properties and situational reactions of the other. On the basis of this type of communication *alone*, however, the pair would not be likely to reach a common understanding, for neither member would know what he had expressed to the other nor even know definitely that he had expressed anything at all.

Although there are various verbal and paralinguistic modes of communication *about* the relevant facts of interdependence, the ultimate

---

* This may represent an ancient tradition among Greeks in interpreting presentations of the self, as exemplified in Plato's second letter to Dionysius, Tyrant of Syracuse: "Now as in the beginning, you must show the way and I will follow your leading. If you show me marks of esteem, I will repay them; if I receive no such marks, I shall keep my own counsel. Note, too, that any marks of respect you show me, if you take the lead, will be evidence that you think highly of philosophy, and the very fact that you have examined other teachers of philosophy besides me will cause many to honor you as a true philosopher. On the other hand, any marks of respect that I show you, unless you return them, will be interpreted as evidence of my admiration of and desire for wealth—and such a name, we know, is nowhere an honest one. To put it in a nutshell, if you do homage to me, we both rise in men's esteem; if I do homage to you, we both sink. So much for this subject." (Hamilton and Cairns, 1969, p. 1565.)

channel of such communication is behavior involved *in* the interdependence itself (be it verbal, gestural, or whatever). It is in what a
person does and does not do and in the consequences of those actions
(and actions foregone), both for the actor himself and for his partner, that
the final and crucial evidence is provided about his rewards and costs,
transformations, values, and intentions. Thus we have argued that the
interest in attribution and self-presentation derives from interdependence that has certain properties (irreversibility, extensiveness,
unpredictability). Here, we argue that the processes of attribution and
self-presentation are, in the final analysis, based on interdependence,
that is, on behavior and its consequences. In brief, interdependence
provides both (a) the *reasons* for communication about person attributes
and (b) the ultimate *means* of such communication.

This chapter analyzes these processes. It also attempts to examine in
the same terms the presentation of self and the attribution of other. It is
assumed that the elements that are communicated are those pertaining to
interdependence and that the rules for manipulating these elements in
the service of self-presentation are the same as those rules used in pro-
cessing these elements in making attributions. We discuss the processes
by which the *given* matrix comes to be known by the participants and then
turn to an analysis of how they learn about one another's value transformations.

This sequence of topics may seem to imply that a person first infers the
partner's *given* outcomes and then uses them as a basis for inferring the
partner's transformations. Although that may be an optimal sequence of
events, the actual one may be quite different; for example, when assumptions about the partner's transformations (those that might be based on
the role definition of the partner, as "mother", "enemy", or "lover") form
the basis for inferring the partner's *given* outcomes. Perhaps the most
typical case is that in which the two kinds of knowledge about the *given*
matrix and about the partner's transformations are gained simultaneously. As noted in Chapter 1, the transformation process is the point
in the causal chain for social behavior at which the "person" appears,
both in fact and phenomenally, as a causal agent. The individual is aware
that his partner's behavior reflects not only the necessities of his situation,
circumstances, biological need states, and abilities but also the more
personal and voluntary factors such as attitudes, social values, and intentions. It is this subjective understanding of the transformational link in
the causation of behavior that underlies the common attributional problem of accounting for the other's behavior in terms of situational and
uncontrollable factors versus personal and volitional factors. The same
problem exists with respect to self-presentation (and associated self-

attribution, though we shall not consider this phenomenon). In the solution of these problems there is rarely the clear information about one class of causal factors, hence the relatively simple inferences possible about the other factors, that our discussion may imply.

SHOWING AND INFERRING THE GIVEN MATRIX

It should be clear at this point in the book that accurate knowledge of the pattern of outcomes in the *given* matrix is essential if the interdependent members are to realize the full potentiality of their relationship. How is this knowledge acquired?*

A first reaction to the question is to assert that a frank and open discussion will lead to a correct joint appraisal. In brief, the discussion might go like this: each will describe to the other the various behaviors in his repertory and will indicate the hierarchy of his RC preferences; each will explain his FC preferences among the alternatives that the other's repertory affords; and each will indicate his BC coordination preferences when outcome interferences and facilitations are experienced or anticipated. In addition, information will be exchanged about expectations and what else each person might be doing (their CL's and CL_{alts}).

Undoubtedly this process of open discussion will sometimes occur (in a more relaxed and informal way than we have summarized) and will sometimes lead to consensual understanding of the relationship. Still, by itself this cannot be the general solution. For this open and honest discussion to be appropriate outcomes in the relationship would have to be highly correspondent. (In noncorrespondent patterns untrustworthy, untrusting, deceptive, and evasive interactions would be more common.) If this correspondence were already known to the pair, there must be some basis other than open discussion for making this important attribution about the pattern of the *given* matrix. Furthermore, discussion—whether honest or deceptive—is not always possible because of the circumstances, common tasks, and necessity for action.

Hence our analysis of the process through which the *given* matrix is jointly understood focuses on the production of behavior that is at least partly nonverbal and on attributions made of that behavior. It has to be confessed at the outset that little is known in detail about this process.

* The *given* matrix may be imposed on the dyad by a third party (the experimenter or an industrial supervisor) who explains in detail the behavioral alternatives, the outcomes, and the patterning. We are not concerned here with external imposition.

The Interpretation of Behavior

The man in the street and the scientist share the same general approach to the interpretation of behavior. Both assume that $B = f(P, E)$. Behavior is a function of the person and of the environment. Thus behavior is assumed to convey information about both P and E. Information about P (which is usually, as here, the particular concern) is derived by viewing the behavior in relation to the particular conditions under which it occurs (which include its foreseen consequences). Lewin's *The Conceptual Representation and the Measurement of Psychological Forces* (1938) is an analysis of these interpretive rules as used in psychology. In what follows we assume that essentially the same rules are used, although perhaps less systematically, by common persons in their everyday affairs.

An observer of a person's behavior can make judgments about several different (though interrelated) aspects of its meaning: (a) the positive or negative quality of the consequences of that behavior, (b) the specific nature of the motivation that underlies it (the P factor because there is always some kind of P involvement), and (c) the main type of cause(s) involved in the behavior (the allocation between P and E, the stability of the causal factors, and so on). Aspect (a) has been the domain of preference scaling based on the analysis of choice behavior; (b) is the interpretive aspect emphasized by Jones and Davis (1965) in their theory of correspondent inferences. The P-cause (intention) takes its name from the consequences of the behavior. This identification of the motivation is least ambiguous when the behavior reflects a choice among alternatives and when the chosen action yields a single unique consequence (least noncommon effects). Aspect (c) has been the focus of attribution theory of the type developed by Kelley (1967), which considers the interpretive implications of the distribution of the behavior over actors, time, situations, stimuli, and so on.

The information the observer has on which to base his interpretation of behavior depends on the number of alternatives or conditions pertaining to the behavior and their diversity. Just as the preference scaling will be limited to the set of alternatives the actor considers so also are the causal distinctions limited by the packages of consequences for the various choices (in the Jones and Davis paradigm) and by the different conditions over which the behavior is "distributed" (in the Kelley paradigm). Strictly speaking, causes can be inferred only with respect to the set of consequences examined and the set of factors over which the distribution is determined.

The observer, however, may not limit himself to the explicit comparisons available to him. He may also make mental comparisons. Thus he may locate the actor's preferences among a limited set of alternatives on a broader scale by assuming that all the alternatives would be preferred to certain bad ones and that none would be preferred to certain good ones. He may even imagine the preference before it is expressed; for example, when he applies a simple causal schema (Kelley, 1972)—a social-cultural stereotype—that causally links types of actor to particular preferences. Similarly, he may take a given condition as being strongly determinative of the behavior (even though the proper comparison, involving the absence of that condition, has not been made) and make an external attribution for the behavior. In these "mental experiments" the person draws on his own experience as an actor and on his observations of other actors.

Means-End Ambiguity of Choice

Simple choice behavior of the actor is ambiguous in regard to locus of cause. To yield dependable interpretations it must be supplemented by a (real or imagined) comparison of conditions. Consider the choice behavior of a person who lives in a small town in which there are three similar movie theaters, all under the same management. On a particular evening the person is inspired to see a film. Although he makes a choice among the three possible actions (he goes to one of the theaters), he has no preferences among the actions per se but only about the films being shown. The films, however, bear no necessary relation to the actions themselves: the film he wanted most to see *might* have been shown at a different theater. The means-ends relations were established more or less arbitrarily by the manager of the theaters. In fact, the person's choices might be best described as preferences about the manager's behavior. There would be no essential change in the situation if the choice were replaced by a request to the manager for a particular film.

Thus, when the relation between a person's choice and his behavior can be shifted arbitrarily (e.g., by the action of some external agent—a theater manager), the choice reveals nothing about the actor's evaluation of his behavior per se and the observer can draw no conclusions about causes for the behavior—that the behavior is in itself pleasing. The choice reflects something *extrinsic* to the behavior. Only when the relation between choice and behavior is relatively invariant does choice reflect causes intrinsic to the behavior.

The example of choice among movie theaters is useful in illustrating some of the ways in which a person's RC, FC, and BC can be distinguished by an observer. RC reflects the intrinsic consequences of a person's own behavior—the consequences for him that it dependably yields without arbitrary external intervention. In the example presented the person has no RC: in their intrinsic qualities one action is like another. Evidence of RC would require that the choice of theater be relatively constant and independent of type of film (which would be true if one of the theaters were discriminably closer to his home or had more comfortable seats).

To pursue the original example the manager's decisions create BC. The person's preferred action will shift according to the ways in which the manager distributes the films among the three theaters. This process, however, really represents a conversion of managerial FC to BC: the more basic fact is that the manager controls attractive objects that he can offer or withhold from the person. Because these objects could potentially be separated from the manager's control (he could be replaced), an observer is not likely to attribute the FC to intrinsic properties of the manager's behavior. Other types of reward (praise, affection) would not be so separable. The separability of actions and consequences affords the means by which attributers distinguish different kinds of reward: object-rewards have a transportable value as a currency that is relatively independent of the identity of the donor, whereas the very meaning of affectional rewards is dependent on and closely associated with the identity of the donor.

The example of the theaters also illustrates the problem of perceiving concordance-discordance in the *given* matrix, hence outcome correspondence. If it becomes profitable for the manager to place in his theaters just the type of film that the person most prefers, then his RC is concordantly related to the FC he exercises over the person and the *given* matrix has high outcome correspondence. The person is not likely to misperceive this harmony of interest, but again there may be ambiguity in identifying its causal locus. The person may attribute the concordance to his own good taste and economic power and those of his neighbors in the community or he may locate the cause in dispositional properties of the manager (as a value transformation).

Ambiguity of Valence

Simple choice behavior may also have some ambiguity regarding the positive or negative valence of the consequences. The chosen action may be more positive or less negative than the nonchosen one or both and the observer may find it difficult to make the discrimination. The distinction, however, can usually be made on the basis of response latencies. Response to the more positive alternative is made with greater alacrity (an approach response) than to the less negative alternative (an avoidance component). Further cues are supplied by the conditions necessary to induce the choice behavior. As Lewin showed, conditions of external constraint—to prevent the chooser from "leaving the field"—are necessary to induce a choice between two negative consequences. Emotional behavior also offers cues for inferring the reward-cost level of the choice alternatives—eager joyfulness accompanying the choice of the more positive alternative in contrast to the protesting and reluctant compliance in choosing the less negative alternative.

The Interpretation of Behavior in Social Interaction

The special problems of inference that arise in ongoing social interaction are now considered. So far, as in the extended example of the movie theaters, an experimenter (the manager) has intervened to structure the assessment of preferences in terms of controlled sets of choices confronting the person as actor. Without this intervention, as in everyday social interaction, the attributional problem for an observer (the partner) becomes more difficult. The comparison information that he would need in order to make dependable inferences is not routinely available.

How does the observer, now as an interacting partner, obtain information about the elements of the *given* matrix—the actor's RC, own FC over him, and the BC contingencies? The actor's RC is again most likely to be manifested in choicelike behavior. In drawing inferences from these choice behaviors, however, the observer-partner must somehow manage to minimize his own possibly contaminating influence over them by withdrawing from close interdependence (a "time out") during the observational period. This lapsing of interdependence permits the actor to exhibit his preferences spontaneously and to free the consequences of his choice from interpretive confoundings. This source of confounding—between one person's RC and the other's FC as contributors to outcome consequences—is discussed below in regard to perceptions of relative control.

In assessing his FC effects on the actor, the observer-partner will rely on expressive cues or, the relationship permitting, on choicelike requests about what the observer-partner should do. Even when the observer has no means of directly monitoring his effects on the actor, the observer has a basis for understanding his FC by applying a simple covariation rule (Kelley, 1971). This principle is illustrated in an experiment on MFC (Kelley, Thibaut, Radloff, and Mundy, 1962).

In the experiment two subjects were placed before identical pieces of apparatus that provided each of them with two responses—a left button and a right button. On each successive presentation of a signal the subjects simultaneously pressed one of the buttons. After each response they received a gain or a loss. The response buttons of the two subjects were wired so that each of the responses controlled the other's gains and losses. Thus each exercised total FC over the other. In the part of the experiment of present concern the interdependence was fully explained, except that subjects were not told which response had which effect on the other's outcomes. Subjects occupied separate cubicles and no explicit communication was possible.

The attributional problem facing the subjects is a difficult one: how to identify the response that helps the other so that an exchange of gains might be effected? The experimental results suggest that subjects are able to solve this problem: over the series of successive trials 26 of 34 pairs attained a stable sequence of exchanging gains. Approximately 40% of the subjects reported that they used a simple covariation rule to distinguish the effects of their responses: if one of their buttons was associated with trial-to-trial stability in their partner's behavior, this meant that button-press yielded him gains, but if the button was associated with variability in the other's behavior this meant that it gave him losses. (Note that one subject's use of the covariation rule affords the other subject an opportunity to encode expressive behavior.) That applying and so interpreting the rule played an important part in solving the interdependence problem is indicated by the fact that it was reported in more of the pairs attaining a stable exchange of gains than in those failing to do so.

The diagnosis of own FC effects on the other by use of the covariation rule requires the user to set aside his interest in gains and losses temporarily and to adopt an orientation aimed exclusively at acquiring information. Instead of *responding* to the other, he tentatively suspends the *inter*dependence by deciding unilaterally to press one of his buttons repeatedly to gauge its effects on the temporal patterning of the other's responses. (This strategy seems similar to that of the observer-partner who creates a lapse of interdependence in order to interpret the actor's RC.) It is plain that both persons cannot adopt this strategy effectively at the same time: the programmed behavior of the attributor (who stabilizes his behavior to test its effects) will develop valid information only if the other responds "naturally" (attempts to maximize his gains). Simultaneous use of the attribution strategy—putting both on a self-programmed stability—would mislead both persons into believing that they are pressing the correct button.

Making a clear attribution of RC and FC in the *given* matrix is probably easier than making one of BC, for it would appear to be simpler to attain the concept of main effects than that of conjunctivity or contingency. Again, though, as in identifying FC, the observer-partner tests for BC by assessing the consequences of his own behavior for the other person. The attributor again takes the initiative, in this case by changing his behavior (or by making a move), and then waits for the other to follow by matching it. (This implies, of course, that there must be some means of monitoring the other's behavior.) The attributor's action thus constitutes a signal that invites coordination.

Relative Contributions of the Interacting Members

It will sometimes be difficult for the observer-partner to interpret the relative causal contributions made by himself and the other to consequences they jointly produce. Who has the control, the causal responsibility, and in what degree? In a series of experiments Horvitz and Kelley (unpublished) have investigated this question with respect to subjects' assessments of own RC in relation to the other person's FC over them. In these experiments the subjects believed that they were interdependent with another person in determining a numerical outcome. In fact, they were interdependent with a "person" simulated by the computer. Each person (real or simulated) had two alternative responses, each of which generated a fixed numerical value. On successive trials, as the two persons responded independently, the subject's outcome was always the sum of the two values produced by himself and his partner. The difference between the values of the subject's two responses (his RC) was varied and, independently, the partner's control (his FC) was similarly varied. The question is the degree to which the subject forms an accurate assessment of how much his own choices (his RC) affect his total outcome score in relation to how much the partner's choices (his FC) affect it.

Over the series of experiments the results are consistent in showing that estimates of own control in relation to that of the partner are approximately accurate when own control is objectively equal to or greater than the partner's. When own control is less than the partner's, however, own control is overestimated. It is not clear just why this overestimation occurred nor (the related puzzlement) to what classes of situation its occurrence can be generalized. There is a hint in the data that suggests a tentative interpretation of the effect. The data show that *absolute* judgments of own control vary directly with FC when RC is very small. This can be taken to mean that, with small RC, the variation produced by the partner is often mistakenly attributed to oneself. More generally, one may notice some particular chance-produced subset of events that leads one to experience a sense of control and then evaluate the degree of control according to the magnitude of variation in the outcome.

Another kind of error in estimation concerns judgments of CL_{alt}. Evidence of this bias comes from experimental studies of bargaining in which each of the two bargainers knows the level of outcome he must attain if he is to realize any profit. Neither knows the value specified for the other. This assigned value (the break-off value or CL_{alt}) constitutes the main external cause for each bargainer's behavior—how resistive or accommodative he will be. In two experiments, when subjects were asked at the end of the bargaining session to estimate their opponent's value (his CL_{alt}), they consistently *underestimated* it (Pruitt and Drews, 1969; Kelley, Shure, et al., 1970). Similar results were obtained by Shure and Meeker (1969) for a game involving the division of a set of territories. The conclusion to be drawn from these three studies is that the causal contribution of an externally imposed factor (the opponent's CL_{alt}) as a source of experienced conflict is systematically underestimated. From these studies alone it is not possible to assert that the opponent's personal contribution to the conflict (by his intractable behavior) is overestimated, although this may appear to be a plausible inference. The attribution of such dispositional properties to the other person as proximal cause for his behavior is the topic of the next section on the perception of value transformations.

PRESENTATION AND ATTRIBUTION OF VALUE TRANSFORMATIONS

Often an observer-partner can assume that the actor in a social relationship has knowledge of the pattern of outcomes in the *given* matrix—of his own preferences, of his partner's preferences, and the degree of correspondence between the two sets of preferences. When, in addition, the observer-partner has similar knowledge (it need not be the same, but he must assume it to be), he is able to discern how the actor's choices relate to the *given* matrix.

As we noted in the preceding section, the distinctions the observer-partner can make are limited by the set of choices available to the actor. As McClintock and Messick (McClintock, 1972a; Messick and McClintock, 1968) have shown, there are enough different plausible social motives that a choice between two simple alternatives, each with consequences for both self and partner, is likely to be ambiguous in its interpretations. These authors have worked out the logic of distinguishing among three of the motives that we have discussed as representing important outcome transformations by means of choices among alternatives (Figure 8.1). They point out that by increasing the number of alternatives (as in the third set of choices in the figure) evidence can be provided separately for

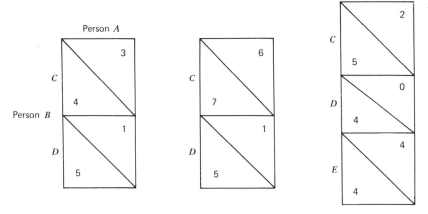

Figure 8.1   Some sets of alternative actions for person *B* differing in their attributional implications.

each of the three social motives (which are always confounded in such two-alternative choices as those to the left): maximizing own (illustrated by the *C* choice), maximizing the relative gain (illustrated by *D*), and maximizing joint gain (illustrated by *E*).

McClintock and his colleagues have developed these choices as means of assessing subjects' orientations to experimental games. These investigators themselves, the attributers in this case, use the chosen options and their consequences to infer the typical reasons behind a subject's behavior. For our purpose the assessment rules McClintock and his group have developed are important in that they suggest the rules that people in general use in showing and inferring their orientations in various social relationships. Although it remains to be shown, there is little doubt that the man in the street uses much the same information and interpretive principles here as the psychologists do.

Self-Presentation in Interaction

Messick and McClintock demonstrate that, with the proper comparisons, experimenters can decode social motives (outcome transformations). We now turn to evidence of whether and how outcome transformations can be presented by partners in social interaction. Subjects *can* report their conscious motives for making particular choices in interaction with others. McClintock (1972a) asked subjects to set down verbal reports of their reasons for their choices during the course of playing the MDG. The following categories summarize the principal reasons given for their choices:

1. To try to get as many points as possible for myself.
2. To keep the lead.
3. To catch up with the other player.
4. To help the other player get more points.
5. To get as many points as possible for both of us.
6. To get the other player to play differently.
7. To try something new.
8. To learn something about the game or the other player.
9. For no precise reason.
10. For another reason (explanation given).

In a later study based on this list McClintock asked subjects in Belgium and the United States to indicate on each of 100 trials which cell in the MDG matrix they preferred and for which of the 10 reasons. Across the Belgian and American samples 85% of the reasons given for preferring a cell fell in the first five categories—those most indicative of the major outcome transformations as defined here.

Although it is plain that interactors can report their motives for choices (at least in the MDG), some patterns in the *given* matrix may be better vehicles than others for the expression or presentation of personal dispositions. In a questionnaire study (Kelley, Jaffe, and Oliver, unpublished) subjects were asked to show how they would express various traits in moves they would make in a set of matrix patterns. The four traits they were asked to exemplify were fair-just, considerate-altruistic, achieving-competitive, and brave-courageous. The patterns in which they were asked to demonstrate each of the traits were perfectly correspondent MBC, PDG, Chicken, and perfectly noncorrespondent MBC. Subjects found correspondent MBC to be the least useful of the four patterns for expressive purposes: it provides fewer ways than the others of distinctively presenting the traits. For example, the considerate-altruistic trait is generally expressed by taking negative outcomes while giving the partner a positive one. This is not possible in the correspondent pattern, and the encoding of this trait gets maximally confused with the others. In the three other patterns the considerate-altruistic trait is one of those most clearly differentiated from the rest. Similarly, the achieving-competitive trait (expressed by taking a positive outcome while giving the partner a negative one) is well differentiated from the other traits in all of the patterns except correspondent MBC. Achieving-competitive is most differentiated from its closest neighbor (brave-courageous) in the noncorrespondent MBC pattern, apparently because of a clear separation between the choice that yields self a negative outcome (for bravery) and the choice that yields self an advantage (for competitiveness).

At least for 2×2 matrices, most patterns are probably constraining with respect to (a) the single dispositions that are difficult to encode and (b) the particular pairs of dispositions that are easily confused. One criterion for "optimality" of pattern would be the degree to which the pattern permits the clear expression of traits; for example, the optimal form of Chicken would presumably permit the clearest display of courage (see Chapter 5 and next section). PDG is a relatively poor vehicle for self-expression, considering the ambiguity of its moves (a point that we discuss further). Still, although its language is ambiguous, it is superior to correspondent MBC which provides hardly any language at all.

The research of Kelley and his colleagues shows that patterns differ in the ease and precision with which they may be employed to reveal dispositions. It is also possible, although Kelley's research cannot help with this question, that some dispositions are more difficult to encode than others—that there is less of a language available to express them or to express them in a way that distinguishes them clearly from other dispositions. In any case, once motivational dispositions are encoded it is important to know whether there are differences among them in the ease with which they can be decoded. This is one of the questions addressed by the research of Thorngate (undated).

In his experiment Thorngate asked subjects to predict the choices of a target person (the "chooser") who was programmed to make Pruitt-decomposed choices expressing one of seven different orientations. The orientations of choosers remained constant throughout the experiment and ranged from one that was highly competitive (reflecting a goal of maximizing relative gain) to one that was consistently altruistic (reflecting a goal of maximizing other's gain). On each trial subjects were shown the decomposed choice-alternatives. During the first 10 trials, however, they received no feedback about the chooser's actual choices; hence predictions during these trials were merely guesses that can be taken to reveal expectations about the most likely or most plausible behavior of a chooser. These results show that subjects make fewest errors predicting the choice behavior of the perfectly individualistic orientation (goal: to maximize own gain). A priori, then, subjects found the individualistic orientation most plausible. Other orientations, as they diverged in either direction (toward competition or toward altruism), were progressively less easily inferred. During the last 30 trials subjects were given feedback after each trial about the correctness of their predictions of the choices made by the chooser. The subjects generally showed improvement in their ability to predict the chooser's behavior. There were striking differences, however, depending on the chooser's orientation, in the level of accuracy attained. When the orientation of the chooser was any of those ranging from individualistic to competitive—when the chooser weighted his own interest above that of the other—subjects learned to predict the behavior almost perfectly; but, when the chooser's orientation was any of those ranging from cooperative to altruistic—when he weighted the other's interest at least as heavily as his own—subjects were significantly less able to make accurate predictions.

In commenting on the implications of his research, Thorngate observes that his subjects were adept at learning to discern the motivational orientation underlying the chooser's behavior and that this high level of accuracy leaves unanswered the question why, in real life, certain decision-maker motives seem to be widely misperceived. As one possible answer he speculated that misinformation about the *given* situation may be responsible for these errors.

> Political leaders, for example, may purposely withhold information about the personal outcomes accruing from their decisions and/or emphasize only the benefits which accrue to others in hopes of demonstrating that these decisions resulted in maximizing the other's gain and hence that they are truly beneficent.

This underlines our point, made earlier, that valid inferences about value transformations are promoted by a more or less accurate understanding of the *given* matrix. Otherwise it is difficult to decide whether a given behavior represents a response to the *given* matrix or is causally grounded in personal dispositions.

The Sequence and Timing of Choices

As shown in Chapter 6, certain social values can be satisfied only by particular sequential patterns of choice. This is especially true for certain patterns of interdependence, namely those having an important component of MBC; for example, in the turn-taking game (Figure 4.8) turn taking by the pair will maximize the joint outcomes and minimize the difference between the individuals' respective outcomes. One person's alternating pattern of choices would afford a basis for inferring that he holds the social values corresponding to these two criteria. Here, as in general, the inference depends on the distribution of consequences. In certain cases, for example, those requiring 4:1 alternation for equal outcomes, an alternating pattern might indicate only a weak interest in equitable sharing of outcomes.

Going first in a preemption game and thereby changing the partner's choice alternatives can also form the basis for inferences about value transformations. The game of Chicken (discussed on p. 134) is particularly interesting in the present connection because the testing of the observer-partner is an explicit and necessary part of the actor's self-presentational strategy. We can assume that to provide a setting for the display of courage the game must involve one option that is safe and another that is risky. This is shown for the actor A in Figure 8.2 in which his choice of C yields a medium outcome no matter what B (the observer-partner) does, but the D choice yields a high or low outcome, depending on what B does. By making the D choice A puts his fate in B's hands; thus the choice of D is evidence of willingness to take a risk. The D choice, however, can indicate this willingness only if there is no other basis for its choice. This requires that the high and low outcomes be equally likely; therefore there can be no expectation of a higher or lower outcome on the average for the D choice than for the C choice. The latter requires that, when A chooses D and confronts B with that choice, A must be maximally uncertain about what B will then do. The preemptive choice of D is evidence of stupidity if the other person is certain to reciprocate with D and evidence of an inane exhibitionism if he is sure to reciprocate with C. To present self as willing to face risky uncertainty the preemptive choice must put the partner in a situation in which his choice is a close one. In other words, A's presentation of his courage requires the creation of a special set of causal conditions for the partner's subsequent behavior, conditions that place that partner in maximum conflict.

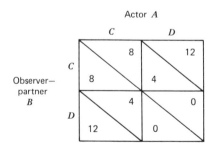

Figure 8.2   The game of Chicken.

Attributions of value transformations may also depend on the context provided by the other person's concurrent behavior. Kelley and Stahelski (1970a) show that an actor's intentions (the goal he has set for himself) in the PDG is inferred not only on the basis of his own successive actions but on the actions of his partner in the meantime. Thus an actor who shifts from C to D on successive occasions is judged more competitive if his partner's first response is cooperative than if it is competitive. In the MDG the partner's move makes little difference in the interpretation of the C to D shift, and (consistent with the McClintock and Messick analysis) the rate of a competitive attribution for this shift is rather high (Kelley, unpublished data). However, there are probably some rules common to all patterns with a degree of outcome noncorrespondence. In both the PDG and the MDG the shift from D to C that consists of "giving up an advantage" is judged to be more cooperative than the similar shift not subject to that interpretation (unpublished data; only weakly true in the Kelley and Stahelski data). Similarly, in both Hero and Battle of the Sexes, which require turn taking for equal outcomes, the move that consists of "offering" to give the partner a turn after having had one is seen as more cooperative than the move interpretable as "asking" for one's turn after the partner has had his.

Biases in the Attribution of Transformations

An unpublished study by Kelley and Patterson suggests that even in close, romantic relationships there may be a tendency to perceive oneself as making a *max joint* transformation to a greater degree than the partner does. Members of young heterosexual dating couples rated their satisfaction-dissatisfaction with common events in their relationship. For the example shown in Figure 8.3:

> You and your partner want to see different movies. Rate your satisfaction for the four cases in which (a) you go together to the movie *you* prefer, (b) you go to your preferred movie and your partner goes to his/hers, (c) you go together to the movie your partner prefers, and (d) you go to the movie your partner prefers and he/she goes to the one you prefer.

Ratings were made on a -10 to $+10$ scale for both self and partner, the latter affording evidence of how the partner is perceived to react to the four situations. It is not surprising that the pattern of results (Figure 8.3) shows a large correspondent MBC component: the person has a strong interest in going with the partner, regardless of the movie, and attributes the same interest to the partner (shown by the estimates of the partner's ratings in parentheses). Moreover, the person reports somewhat more satisfaction if the jointly selected movie is the one preferred by the partner rather than the one preferred by the self. This evidence that the person's satisfaction depends in part on the partner's does not find its parallel in the outcomes imputed to the partner. The partner is seen to derive more

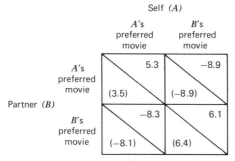

Figure 8.3   Own outcomes and estimates of partner's outcomes (in parentheses) for choice of movies.

satisfaction from the joint attendance at his/her preferred movie than from going together to the movie preferred by the self. In other words, the typical subject sees himself/herself as giving more weight to the partner's outcomes than the partner gives to the subject's outcomes. This result was replicated for five other interdependence situations similar to that in Figure 8.3. It was also apparent in a direct rating procedure in which the person rated the overall desirability of various combinations of own and partner's "outcomes" and made estimates of the desirability for the partner of the same combinations. Own sense of desirability reflected to a greater degree the partner's "outcomes" (relative to own "outcomes") than was perceived to be true for the partner's experience of desirability.

A rather similar result has recently been obtained by Michael Ross (personal communication). When members of couples are asked to estimate their percent contributions to various activities (What percent of the breakfasts do you prepare? What percent of the waiting do you do?), the two estimates consistently add up to more than 100%. In other words, one or both persons overestimate the contributions the self makes to the welfare of the couple. Although this result is subject to a variety of interpretations, Ross suggests the plausible idea that it may reflect differential availability in memory of relevant events (Tversky and Kahneman, 1973). When the person makes a judgment of own versus partner's contributions, instances of the former come more readily to mind. A similar interpretation may be made of the Kelley and Patterson results. Each person may generally be more aware of instances in which he/she does things out of consideration of the partner's preference than of instances in which the partner reciprocates. The counter self-interest (discordant RC) makes such actions salient to the actor, but a desire to reflect a genuine considerateness in the action inhibits explicit expression of the overridden self-interest. (Such expression would threaten to define the action as an instrumental move to elicit a reciprocation of the benefit.) Thus the considerate act may often be salient for the self but go unnoticed by the partner.

Strategy or Social Motive?

McClintock (1972a) has observed that subjects' choices in mixed-motive games may have proximal (immediate) or distal (ulterior) goals and that the ambiguities involved in deciding which goal is being pursued pose a major interpretive problem for the scientist. It is not only for the scientist that this constitutes a problem but also undoubtedly for the naïve participant, the observer–partner.

As noted in Chapter 7, McClintock draws the distinction between choices that represent a simple and direct expression of a motive or goal and those that are an indirect expression of a goal. The latter are instrumental or strategic acts; for example, ". . . a strategy devised to convince the other player to make choices which will permit you to realize your goal of maximizing own gain" (p. 281). Thus an observer may be deceived into believing that an actor's move reflects a motive of genuinely friendly cooperativeness when in fact it represents a manipulation strategy designed to further his own ulterior interests. The research and theory of Jones (Jones, 1964; Jones and Wortman, 1973) document the use of this kind of strategy by the ingratiator who attempts to protect his long-time interests by disarming interdependent others.

It will be noticed that McClintock's distinction between social motive and strategy is analogous to the one we have made between two kinds of transformation (cf. Chapter 6): mathematical operations performed on the *given* matrix values (outcome transformations) and sequential rules (or sequential transformations). The success of an instrumental strategy, for example, one of ingratiation, can be said to depend on confusing one type of transformation with another. Specifically, the strategy depends on mistakenly identifying a sequential transformation as being a transformation of the outcome values. In McClintock's analysis (and also in Jones's) the sequential transformation is typically in the service of an "antisocial" motive—self-aggrandizement, exploitation—whereas the outcome transformation simulates a "prosocial" intention—a compliment or a gulling gambit of cooperation. More generally, though, there is no reason why strategies (sequential transformations) cannot be guided by motives that are fully as prosocial as those that guide some (but not all) outcome transformations. As we have seen, in some patterns of interdependence involving MBC prosocial values can be realized *only* by sequential rules. Nevertheless, it probably remains true that many attributional *errors* are made when strategies are used in a deceptive way for manipulative ends.

The basic problems of self-presentation and attribution appear to be whether to show one's motives openly and honestly regardless of their "prosocial" or "antisocial" character *and* whether to be suspicious in interpreting what the other has shown. These questions seem to resolve into the larger contextual question of where the interest of the interdependent parties lies. In the next section we try to demonstrate that an answer to this larger question requires an analysis of the degree of outcome correspondence and the stability (or transiency) of the relationship.

DYNAMIC SEQUENCES

We are concerned in this section with self-presentational and attributional processes that accompany the developments or evolutions by which relationships take form and proceed toward stability or, on the other hand, experience increasing conflict that leads to mutually destructive behavior and/or termination of the relationship. In these dynamic sequences the display and correct reading of goals and intentions becomes important not only as a symptom of whether the relationship is moving toward stability or disruption but also as a causal input that accelerates or decelerates the movement. We begin the analysis by considering the tension that exists between mutual and unilateral interest as criteria for action in the relationship.

In Chapter 7 we showed that interdependence patterns provide settings in which both prosocial and egoistic transformations may reward the individual. The consequences for a person of any particular transformation depend on both the pattern of interdependence and the transformations the partner is making or is disposed to make. It is plain, then, that before embarking on a line of action it behooves each member to attain a correct understanding of the degree of correspondence in the *given* matrix. If outcomes are objectively congruent, then the member can make the prosocial overture—show the value he places on cooperation—with some confidence that his partner will reciprocate. On the other hand, if the pattern of the *given* matrix is highly noncorrespondent, each member's unilateral interest, prescribing an antisocial transformation, dominates his decision. If the member incorrectly interprets the *given* matrix as correspondent and accordingly makes a prosocial overture, he will be vulnerable to the other member's self-interested action. However, it is maximally to the member's advantage—when he is confident that the pattern is noncorrespondent—to conceal his intention to move competitively and to encourage the other member to interpret the situation as being truly harmonious.

What is prescribed in the foregoing paragraph for relationships that are grounded in an objective conflict of interest holds clearly only for transient encounters or for relationships in which the worst action available is not seriously damaging. The competitive action of one member may lead to attempts at retaliation by the others but no serious escalation of conflict can develop—the encounter is terminated or the retaliation is as harmless as the competitive provocation. But when the objectively conflicted relationship has a long future and one from which there is no exit, as in a marriage whose partners have very poor CL_{alts} or two powerful nations on a small planet, a common interest may develop in controlling the (possibly) mutually destructive escalation of conflict. This common interest is an objective one; it has definite consequences and it modifies the *given* matrix by adding an element of outcome correspondence. Adding this degree of harmony of interest to the motivational mix makes it adaptive for both members to take accurate account of the noncorrespondence in the *given* matrix (and to show one another that accurate account has been taken). Unless both members have an accurate understanding of the degree of real disharmony of interest, one of them may start an escalation of the conflict by underestimating its true degree (and thus irresistibly inviting the other's escalating move) or overestimating it (and making the move himself) by failing to perceive the element of common interest.

When the relationship involves both common interest and conflict of interest (the mixed-motive game, intermediate between correspondence and noncorrespondence), then problems of presenting and inferring one another's transformational tendencies become severe. As we noted in Chapter 7, these relationships create a tension between prosocial and egoistic or antisocial transformations. As shown in Figure 8.4, there is a *mutual* interest in moving from the latter types of transformation in the lower portion of the figure to the prosocial transformations exemplified by the *max other* and *max joint* outcome transormations. On the other hand, if one person is operating at one of the higher levels, his partner often finds a *unilateral* advantage, at least in the short run, in adopting one of the more egoistic criteria for action.

The processes shown in Figure 8.4 may be taken to represent, by the upward pointing arrow on the right, the formation and development of the relationship through the building of mutual trust and, by the downward arrows on the left, the escalation of conflict. These two processes

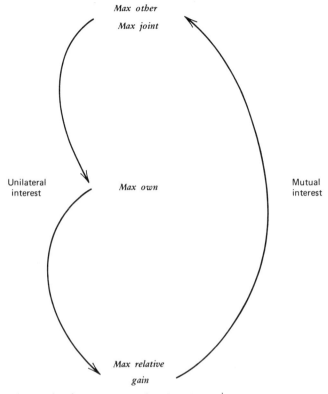

Figure 8.4   The tension between mutual and unilateral interest in various criteria for action.

depend critically on the self-presentations and attributions that are made in the relationship. We will analyze the two processes separately.

Development of the Relationship

The formation process is characterized by a series of decisions by each individual, decisions that are usually, though not always, quite implicit and unselfconscious. At each decision point the individual elects whether to "move further into" the relationship (and how much, at what rate) or to drop out of it. The former involves "giving more" to the relationship and becoming more dependent on the partner's reciprocated benefits. The latter alternative includes physically remaining in interaction but doing so on false terms—appearing to make a further commitment but with no personal intention to fulfill the contractual terms being implicitly evolved.

Because trust-inducing initiatives may be ambiguous when action is taken simultaneously (Swinth, 1967), we present the process as a series of steps involving alternating moves and countermoves.

Step 1. The individual's decision to move further into the relationship is made on the basis of some increase in certainty that (a) the relationship will be rewarding (and low in cost) and (b) he will not be exploited or abruptly abandoned. Increased certainty about the reward qualities and dependability of the other rests on attributions concerning more or less stable dispositions of the other. Has he the *ability* to produce the kinds of outcome that are rewarding to self? From Jones and Goethals (1971) it seems clear that abilities are perceived to be stable over time and that early samples of high-level performance create strong primacy effects that cause the observer to expect future performances to be equally impressive. Hence this research suggests that early samples containing highly valid indicators of talent, especially when direct, unmediated, observation of the other's products is possible (Thibaut and Ross, 1969), should heighten the certainty that early rewards are not accidental or transient. By the same token early samples of inferior performance relevant to the production of rewarding outcomes should lead to decisions to break off the relationship.

Heightened assurance of not being exploited or abandoned is based on cues that the other person can be depended on, trusted to reciprocate appropriately, and to respond in the same terms as are implied by one's own actions. This impression of the other's dependability derives from assessments that (a) he is dependent on the relationship, (b) his interests and your own overlap in a sufficient degree of common interest, and (c) he intends to act out of consideration of your and the common interest, that is, to make a prosocial transformation of the matrix. Workers under the same supervisor exemplify the kind of situation in which cues of this sort abound. The workers are related to one another in a more or less stable "balance" of power and they share large areas of common interest. Their intentions toward one another may be regarded as honest and are supported by commitments to widely shared norms.

Step 2. The decision to "move further into" the relationship was based on some assurance that the relationship would be both rewarding and dependable. At the same time the decision entails actions or moves designed to increase the other person's certainty in the same two respects *and* thereby to induce a reciprocal "confirming" or "validating" move from him. (To say that the decision was so designed does not mean that it may not be motivated and interpreted differently, especially if the move is very large and very fast—"coming on too strong." This consideration is dealt with later.) Thus the latent "message" to the other person is (a) the relationship with me will be rewarding for you and low in cost; and (b) I am dependable and intend to fulfill the terms implied by my behavior. [As above, this implication of dependability may include suggestions that (a) I too am dependent on the relationship, (b) our interests are convergent, hence I will not be tempted to harm you, and (c) I am committed to following the same rules and norms that you are.]

Making the initiating move that reassures the other party and invites his confirming countermove is part of Osgood's (1962) proposal for "graduated reciprocation in tension reduction." A simplified version has been tested in the laboratory by Pilisuk and Skolnick (1968). Subjects played an extended form of the PDG with a scenario that employed the language of international tension; for example, armament, disarmament, mutual inspection. Some of the subjects were paired with programmed opponents who played a matching (tit-for-tat) or a conciliatory strategy that prescribed a play on trial $n + 1$ that was one degree (one "missile") less aggressive (or more friendly) than that of the subject on trial n. Thus both programmed strategies were matching strategies but the conciliatory strategy also contained a unilateral initiative toward disarmament. An additional sample of paired subjects played "naturally," that is, without any programmed intervention. Cross cutting the foregoing treatments was an inspection variation that permitted half the pairs a display of intentions (the programmed "opponents" were always honest) about subsequent moves. The results suggest that the Osgood proposal for integrating small, consistent, unilateral initiatives of friendliness with an honest prior declaration of intentions does produce significantly more cooperation than is found in natural pairs but only marginally more cooperation than is generated by the comparable matching strategy. The evidence in this study for the trust-enhancing contribution of the initiating move is thus only suggestive. (The authors indicate a possible artifact produced by the values in the payoff matrix that might, under the conciliatory strategy, have put a ceiling on further cooperation.) In any case, there is further evidence of the importance of the initiating move.

We might ask about some of the specific cues that could lead the other person to interpret one's initiating move as implying dependability. These cues would seem to include any evidence that the move has involved some cost, that it has been made in the face of risks or other obstacles. [Swinth (1967) shows that accepting risks and incurring costs (foregoing gains) act in the same way to develop trust.] If one's initiating move is perceived to entail some sacrifice of one's own interests, the other person will be more likely to attribute it to a dependable source, hence to make a validating reciprocation. Pruitt's (1968) research suggests that this is so. Subjects receiving a standard reward reciprocated more generously the smaller the resources they imputed to the person rewarding them.

Step 3. The decision to move further into the relationship serves not only to reassure the other person that the relationship will be rewarding and dependable; it also tends to be *committing* in several ways. First, the move constitutes a tacit agreement to continue and to enlarge the relationship, at least in a further exploratory way. Moreover, if the move is public, if it is visible or otherwise communicated to relevant other persons—to the "field of eligibles" (Winch, 1952)—it tends to cause alternative partners to back away and to withdraw any aspirations they might have to form a relationship with either of the dyadic members. This receding of the alternatives has the effect of heightening the costs to the dyadic members of breaking off their interaction. (These comments, of course, apply only to relationships that are mutually exclusive or incompatible with the developing one, this being the conceptual meaning of alternative.) Again, if the move has been public, it may stimulate the surrounding social system to take part in enforcing the continued solidarity of the dyad. This will be true when explicit social rituals—initiation or induction ceremonies—confirm the formation and adjure the preservation of a relationship.

Step 4. The process so far has entailed (in Step 1) the individual's decision to move further in the relationship, based on some increased certainty that it will be rewarding and dependable, and (in Step 2) actions designed to increase the other person's certainty that it will be rewarding and dependable for him. Such actions or moves tend (in Step 3) to commit the actor to the relationship. Now (in Step 4), if the "move further" has been successful in transmitting the promise of a rewarding and dependable relationship, it reduces the other person's uncertainty in this regard and creates the conditions that encourage him to make the next move. Thus, in general, the formation process can be considered as an exchange of actions or messages that reduce uncertainty or increase the mutual assurance that the relationship will endure and be worth enduring.

As the mutual assurance steadily increases during the early formative period, each member may perceive that he is being evaluated by the other in an increasingly positive way. Each person may thus experience the ascending sequence of evaluations studied in the experiment by Aronson and Linder (1965) in which female subjects overheard evaluations being made of them at repeated intervals by another girl (an experimental confederate). Because the subjects were led to believe that the confederate was unaware that she was being overheard, the subjects could not attribute the evaluations to any attempt to flatter or openly insult them. During each of the intervals between the evaluations the subject was required by the ostensible purpose of the experiment to talk with the confederate for a few minutes. Under the various experimental conditions the overheard evaluations gradually improved from initially negative to finally positive, deteriorated from initially positive to finally negative, or were steadily positive or steadily negative. Postexperimental assessments of the evaluator revealed that she was liked best in the first condition when her evaluations gradually changed from negative to positive.

Research on bargaining and gaming has shown some parallel effects in comparing the consequences of different schedules of concessions or cooperative-competitive play. Benton, Kelley, and Liebling (1972) report that a bargaining opponent who commences with extreme demands and gradually moves to more moderate ones is evaluated as having been fairer than one who begins with moderate demands and persists with them throughout. Moreover, with the former opponent the subject feels greater responsibility for the outcome, greater success in influencing the partner, and greater satisfaction with the negotiation. In reviewing research on programmed strategies in the PDG, Oskamp (1971) summarizes the consistent findings that a shift from a low to a high rate of cooperation is more effective in inducing subjects to cooperate than a consistently high rate of cooperation. Although the temptation to exploit the sucker (the consistent cooperator) may account for these PDG results, a more general interpretation would seem to be required to account for the more favorable effect found for all of the foregoing ascending schedules: increasingly cooperative PDG programs, extreme to moderate bargaining demands, and negative to positive evaluations in the Aronson and Linder experiment. The plausible possibility is that the subject may experience the security that derives from a sense of control and mastery over his social environment, attributing to himself the causality for the positive trends in the other person's behavior.

A Dilemma

In taking an action to reassure the other person that the relationship will be both rewarding and dependable (Step 2), the individual faces a dilemma. On the one hand, the move further is not meaningful to the other person if it consists only of what has already been thoroughly justified by the other's prior action. It is necessary, if the other person is to be induced to make his move further (Step 4), that one's own action constitute an initiative, an indication of one's personal intention to move further, and not simply what is demanded by the other's earlier contributions. To ensure Step 4, one's move must embody more than simply matching or catching up with what the other's actions have already justified.

The foregoing observations imply that the process proceeds by *risk taking* and, if both persons are to experience a reduction of uncertainty, ideally both would take risks. (If, however, one person is more secure in his interpersonal relationships than the other, he may have to take the lead in the risk taking and perhaps receive assurance by the other's following; but even this process can constitute symmetrical risk taking. The insecure partner communicates his anxiety and, given that context, even his lower-level increases in commitment are seen and felt as risk taking.)

We have said that one must make a move that is not perceived to be simply the effect caused by the other person's prior actions. *On the other hand*, if in making the move further (in Step 2) the components of the message are emphasized too strongly (capabilities to produce rewards, dependence, and dependability) then the reassurance gained from the other person's subsequent move (in Step 4) is endangered. The sheer size of own move may then suggest his motivation for remaining in the relationship: he only wants to get the reward or to exploit trust and dependence. Another possible consequence of making a move of too great a magnitude is that too large a move, "coming on too strong," may be interpreted by the other as an aggressively dependent overture: he is being overwhelmed with rewards for which he will be asked a costly repayment in the future. That persons are wary of and resist this possibility of future exploitation is suggested by an experiment by Brehm and Cole (1966). When the situation is perceived to be important, subjects who were unexpectedly given a soft drink by a confederate helped the confederate less in a subsequent activity (stacking papers) than subjects who had not been given the soft drink. Similarly, Schopler and Thompson (1968) have demonstrated that when the setting is "formal" (but not when it is "informal") the receipt of a favor (a flower) leads to less willingness subsequently to help the confederate (by assenting to wash blouses) than when no favor was done. Schopler and Thompson interpret their results in terms of the attributions made of the donor's motives: that he is preoccupied with the recipient in the informal condition and with his own requirements in the formal one.

The dilemma then is how to make a move meaningfully greater than the other's prior moves have warranted (to constitute a reassurance to him) but not so great as to put in question to you his subsequent move or to put in question to him *your* intentions.

This process of developing trust, as we have just described it, takes place in the early stages of relationships when dangers and uncertainties abound. If the initial contacts indicate to either of the potential partners that the *given* matrix is too extremely noncorrespondent, then there is too little basis for the development of trust or for the adoption of prosocial transformations (see Chapter 7). On the other hand, if the matrix is extremely correspondent, there is also no basis for the development of trust, for there is nothing to risk, hence no test of willingness to take risks: cooperative overtures will be attributed to the structure of the situation rather than to dispositional (or pattern-transforming) properties of the participants. Therefore it is in the middle regions of the continuum of outcome correspondence, in which elements of both conflict and co-operation are present as temptations, that attributions of trust have their origins. Here, also, conflict can escalate.

Escalation of Conflict

The process by which conflict develops is in many ways the simple reverse of the process of trust building. Competitive and destructive behaviors replace the cooperative and constructive as the directions taken in the processes summarized in Figure 8.4; but there is more to it than that. A crucial difference between the two processes is that whereas the upward movements of trust development in Figure 8.4 require a mutual assent—a conjunctive responsibility—the downward movements of conflict development can be started and maintained by unilateral action.

This process has been analyzed by Kelley and Stahelski (1970b). After subjects had been instructed in the PDG, they were asked to decide what their goal would be in playing the game with another person, whether they wanted to establish a cooperative relationship with him or intended to play competitively. This decision about intentions reflects roughly the dispositional properties of the subjects. In pairs of subjects with different goals, one having selected the cooperative goal and the other, the competitive goal, the cooperator is poorly equipped to show his cooperative intention. His cooperative play will be exploited, and if he plays the other (D) alternative it will be interpreted not as an attempt to defend himself but as an act of aggression. Thus, faced with a determined competitor in the PDG, the cooperator has no way of turning the play toward co-operation. He must play the competitive alternative in self-defense and the relationship rapidly becomes one of mutual punishment. The competitor, meanwhile, is quite unaware of his causal role in producing the conflict, mistakenly assuming that everyone else, like himself, has competitive intentions.

Although the basic experiment of the Kelley and Stahelski research is the PDG, the authors report similar effects from other studies, using, for example, the game of Chicken and another (modeled after the Deutsch and Krauss trucking game) in which the two players must share a limited facility that only one at a time can use. In these games, as well, the cooperator's behavior rapidly assimilates to that of the competitor: competition dominates. These two games share with the PDG a critical property: the cooperator has no unambiguous way of communicating his cooperative intention. He has only the choice between being systematically exploited or making a move in which his effort to defend himself is likely to be attributed to an aggressive intent. In these circumstances, and the real world situations to which they generalize, one determined aggressor can start a process that irresistibly generates reciprocal aggression.

The assimilative effects we have described may not occur if the repertory of possible behaviors is expanded. Miller and,Holmes (1975) have studied this possibility in the context of an expanded PDG (see Figure 8.5) in which a withdrawal alternative is added to the PDG. This alternative permits the cooperator to protect himself from severe damage while clearly communicating his lack of aggressive intent. Miller and Holmes show that the withdrawal response does indeed protect the cooperator from being assimilated to the competitor's aggressive overtures. Unilateral aggression does not start an irresistible escalation of conflict.

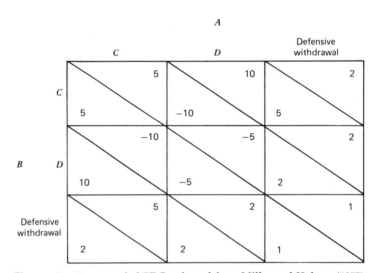

Figure 8.5   An expanded PDG, adapted from Miller and Holmes (1975).

We have commented earlier on other factors that may inhibit the escalation of conflict. When the relationship contemplates a long future of coexistence from which exit is difficult and in which uncontrolled conflict can be damaging to both sides, a perception of the common interest may produce caution. Then, it can be hoped, rashness in initiating aggression will be curbed and, if aggression occurs by mistake or momentary impulse, the response will not be immediate retaliation in kind but rather the functional equivalent of a defensive withdrawal.

9

Interdependence in Triads

ABSTRACT

An analysis is made of the components of triadic interdependence. This analysis provides the basis for a discussion of the third person's possible effects on the dyad—how the dyad can be strengthened, changed, or disrupted by a representative of the social environment. Attention is then focused on the consequences for the third person of the dyad's behavior, viewed in terms of the power of the dyad over the "outsider." In final sections consideration is given to full-blown, three-way interdependence with special emphasis on some phenomena unique to the triad (relative to the dyad).

We now consider the consequences for the dyad of the actions of a third person. In adding the third person to our analysis, we are not simply interested in its generalization to the triad, although that is one of our purposes. We also view the third person as epitomizing the social context in which the dyad exists. The ways in which person C can affect the A–B pair reveal how the dyad can be strengthened, changed, or disrupted by its social environment. The ways in which the pair can cope with C's interventions reveal their resources for dealing with external social opportunities and threats.

Among the many ways in which C can affect the interaction between A and B only certain ones are considered here. An important distinction is whether C affects the *interdependence* between A and B or whether he merely affects the process by which they cope with a particular pattern of interdependence. As an example of the latter, he may provide signals to help them to solve a coordination problem (just as the coxswain performs this function for larger groups). Another example would be the escrow officer at a bank who handles the process details that ensure that the terms of a contract are met by both sides before an exchange is made. In a sense his role is to guarantee simultaneity of action according to agreement. Other examples would involve C's aid to the pair in understanding their interdependence, his help in the intercommunication of intentions, and his decisions on their behalf as an arbitrator when the conflict prevents them from making their own (see Thibaut and Walker, 1975, for further analysis of this process). Our analysis excludes such contributions to process and is restricted to the third person's effect on the interdependence between A and B. It does, however, include examples in which C plays a role in the evocation of values, for, as we have seen, they affect the way in which A and B are effectively interdependent.

Patterns of interdependence in the triad are far more complicated than those in the dyad. In the interest of clear presentation we focus first on A's and B's respective outcomes and the impact on them of C's actions. This forms the basis for considering the interplay between A and B as an ongoing dyad and C as an intervening "outsider." Subsequently we consider how C's outcomes vary within the three-way relationship. This focuses our attention on the consequences for him of A's and B's actions and affords the means of analyzing their power over him. Then, the two-versus-one perspective is set aside for a full-blown, three-person analysis and we consider some phenomena unique to the triad. This constitutes the first step in generalizing the dyadic analysis to larger multiperson groups, although we have left that for others to do.

COMPONENTS OF TRIADIC INTERDEPENDENCE

It is necessary first to orient ourselves to the complexities that are introduced, at least potentially, by extending the analysis to the level of the triad. This is conveniently done in terms of the components of interdependence that exist in the triad. Figure 9.1 reminds us of the relation between the components of interdependence in the dyad and the analysis of variance paradigm. As we stated in Chapter 2, dyadic interdependence is analogous to an experimental design in which there are two independent variables (the two persons A and B) and two dependent variables (A's and B's respective outcomes). The analysis of variance model reveals that there may be three sources of variance in each person's outcomes, his own main effect (RC), the partner's main effect (FC), and their joint effect (BC). These three sources account for the variance of each set of outcomes

Source of Control	Person affected	
	A	B
A	RC_A	FC_B
B	FC_A	RC_B
$A \times B$	BC_A	BC_B
Average	GM_A	GM_B

Figure 9.1 The components of dyadic interdependence expressed in terms of the analysis of variance.

around its particular average level or grand mean (GM). The three sources of variance are referred to as types of control. The subscript following each control term in the figure denotes the person affected by it.

Figure 9.2 shows the same analysis made for the triad. There are now three independent variables, corresponding to the three persons, and three dependent variables, corresponding to their respective outcomes. The number of possible sources of variance in each person's outcomes is increased to seven. It becomes necessary to supplement the subscripts following each control term (which indicate the person affected by it) with subscripts *preceding* each term to indicate the person or persons who exercise the control. Thus $_AFC_C$ refers to fate control exercised by A over person C. The necessity for this double coding is apparent. *Three* possible sources of fate control act on A, one exercised by B, a second, by C, and a third, by B and C, acting jointly ($_{BC}FC_A$). The same is true for each person and for BC as well. If the reader finds it confusing that the three-way interaction terms translate into BC exercised over a person by the joint actions of his two partners, it might be well to review the meaning of BC in the dyadic components. The $_BBC_A$ term reflects the *joint* effect on A's outcome of his and B's actions. By virtue of this joint effect, when B modifies his action, the BC component creates a reason for A to modify his also, hence, the behavior control. Similarly, the effect of the $A \times B \times C$ interaction on A's outcomes ($_{BC}BC_A$) implies that because all three persons jointly exercise an effect on A's outcomes, if B and C *jointly* change their actions his distribution of outcomes provides a reason for A to make a corresponding shift in his action. The reader will note that the subscripts preceding the RC terms have been omitted. They are made unnecessary by the definition of RC: only A can exercise reflexive control over A.

Source of Control	Person affected		
	A	B	C
A	RC_A	$_AFC_B$	$_AFC_C$
B	$_BFC_A$	RC_B	$_BFC_C$
C	$_CFC_A$	$_CFC_B$	RC_C
$A \times B$	$_BBC_A$	$_ABC_B$	$_{AB}FC_C$
$A \times C$	$_CBC_A$	$_{AC}FC_B$	$_ABC_C$
$B \times C$	$_{BC}FC_A$	$_CBC_B$	$_BBC_C$
$A \times B \times C$	$_{BC}BC_A$	$_{AC}BC_B$	$_{AB}BC_C$
Average	GM_A	GM_B	GM_C

Figure 9.2   The components of triadic interdependence expressed in terms of the analysis of variance.

It is apparent that the introduction of a third person greatly increases the complexity of the analysis. Compared with the six control components to be considered in the dyad (in Figure 9.1), there are twenty-one such components for the triad (Figure 9.2). To facilitate our thinking about this extensive array of components we first limit our consideration to A's and B's outcomes, that is, to the A and B columns of Figure 9.2. Here are listed the original six terms local to the A–B dyad and the additional eight terms that in one way or another involve C's exercise of control. Then, when questions are raised about the power of A and B over C, it will be necessary to take account of the seven terms in the C column of Figure 9.2, in which C's outcomes are subject to various types of control.

PERSON C's EFFECTS ON THE A–B RELATIONSHIP

Analysis of A's and B's Outcomes in the 2 × 2 × 2 Relationship

The pattern of A's and B's outcomes in a triadic relationship in which each person has two response alternatives can be represented by the pair of matrices in Figure 9.3. These are simply the two halves of the 2 × 2 × 2 cube, corresponding to C's separate responses, c_1 and c_2. This mode of representing the relationship is convenient because it highlights the change in the A–B relationship produced by C's shifts in behavior.

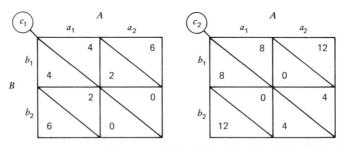

Figure 9.3   Representation of the 2×2×2 relationship as it involves A's and B's outcomes.

Figure 9.3 shows a case in which C can by his choice of actions determine whether A and B are related in the manner of Chicken (c_1) or PDG (c_2). As can be seen, C's action also affects the variance and the average

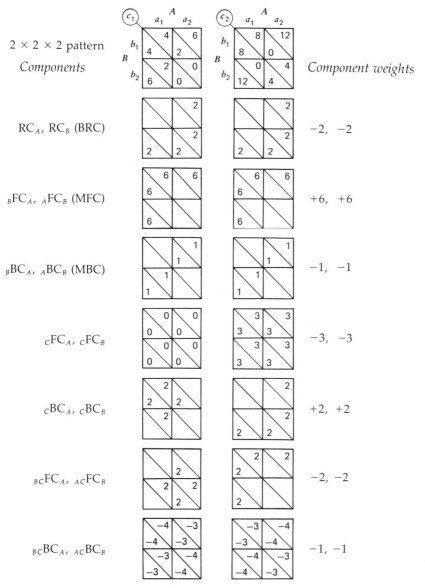

Figure 9.4   Analysis into components of the 2×2×2 pattern from Figure 9.3.

level of outcomes between the two patterns. A complete analysis of this three-way relationship appears in Figure 9.4, the original $2 \times 2 \times 2$ pattern at the top and its components arrayed below it. Whereas in the analysis of 2×2 relations the components are portrayed in successive 2×2 matrices, here the components of the $2 \times 2 \times 2$ pattern are shown in successive *pairs* of 2×2 matrices. The components of the analysis correspond to the seven pairs of terms in the A and B columns of Figure 9.2, although in a slightly different order. The first three terms are the familiar ones involving only A and/or B and can be readily calculated by averaging the c_1 and c_2 matrices and analyzing the average matrix. The remaining four terms involve C's sole or joint control over A's and B's outcomes. The fate control C exercises over the others reflects the difference between the two matrices in average outcomes. Thus $_cFC_A$ is readily calculated by averaging A's outcomes in the c_1 and c_2 matrices and taking the difference. The next two terms can be calculated by averaging separately over A and over B. The $B \times C$ matrix obtained by averaging over A can be analyzed into its components to show $_cBC_B$ and $_{BC}FC_A$. Similarly, the analysis of the $A \times C$ matrix obtained by averaging over B reveals $_cBC_A$ and $_{AC}FC_B$. Once all the terms are calculated $_{BC}BC_A$ and $_{AC}BC_B$ can be calculated as a remainder in a manner similar to that used for determining the MBC component of a 2×2 matrix; that is, values are entered in the lowermost matrices of Figure 9.4, as needed, to make the seven pairs of component matrices add up to the original ones. The clue that the books are balanced is that the matrices for $_{BC}BC_A$ and $_{AC}BC_B$ have regular behavior control patterns, although reversed in direction between the left and right matrices, as in Figure 9.4.

Alternative Method of Analysis

An alternative and simpler way to calculate the components of the $2 \times 2 \times 2$ matrix begins with the components of the c_1 and c_2 matrices (Figure 9.3). This method is important because it highlights the precise ways in which C, by the controls he exercises, can alter the pattern of the relationship between A and B. The notation and formulas are given in Figure 9.5. The analyses of c_1 and c_2 matrices proceed as usual; the terms are given signs according to their orientation with respect to the a_1b_1 cell of each 2×2 matrix. (The formulas yield signs according to the components' orientations to the $a_1b_1c_1$ cell of the $2 \times 2 \times 2$ matrix.) Components that yield high values in that cell are given positive signs and those yielding low values are given negative signs. (This rule has been followed in giving signs to the component weights in Figure 9.4). The seven pairs of formulas are then applied to yield the indicated seven pairs of components.

The reasonableness of the first three pairs of formulas will be apparent to the reader. Person A's RC_A for the entire relationship is simply the averaging of his RCs for its two halves. These formulas accomplish the averaging over c_1 and c_2. The fourth pair of formulas takes account of the fact that C's fate control is reflected in any change between c_1 and c_2 in average level of outcomes. The rationale underlying the last three formulas can be seen by referring to the corresponding component matrices in Figure 9.4. The $_cBC_A$ term refers to the fact that A's RC shifts from one side to the other with a shift between c_1 and c_2. Thus C's behavior control over A is greater when A's RC in the two matrices operates in different directions than, for example, when it operates in the same direction. In the formula the difference between RC'_A and RC''_A takes account of this fact. Similarly, $_{BC}FC_A$ is larger to the degree that when C makes one choice B's fate control over A is strong in one direction, and when C makes the other choice it is strong in the other direction. Again, the difference between FC'_A and FC''_A reflects this fact. The same reasoning applies to the $_{BC}BC_A$ component, which is large when B's behavior control over A is reversed in direction by a shift in C's choice.

Matrix	Terms for the Components
c_1	RC'_A, RC'_B, FC'_A, FC'_B, BC'_A, BC'_B, GM'_A, GM'_B
c_2	RC''_A, RC''_B, FC''_A, FC''_B, BC''_A, BC''_B, GM''_A, GM''_B

1.	$RC_A = 1/2\,(RC'_A + RC''_A)$	$RC_B = 1/2\,(RC'_B + RC''_B)$
2.	$_BFC_A = 1/2\,(FC'_A + FC''_A)$	$_AFC_B = 1/2\,(FC'_B + FC''_B)$
3.	$_BBC_A = 1/2\,(BC'_A + BC''_A)$	$_ABC_B = 1/2\,(BC'_B + BC''_B)$
4.	$_cFC_A = GM'_A - GM''_A$	$_cFC_B = GM'_B - GM''_B$
5.	$_cBC_A = 1/2\,(RC'_A - RC''_A)$	$_cBC_B = 1/2\,(RC'_B - RC''_B)$
6.	$_{BC}FC_A = 1/2\,(FC'_A - FC''_A)$	$_{AC}FC_B = 1/2\,(FC'_B - FC''_B)$
7.	$_{BC}BC_A = 1/2\,(BC'_A - BC''_A)$	$_{AC}BC_B = 1/2\,(BC'_B - BC''_B)$

Figure 9.5 Formulas for calculating components of the $A \times B \times C$ matrix from the components of the c_1 and c_2 matrices.

In the example shown in Figure 9.4 the last three terms act to change the magnitude of components between c_1 and c_2, serving (a) to introduce the RCs in c_2, although there was none in c_1, (b) to increase the magnitude of the FCs in c_2, and (c) to eliminate the BCs present in c_1. The first and last of these changes are necessary, of course, to shift the relationship from the pattern of Chicken to that of PDG.

C's Control Components

Figure 9.5 tells us how to calculate the components of the $2 \times 2 \times 2$ relationship from the components of the two halves c_1 and c_2. Alternatively, we can view the formulas in terms of what they show about how C's control terms change the A–B relationship; that is, we can examine the formulas to see what C control term must exist to form a shift between c_1 and c_2 in any aspect of the A–B relationship. Similarly, the formulas show the aspect of the relationship that is changed if any particular C control component is present. The effect of C's control components may be summarized as follows:

1. The $_cFC_A$ and $_cFC_B$ components do not change the *pattern* between the c_1 and c_2 matrices because they do not affect the RC, FC, or BC components of those matrices; C's fate control simply changes the general level of outcomes.
2. In contrast to $_cFC_A$ and $_cFC_B$, the lower three pairs of components in Figure 9.5 do serve to change the nature of the relationship between A and B as C shifts between c_1 and c_2. Thus any change in the pattern of the relationship between A and B can be traced to one or more of the last three types of C's control.
3. The $_cBC_A$ and $_cBC_B$ components change the direction and/or magnitude of A's and B's RC, between the c_1 and c_2 submatrices.
4. The $_{BC}FC_A$ and $_{AC}FC_B$ components change the direction and/or magnitude of B's fate control over A and A's fate control over B, respectively, between the c_1 and c_2 submatrices.
5. The $_{BC}BC_A$ and $_{AC}BC_B$ components permit C to change the magnitude and/or direction of $_BBC_A$ and $_ABC_B$. One possible consequence of this kind of control is that C's choice determines the nature of the co-ordination required between A and B. This is true when the $_BBC_A$ and $_ABC_B$ terms are correspondent, as in the lower-most matrices of Figure 9.4.

Specific Interventions by C

Changing the Value and Meaning of Behavior

No attempt has been made systematically to examine the possible antecedents of C's types of control over the A–B relationship. Some examples, however, will serve to suggest types of antecedent and the consequences of C's possessing various types of control.

It is easy to imagine the circumstances under which C would have $_cFC_A$. This component merely requires his possession of commodities that A desires, his ability to act in ways A finds rewarding, or his effectiveness in raising or lowering A's costs of interaction. Equally familiar are the generic bases for $_cBC_A$. Special combinations of A's and C's behavior must be compatible from A's point of view, these capabilities reflecting facilitation effects with heightened reward and/or reduced costs, or absences of interference effects with reduced rewards and/or increased costs. (See Chapter 3 on Antecedents of the Given Matrix and Chapter 4 in Thibaut and Kelley, 1959.) For example, without C's help (in state c_1) A may prefer doing a_1 to a_2. However, when C provides him with a special tool for performing a_2 or guidance in its appreciation (this help constituting c_2), A's preference may shift to a_2 in view of the lower costs and/or greater rewards associated with it. A common phenomenon is that the mere presence of another person interferes with the performance of certain behaviors, increasing their costs and reducing the satisfaction the actor derives from them. C's two actions, c_1 and c_2, may refer to C's presence and absence. If his presence interferes with one of A's actions but not the other, then the shift from c_1 to c_2 may change whether A prefers a_1 or a_2.

The other two of C's control components are more complexly determined. The term $_{BC}FC_A$ means that C selectively affects A's preferences for B's behaviors. (It also, of course, means equally that B selectively affects A's preferences for C's behaviors, but here we are viewing these terms in relation to C's effects on the A and B relationship.) A simple example is one in which both B and C give A one of two items and the items are such that each has greater value if a person also possesses the other. Thus b_1 and c_1 may consist of giving A a small dinghy and b_2 and c_2 giving A a nylon sail for the dinghy. Obviously, if C does c_1, A will prefer b_2, but if C does c_2 A will prefer b_1. Similarly, A may prefer a glass of wine and a piece of cheese to two glasses of wine or two pieces of cheese. Consequently, b_1 (wine) will be preferred to b_2 (cheese) if C gives cheese, but the preference will be reversed if C gives wine. In general, $_{BC}FC_A$ requires that C be able selectively to interfere with or facilitate A's enjoyment of B's behaviors. Other examples similar to those for $_cBC_A$ can be given except that the selective effect of the tools or tutelege that C provides is on A's appreciation of B's actions rather than his own.

The $_{BC}BC_A$ component, representing the most complex configuration of outcomes, is the most difficult to illustrate. In general, C's shift from c_1 to c_2 changes or redefines what is compatible or incompatible behavior between A and B. If a_1 and b_1 represent one opinion on a controversial polarized issue and a_2 and b_2, the opposing opinion, then C's successful induction of pressure toward agreement (c_1) would place value on a_1b_1 and a_2b_2 combinations but his eliciting a norm of independent expression (c_2) would place value on a_2b_1 and a_1b_2. A more trivial example in which C changes the meaning of similarity between A and B is the invitation to a costume ball with a prize for the most striking couple. This invitation (c_1) makes it desirable for a husband and wife to coordinate their dress in contrast to the usual party invitation (c_2) which carries no such implication. Many examples of $_{BC}BC_A$ can be developed from the idea of optimal combinations of two and three tools or instruments. To make music two roommates require an instrument and a score. If C contributes nothing (c_1), it is necessary for A to contribute one item and B the other (i.e., a_1b_2 or a_2b_1 are the preferred combinations.) If C contributes the score (c_2), inasmuch as only one score is needed, the preferred combination for A and B now becomes one in which both provide instruments (a_1b_1), assuming both enjoy playing more than listening. (Example is imperfect insofar as the a_2b_2 cell, everyone providing a score, is still unrewarding.)

Alternative methods of Changing Patterns. We have seen that $_CBC_A$ changes the direction of RC_A between the c_1 and c_2 matrices (RC'_A versus RC''_A) and $_{BC}FC_A$ changes the direction of $_BFC_A$ between the two matrices ($_BFC'_A$ versus $_BFC''_A$). Thus the concordance between the RC and FC terms in the c_1 and c_2 matrices can be changed in two ways, either by $_CBC_A$ and $_CBC_B$ which affect the RC terms or by $_{BC}FC_A$ and $_{AC}FC_B$ which affect the FC terms. From this it follows that there are alternative ways, shown in Figure 9.6, in which C can change the A–B relationship from, for example, PDG to MDG. Beginning with discordance between the RC and FC terms in the PDG (c_1) matrix, C's actions can create concordance either by reversing the direction of the RC terms (as in Case I by means of $_CBC_A$ and $_CBC_B$) or by reversing the direction of the FC terms (as in Case II by means of $_{BC}FC_A$ and $_{AC}FC_B$).

The actions of A and B in Figure 9.6 might refer to those of two small boys who possess different pairs of baseball trading cards. They agree to give each other one card. In the c_1 matrix, of his two possible actions, boy A slightly prefers (to the extent of 4 units) to give Y and keep X but B strongly prefers (8 units worth) the opposite, that A give X and keep Y. Symmetrically, B somewhat prefers that he give Q and keep P but A strongly prefers that B do the opposite. Thus at c_1, without C's intervention, they are in the typical PDG situation. In Case I C's intervention is to make each boy value more the one of his *own* cards that the partner values less by pointing out (though separately to their owners) the virtues of cards Y and Q. This shifts each boy's preference to giving the other boy the card that boy prefers. In Case II C's intervention is to make each boy

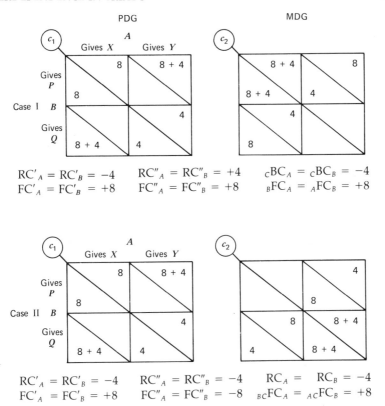

Figure 9.6 Two different ways for C to change the A-B relationship from PDG to MDG.

value more the one of his *partner's* cards that the partner values less. Again, the value-changing information (e.g., about rarity or quality) would have to be given separately to the two boys or both would change their preferences and the conflict aspect of the PDG would remain. [The example is interesting in that it shows the basis of the PDG in shared preference orderings in the context of agreement to exchange something. In this context C's RC- and FC-shifting interventions might be communicating preference-shifting information to the interdependent persons but separately so that the preference orders become negatively correlated.]

Alternatively, in this example C might accomplish the shift in Case I by invoking the value of *generosity* and pointing out its implication for giving away to one's friends the things one likes best. This would decrease each boy's satisfaction in keeping the card he most prefers and create a reward for giving it. Along the same lines C's intervention in Case II might consist of emphasizing the *altruistic* satisfactions to be gained from observing that one's friends possess valuable things. If this appeal were effective, each boy would then prefer the other to keep the better card and give away the less valuable one.

In any such situation inasmuch as the FC terms are the larger ones in the c_1 and c_2 patterns, a stronger degree of control is required of C if he is to succeed in the method illustrated by Case II. In the example given Case II requires that C succeed in reversing a stronger initial preference than that required for Case I. This is shown in Figure 9.6 by the relative absolute magnitudes of $_{BC}FC_A$ for Case II and $_cBC_A$ for Case I.

It will probably be apparent to the reader that if C reversed the direction of *both* the RC and FC terms of the PDG his effect would be simply to interchange the meanings, *defined in terms of the pattern*, of each person's response alternatives, the "cooperative" choice becoming the "defecting" choice and vice versa. Thus, if C were able to produce *both* effects described by Cases I and II by independently changing each boy's preferences about his own possessions and the partner's, then the "cooperative exchange" would shift from the X and P cards to the Y and Q. If accomplished by the invocation of generosity and altruistic values, the cooperative exchange would, oddly enough, involve giving the partner the least preferred card so that he could satisfy his altruistic interest but at the expense of being able to satisfy one's own interest in generosity. Indeed, the "exploitative" person would be one who managed to be generous by giving a valuable card while also feeling altruistic from having received a less valuable one from the partner!

We have used the PDG and MDG to illustrate the alternative ways in which C can shift certain A–B relationships from one pattern to another. Similar illustrations can be provided for other shifts; for example, between perfectly noncorrespondent combinations of BRC and MFC and perfectly correspondent ones, or between Battle of the Sexes and the matrix to its right in Figure 4.3.

Reversible and Irreversible Effects. Not all the ways in which C can affect A's and B's outcomes permit him to move back and forth between c_1 and c_2 at will. This is not a question of which control component he exercises but of the method by which he does so. For example, if C changes A's preferences regarding his own or B's action by tutelage in appreciation or by invoking norms about good or valued behavior, C will have no dependable means of undoing what he has done. Some of his effects, then, are likely to be irreversible, with the consequence that the power represented by the relevant control component no longer exists.

Changing the Correspondence between A's and B's Outcomes

One important aspect of C's effect on the A–B relationship is his impact on the correspondence between their outcomes. This is basic to whether they have a common interest in his actions or conflicting preferences about what he does. This aspect of the analysis is essential to determining whether his influence will be to strengthen their relationship or to weaken it.

The analysis of this aspect of C's effects begins by examining the relevance of each of his types of control to the correspondence or non-correspondence between A's and B's outcomes. If C has fate control over both A and B, he controls a source of positive or negative covariation between their outcomes. If $_cFC_A$ and $_cFC_B$ are large and have the same sign, they serve to increase markedly the correspondence between A's and B's outcomes *as calculated over the entire 2 × 2 × 2 matrix*. This is illustrated in Figure 9.7 in which the A–B relationship is a PDG at each

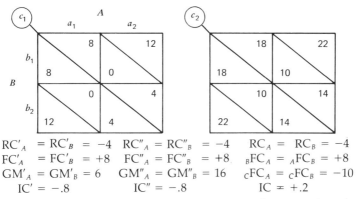

$$RC'_A = RC'_B = -4 \quad RC''_A = RC''_B = -4 \quad RC_A = RC_B = -4$$
$$FC'_A = FC'_B = +8 \quad FC''_A = FC''_B = +8 \quad _BFC_A = {_A}FC_B = +8$$
$$GM'_A = GM'_B = 6 \quad GM''_A = GM''_B = 16 \quad _cFC_A = {_c}FC_B = -10$$
$$IC' = -.8 \quad\quad IC'' = -.8 \quad\quad IC = +.2$$

Figure 9.7   Effect of C's fate control to increase the degree of correspondence between A's and B's outcomes over entire 2×2×2 matrix.

level of c; the index of correspondence in each case is $-.8$. For the entire 2 × 2 × 2 matrix IC $= +.2$. When $_cFC_A$ and $_cFC_B$ have opposite signs, they serve to increase the noncorrespondence for A and B over the entire matrix. This is illustrated in Figure 9.8. The point of these examples is that as C varies his behavior he either affects A and B in the same way (as in 9.7) or differently (as in 9.8). In the first case they have a common interest to induce C to remain at c_2. In the second case A wants him to remain at c_2 but B prefers him to enact c_1. In Figure 9.7 the higher correspondence for the total matrix compared with the separate matrices implies that by intermittent variation in his action C keeps the entire range of outcomes salient for A and B. They are likely, then, to perceive their common interest (in having C enact c_2) rather than their more conflictful relationship at each level of c. The high degree of noncorrespondence for the entire matrix in Figure 9.8 implies that to their partial conflict in the PDG pattern at each level of c has been added a conflict about which action to induce C to take.

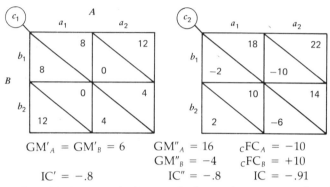

$$GM'_A = GM'_B = 6 \qquad GM''_A = 16 \qquad _cFC_A = -10$$
$$GM''_B = -4 \qquad _cFC_B = +10$$
$$IC' = -.8 \qquad IC'' = -.8 \qquad IC = -.91$$

Figure 9.8   Effect of C's fate control to increase the degree of noncorrespondence between A's and B's outcomes over entire $2 \times 2 \times 2$ matrix.

It may be noted that it is meaningful in these situations to refer to the concordance or discordance between $_cFC_A$ and $_cFC_B$. Just as there may be concordance or discordance between a person's control over his own outcomes and his control over another's (e.g., RC_A may be concordant or discordant with $_AFC_B$), there may also be concordance or discordance between a given person's control over a second person's outcomes and his control over a third person's outcomes. Both types of concordance affect the correspondence between the outcomes of the two affected persons (A and B in the examples).

In the case above, the effect of C is to *contribute* to the correspondence or noncorrespondence between A and B by variation in his action. In the cases to follow C's change of action *produces* a *change* in the correspondence between A and B. In Figure 9.9 C changes the A–B relationship from a noncorrespondent pattern of BRC + MFC to a correspondent one. In the example the means of producing this change is $_cBC_A$ and $_cBC_B$. However, as we have seen, the same shift can be produced alternatively by $_{BC}FC_A$ and $_{AC}FC_B$. It is simply a matter of

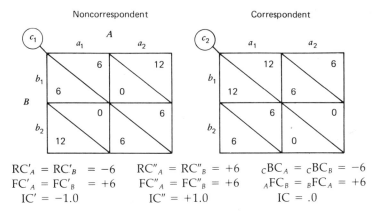

$$RC'_A = RC'_B = -6 \qquad RC''_A = RC''_B = +6 \qquad {}_cBC_A = {}_cBC_B = -6$$
$$FC'_A = FC'_B = +6 \qquad FC''_A = FC''_B = +6 \qquad {}_ABC_B = {}_BFC_A = +6$$
$$IC' = -1.0 \qquad\qquad IC'' = +1.0 \qquad\qquad IC = .0$$

Figure 9.9   Effect of $_cBC_A$ and $_cBC_B$ in shifting the A-B relationship from noncorrespondent to correspondent.

whether C's shift reverses the direction of the RCs or FCs between c_1 and c_2. In Figure 9.10 C shifts the A–B relationship from noncorrespondent MBC to correspondent MBC. This can be accomplished by using either $_{BC}BC_A$ or $_{AC}BC_B$, the latter being shown in the figure. In both cases the degree of conflict between A and B is higher for one of C's actions than for the other. By shifting his behavior C can determine whether it is possible for A and B to enjoy their best outcomes at the same time. Obviously, in this manner his action determines the maximum joint outcomes they can achieve. They are likely, then, to have a common interest in inducing C to take the action that heightens the correspondence of their relationship.

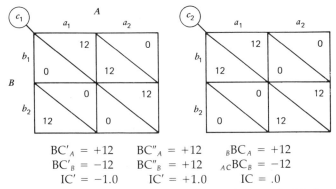

$$BC'_A = +12 \qquad BC''_A = +12 \qquad {}_BBC_A = +12$$
$$BC'_B = -12 \qquad BC''_B = +12 \qquad {}_{AC}BC_B = -12$$
$$IC' = -1.0 \qquad\quad IC' = +1.0 \qquad\quad IC = .0$$

Figure 9.10   Person C changes the correspondence of the mutual behavior control relationship between A and B.

(It is not meaningful in these last cases to describe C's effects as concordant or discordant. His effect is to *vary* the concordance or discordance between, say, RC'_A and $_AFC'_B$ or to vary the correspondence or non-correspondence between, say $_ABC'_B$ and $_BBC'_A$.)

In summary, A and B may have a common interest in C's taking a particular action for either or both of two reasons: (a) It increases both their outcomes and (b) it places them in a situation of high correspondence in which both are able to attain their high outcomes at the same time. The first is true when C's two actions affect their rewards and costs in the same way, $_cFC_A$ being concordant with $_cFC_B$; for example, the adult chaperone may by her presence disrupt the young couple's uninhibited and rewarding love making. The second is true when C is able to determine (a) the degree to which A's and B's RCs and FCs are concordant (e.g., the fond parents of a young bride provide her and her husband with household equipment that makes it easier for them to do the chores they expect of each other, thus reducing RC discordant with FC) *or* (b) the degree to which A's and B's BCs are correspondent [e.g., the friend who (c_2) provides piano accompaniment to the pair of violinists, one of whom must otherwise (c_1) do the unrewarding job of providing the accompaniment while the other enjoys playing the violin].

Facilitating the A–B Relationship

By his effect on the correspondence between A's and B's outcomes C can strengthen or weaken their relationship. Further aspects of this phenomenon are examined in Chapter 10's discussion of coalitions. Meantime we shall look at some rather specific ways in which he can promote or facilitate their relationship.

The Circular Relationship. Person B may be unilaterally dependent on A, affected by $_AFC_B$ or $_ABC_B$ but without any power over A. Person C can transform this into a relationship of mutual dependence if he is able to exercise some form of control over A, either $_cFC_A$ or $_cBC_A$. We might wonder why C would do this on B's behalf, but one clear case would be when B has similar control over him, either $_BFC_C$ or $_BBC_C$. Thus in one simple case C makes possible a circular pattern of fate control; he is willing to help A if A will then help B because B will then help him. An example is provided by three roommates with different needs and skills. Albert, the astronomy student, can help Bob with his calculus problems while Bob, son of a garage mechanic, can repair the clutch in Carl's BMW if Carl, a major in Romance languages, will tutor Albert for his French exam. The circular nature of the pattern is indicated by the subscripts of the three terms: $_AFC_B$, $_BFC_C$, and $_CFC_A$.

It can be seen that C does more than simply facilitate the A–B relationship. He actually makes it possible. A and B have a common interest in having C enact c_1. A's interest is direct—he profits directly from c_1. B's interest is indirect—he wants C to enact c_1 because A does and he wants to please A. Furthermore, A and B have means of satisfying their interests; A by inducing B to benefit C and thereby to induce C to benefit A, and B, by inducing C to benefit A so that A will benefit B.

In this situation any reciprocated FC (e.g., $_CFC_B$ as a reciprocation for $_BFC_C$) would render superfluous the other two FCs (in the example $_AFC_B$ and $_CFC_A$). The two persons with mutual fate control could do as well without the third person as with him; therefore his inclusion would be in doubt. In general, we might expect that arranging the exchange of benefits between two persons would be simpler than managing the circular "pass it on" pattern with the three persons and would therefore tend to be preferred.

A circular pattern of dependence may also be based on BC; for example, the operative controls would be $_ABC_B$, $_BBC_C$, and $_CBC_A$. Here each term might imply that the second person (the one "controlled") would get satisfaction from comparing his own behavior with that of the first person (the one exercising the control). Without C, A has no reason to remain in a relationship with B, but if C is oriented toward comparison with B and A is oriented toward comparison with C then a three-way relationship is possible. In each case the satisfaction may come from similarity (matching the comparison person) or from dissimilarity (mismatching). Not all combinations of these preferences, however, are equally good for the trio. It is fairly easy to show that for maximal correspondence among the three persons' outcomes in the $2 \times 2 \times 2$ case (for all three to be able to gain reward at the same time), either all three must prefer matching their comparison persons or one must prefer matching and the other two, mismatching. The proof of this statement is found in the simple demonstration that with only two responses each there is no pattern of their three choices that will fulfill the requirements of either two matches and one mismatch or three mismatches. We analyze this phenomenon in greater detail when we consider the relation between outcome correspondence and cognitive balance.

Improving the Reward-Cost Balance. Consider the case in which the A–B relationship is of marginal benefit to its participants because their costs in delivering rewards to each other are almost as great as the value of those rewards (e.g., RC_A is discordant with $_AFC_B$ and almost equal in magnitude). C can increase the profitability of the interaction if (a) he is rewarded by the same actions by which A and B reward each other, (b) A's and B's costs are increased very little in the triad, and (c) C has means of rewarding them. This is best exemplified by informative or entertaining actions that lose little of their value by being performed for the benefit of more than one person and the costs of which increase little with small increment in the number of recipients. A's costs are reduced by the addition of the third person, at least in relation to the rewards he delivers. In general, if the rewards are such (shareable and mutually enjoyable) that the total reward value of A's action increases more with the addition of the third person than his costs do and if the same is true for B, then a C who is able to reciprocate the rewards will make possible a triad that is more satisfying to all than any dyad would be. Thibaut and Kelley provide other illustrations of this and related functions of the third person (1959, pp. 196–197).

The Middle Man.   Some aspects of the preceding cases are involved in the third person who, in the interests of reward-cost improvement, is the middle man in certain aspects of the A–B exchange. Consider the lonely woman (A) who wishes to employ an escort (B) for occasional social events. For reasons given in the Chapter 3 discussion of the incompatibility of such rewards as money and affectionate attention it may be mutually interfering (cost raising and reward reducing) for her to give money directly to the escort. A third person, the agent for an escort service, can intervene to pass the money along from the employer to the escort (while taking a small commission). This serves to conceal the economic aspect of the A–B interaction and, by permitting them to limit their direct exchanges to social–emotional resources, to maintain the reward value of these resources at a high level.

A middle man may also handle the exchange between A and B of all the relevant resources. This usually occurs for reasons of cost cutting. If A and B find it too costly to transmit rewards to each other but, for some reason, economical to transmit them to C, *and if* they are the kinds of reward that can be passed along, then C may make possible an indirect exchange where no direct one is possible. The examples in economic relations (wholesaler, retail distributor) are commonplace. In informal social relations a symmetrical version of Longfellow's story about Miles Standish and Priscilla Mullens, with John Alden as the middle man, would serve as an illustration.

Facilitating Turn Taking.   In the turn-taking game, if A and B persist in pursuing their immediate interests, neither gains anything. A third person can sometimes modify the problem by pointing out the wisdom of turn taking, perhaps supporting the argument with reference to the values of *max joint* and *min diff*. The effect is to induce a shift in the A–B relationship from a 2×2 pattern of high conflict to an extended pattern of sequential play in which, with the value transformations, A and B have high correspondence of outcomes. An experimental example is provided by Deutsch's research (1966) on tutored communication in the trucking game.

Disrupting the A–B Relationship

Inducements to Discordant Behavior. C may have more fate control over B than A. If so, and if he so desires, C can induce B to take actions that are discordant in the A–B matrix. C's interest in doing this would reflect some divergence between his own preferences about B's behavior and A's preferences (e.g., $_BFC_C$ is discordant with $_BFC_A$). For example, a daughter has been pursuing her school work (which her mother wants) and her mother has been providing additions to the girl's wardrobe. A young man whose "hold" over the girl is greater than that of the mother may make his presence contingent on a different activity, one he finds rewarding but that the mother does not. This is illustrated in Figure 9.11 where the cells to which the young man (C) restrains the interaction (by his contingency rule) are heavily outlined. The matrix analysis suggests that the young man does not increase the noncorrespondence between mother and daughter over the entire $2 \times 2 \times 2$ relationship, but he does create a sharp conflict between them in the portion to which he limits the interaction in converting his fate control to behavior control.

Invoking Antisocial Values.   If two boys are in a Chicken situation (e.g., armed and surely able to hurt each other if they fight), a third person can

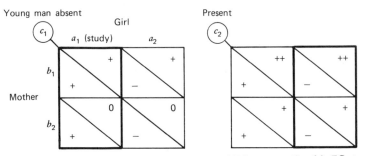

Figure 9.11   Person C creates conflict between A and B by converting his FC_B to BC_B.

sometimes strengthen the hand of one against the other; for example, if a close friend of A makes it clear that he will disdain A if he backs away from the danger, B knows that A now has strong RC operating on him to take the risky action. The friend's presence and comment increases the plausibility that A will pursue the dangerous course. This, of course, makes a similar course more dangerous for B and indirectly increases A's chances to come out the winner.

Because of the advantage C's action gives him, A may be tempted to create the same situation himself by making statements to his friend which imply that he (A) is to be considered a coward if he does not follow through with his aggressive intentions. The problem in either case is that the evocation of the value of bravery may be effective for B as well, acting to make the risky course more desirable than the safe one, regardless of its outcome. Indeed, a third person's general labeling of the challenge situation in such value terms may push the pair into a mutually destructive (though, in terms of transformed RC, mutually rewarding) course.

Asymmetrical Invocation of Prosocial Norms.   In a threat game C may invoke a loyalty norm for the threatener. This increases his reluctance to use his threat power (increases the RC against taking the mutually destructive action) and renders him more susceptible to the allocator's exploitation. Thus, although invoking the prosocial norms relevant to both the allocator and the threatener (fairness as well as loyalty) may work to the long-term advantage of the pair (by helping them to avoid a costly series of disruptions in the interests of justice), the asymmetrical invocation of loyalty may set the stage for exploitation and eventual disruptive rebellion.

THE DYAD'S POWER OVER C

Analysis of C's Outcomes in the $2 \times 2 \times 2$ Relationship

Figure 9.12 describes the outcomes for C, one of three young men sharing an apartment. His outcomes are shown as they are affected on a typical evening by his own actions (whether he sings or reads) and the actions of his two roommates (whether A sings or reads and whether B plays the piano or reads). The format is similar to that in Figure 9.3 except that the only outcomes in the matrix are those of C. The sources of variance in C's outcomes for this situation are analyzed in Figure 9.13. This analysis suggests the main reasons underlying the distribution of C's outcomes. It

Figure 9.12   Person C's outcomes as affected by his own actions and by those of A and B.

makes little difference to him, on the average, whether he sings or reads (RC_C is small). He has some slight preference for A to read rather than sing and a somewhat stronger preference for B to play the piano rather than read ($_AFC_C$ and $_BFC_C$ terms). The most important component of his interests is that he prefers to sing when A does and not to sing when A does not (to read when A reads). This is the $_ABC_C$ component. He has a very slight preference not to sing when B plays the piano and to sing when B reads ($_BBC_C$). He has a moderately strong preference for A and B to act in a "similar" manner, that is, both to make music or both to read ($_{AB}FC_C$), and this preference is particularly strong when he himself is singing (i.e., when he is reading he would prefer that one of the others be making music). The latter is indicated by $_{AB}BC_C$.

A and B's Controls over C

C's preferences mean, of course, that A and B have certain kinds of control over him. Our example indicates all the possible kinds of control. *Individually*, A and B have FC and BC which can be used cumulatively. Thus in our example A and B can vary C's outcomes over a 5-unit range by coordinated use of their FCs, moving from a_1b_2 to a_2b_1. Similarly, they can combine their respective BCs to exercise a 7-unit degree of BC over C, although most of the effect here is A's. This process also requires that A and B coordinate on the a_1b_2 versus a_2b_1 combinations of their actions. (The former motivates C to do c_1 for 7 points or take 0 points with c_2, and so on.) These examples point to an important fact: the cumulative use of their *individual* controls over C, either FC or BC, requires A and B to coordinate their actions. To combine their respective controls they must limit themselves to two of the four possible combinations of their actions.

Jointly, A and B also have FC and BC over C. As shown in Figure 9.13, however, these are exercised by varying whether they "match" their actions; that is, by which of the two diagonal pairs of combinations of

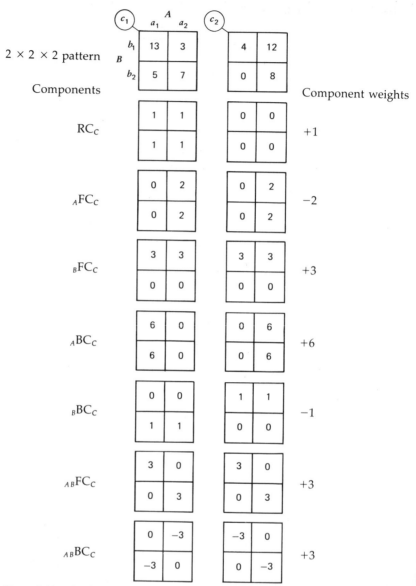

Figure 9.13   Analysis of C's outcomes in the 2×2×2 pattern from Figure 9.12.

their actions their choices represent. Thus in the example A and B can use their joint fate control to give C 3 units simply by doing behaviors with matching subscripts. Similarly, via $_{AB}BC_C$, their matching behaviors motivate C to do c_1 and their mismatched behaviors motivate him to do c_2.

The cumulative and joint components of A's and B's control over C can be contrasted in the following ways:

1. In the *cumulative* use of their *separate* powers A and B must coordinate between two specific combinations of their actions if they are to have *maximum* effect. Failure of such coordination, however, does not preclude *one* having *some* effect.
2. In the use of their *joint* power, A and B must coordinate between two specific *pairs* of combinations of their actions (the pairs defined by the two diagonals). Either member of a certain pair will have the desired effect. Failure of such coordination *totally precludes* having the desired effect. In short, in (1) the coordination requirements are more severe but may be partly fulfilled, whereas in (2) the coordination requirements are less severe but are absolute.

One common kind of power combines the worst properties of cumulative and joint power. Referred to by Thibaut and Kelley (1959) as conjunctive power, it is illustrated in Figure 9.14. A and B deliver a reward to C only if they coordinate on a_1b_1. Thus the coordination requirement is both severe and absolute. The analysis of the components reveals the reason. Although each person's contribution to the requirement is rewarding to C ($_AFC_C$ and $_BFC_C$), each partial contribution is negative for him in the absence of the other part ($_{AB}FC_C$). The mirror image of conjunctive power is *disjunctive* power in which C is rewarded, unless, say, the single a_2b_2 combination occurs. Here the best aspects of cumulative and joint power are combined: the coordination requirements are mild and the effect is maximal with their fulfillment. The analysis of this pattern (in Figure 9.15) shows that the joint power of A and B ($_{AB}FC_C$) compensates for any partial failures to coordinate optimally in the cumulative use of their separate powers.

The analysis of C's outcomes reveals the means that A and B have of controlling them, and potentially, of controlling C's behavior. In the preceding section we discussed the reasons that A and B may have for wishing to control C's actions, and in this section we cover the resources they have for doing so. We now take up the three sets of outcomes simultaneously and consider some phenomena unique to the triad. Later we return to the interaction between A and B on the one hand and C on

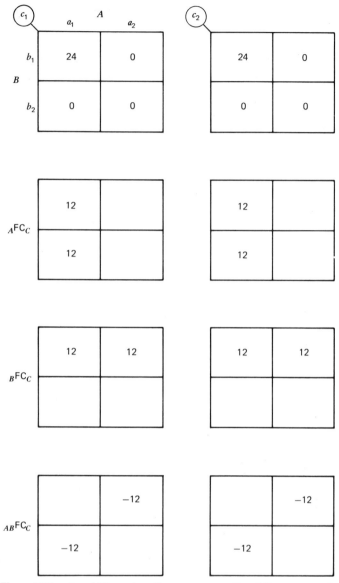

Figure 9.14 *A* and *B*'s conjunctive power over *C* and its components.

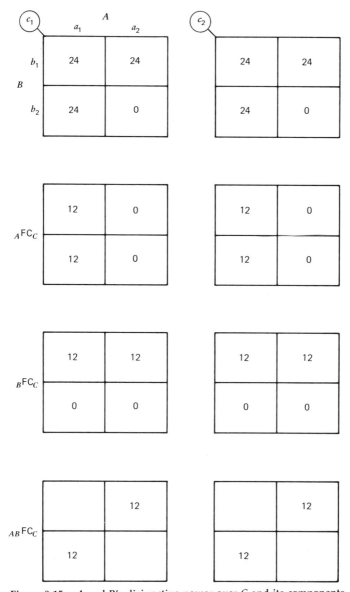

Figure 9.15   A and B's disjunctive power over C and its components.

the other, as we analyze a possible coalition against C or his coalition with one of them against the other.

TRIADS BASED ON COMPOUNDED DYADIC RELATIONS

Because a triad includes three dyads, one possible special form of triadic interdependence is that in which a certain two-person game is played simultaneously and in synchrony in each of the three pairings. Thus, if A and B are in a PD game, each also, separately but simultaneously, plays the same PD game with C; the single constraint is that the choice a person makes in one relationship is also the choice he makes in the other.

Following Hamburger (1973), we describe as a *compound* game one in which each person of the triad plays "several 2-person games simultaneously" (p. 33) and "is required to make the same choice in each of these . . . 2-person games he is playing" (p. 38). The first limits us to relationships based on components found in the dyad (e.g., $_AFC_C$, $_BBC_A$, and RC_C, but not $_{BC}FC_A$ or $_{AC}FC_B$) and the second property permits us to characterize the relationship in a $2 \times 2 \times 2$ matrix.

From the point of view of the A–B relationship, compounding has the consequences that (a) the relationship between A and B at c_1 and c_2 may be different from the relationship that is compounded and (b) their relationship at c_1 may be different from that at c_2. The implications of these facts are that A and B must treat their relationship in a different way when it is part of the three-way interaction and further, when (b) is true, that the nature of their relationship may depend on what action C takes.

Let us begin with examples of the *first* phenomenon. We asserted in Chapter 5 that in the optimal dyadic PDG the amount a person benefits the partner by the C choice is about twice as big as the self-benefit he forgoes by doing so. Therefore for a proper compounding of PDG it is necessary to have the person's RC equal to half the *total benefit* he delivers to his partners. A $2 \times 2 \times 2$ relationship based on this idea is shown in Figure 9.16. A's and B's outcomes are shown in the upper portion of the table and C's, in corresponding locations in the lower portion. The outcomes reflect the facts that each C response yields each partner one unit of reward, or a total of two units, and that each D response gives the actor one unit of reward. That this is a proper triadic PDG relationship is shown by the fact that the more persons choosing C, the higher the total score,

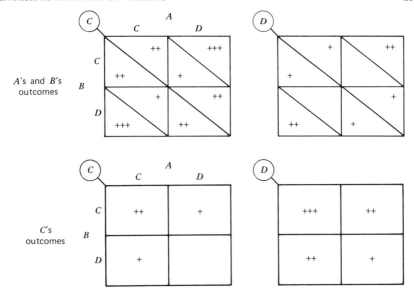

Figure 9.16   Compound PDG.

but, whatever the other persons' choices are, an individual always gets a higher score by choosing D than C. The reasons are apparent:

1. By his choice of C a person puts more into the system than by a choice of D.
2. As far as his *own* interests go, a person is always better off to give himself the smaller benefit than to generate the larger one for his partners.

It will be noted in Figure 9.16 that, whatever C's choice, the relationship between A and B is a constant-sum game. They divide up two units (if C withholds his benefits) or four units (if he delivers them). Thus the three-way PDG is not reflected in a PDG between each pair of persons when the third person's choice is held constant. The constant-sum property of the A–B relationship reflects the fact that, for example, $-RC_A$ is equal to $_AFC_B$. If each person's RC is made *smaller* than half the total FC he controls, the A–B relationship is a PDG, whether C chooses his cooperative or his competitive response.

Correspondent MBC provides another example in which the A–B relationships at c_1 and c_2 differ from the dyadic pattern compounded. Figure 9.17 shows a compounding of correspondent MBC. Each person receives

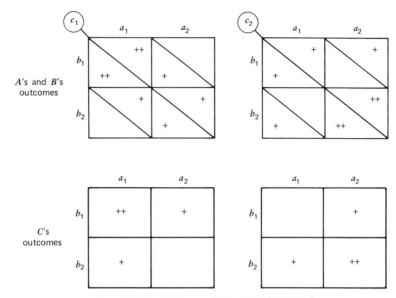

Figure 9.17   Compound correspondent MBC.

a reward from each of his partners whose response he manages to match. In the case shown each person gets two units of reward if the trio enacts $a_1b_1c_1$ or $a_2b_2c_2$. In all other cells two persons get one reward each and the third, no reward. The last is the person who has failed to coordinate. The two fortunate ones get their rewards from matching each other. The "deviate" who fails to match his partners deprives them of a unit of reward and gets nothing himself.

It can be seen in Figure 9.17 that if A and B know what C has done before making their choices they have RC for their own choices. The A–B relationship is the same at c_1 and c_2 but the rows and columns are interchanged; that is, the RCs are reversed in direction. In general, once one person acts in this situation the others find it their best bet to coordinate with him. Such coordination benefits everyone, the first person included, and the relationship encourages the emergence of someone who takes the initiative and thereby "directs" the others in achieving the mutually beneficial coordination.

The *second* phenomenon, that the c_1 and c_2 matrices may differ with compounding, was first noted by Hamburger (1973). This is the more interesting possibility because it implies that if A and/or B can determine what C's choice will be, their strategy for making their decision(s) may differ, depending on what he does. Our analysis reveals that this phenomenon occurs only when the compounded game involves *BC in combination with FC and /or RC*. This is shown by a consideration of the following:

1. Only components from dyadic relationships can be included in the compounding, by definition of the term.
2. The formulas in Figure 9.5 show that the only differences in patterning between the c_1 and c_2 matrices produced by a dyadic C-control term are those produced by $_cBC_A$ and $_cBC_B$. The RC_C term is irrelevant and the $_cFC_A$ and $_cFC_B$ terms change only the average level between c_1 and c_2 and *not* the pattern.
3. $_cBC_A$ and $_cBC_B$ *alone* (applied symmetrically, as they must be in compounding) act, in effect, to reverse the labeling between the c_1 and c_2 matrices. This was apparent in Figure 9.17 in which the c_2 matrix is simply the c_1 matrix with the subscripts interchanged for each person's responses.
4. Given $_cBC_A$ and $_cBC_B$, if the compound game also involves FC and/or RC components, the reversal of the RC terms between c_1 and c_2 produces a change in pattern rather than a mere reversal of labels. This results from the change in concordance between the RC terms and the BC and FC terms of the submatrices.

Some examples that illustrate this phenomenon are shown in Figure 9.18 which presents compound Chicken (MFC and MBC) and compound Hero (BRC and MBC). It can be seen that with the compounding of Chicken the *A–B* relationship shifts from some combination of PDG and Battle of the Sexes at c_1 to a rather cooperative game similar to MDG at c_2. For the compounding of Hero the shift is from a simple coordination game at c_1 to Martyr at c_2.

TYPES OF CONSTANT-SUM GAME IN THE TRIAD

The relationship of perfect conflict in the dyad entails a conflict between the actor's interests and those of his partner. In the one case (NCR MBC) the two persons prefer different combinations of behavior. In the other (BRC equal to and discordant with MFC) there is a perfect conflict between giving reward to the partner and keeping it for oneself. These two kinds of constant-sum game have their parallels in the triad and it may also involve a third type of conflict. Figure 9.19 shows a constant-sum game based on noncorrespondent MBC. In this particular example one person in each pair gains a reward for matching the second and the second gains

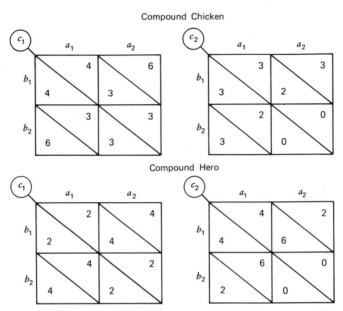

Figure 9.18. A's and B's outcomes for compound Chicken and Hero.

a reward for not matching the first. Thus A tries to match B but B tries not to match A, A tries not to match C but C tries to match A, and B tries to match C but C tries not to match B. The resulting pattern is a game in which the three persons divide three units of reward, according to a $1:1:1$ or $2:1:0$ ratio. The first occurs with a set of responses that lets each person satisfy one of his two requirements (e.g., $a_1b_1c_1$) and the second occurs when one person is able to satisfy both of his requirements (e.g., $a_1b_1c_2$. makes A the lucky fellow). Here as with compound CR MBC, if A and B know what C has done, they have RC. However, when they have this information and act accordingly, C gets no reward (as in $a_2b_1c_1$); therefore no one will want to make a first choice that can be known by the others.

Is there a basis here for two persons to act together, either to gain good outcomes for themselves at the expense of the third or to ensure an equal distribution of rewards among the three? With regard to the first possibility, it may be noted that when A gets two rewards C gets one, but when C gets two rewards it is B who gets one and not A (who gets one when B gets two). (The particular pair-relations here depend on the one of two ways in which the NCR MBCs are fitted together.) Thus there is no basis for a two-person exchange agreement that freezes out the third. In relation to a dyad's ensuring the $1:1:1$ distribution it can be seen that any

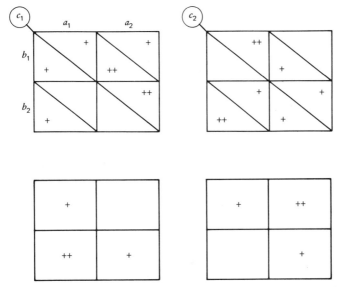

Figure 9.19   Constant-sum game based on noncorrespondent MBC.

pair can make it at least as desirable for the third person to cooperate in such a distribution as not to. If A and B enact a_1b_1, C gains as much by enacting c_1 (which yields $1:1:1$) as by enacting c_2 (which yields $2:0:1$). Of course, if for some reason he believes he can do better than one reward per occasion, C may attempt to disrupt the A–B coalition by favoring A. A and B might guard against a cumulative effect of this sort by alternatively setting up for $a_1b_1c_1$ and $a_2b_2c_2$ were it not for the fact that in both cases C's failure to do his part for equality results in A's advantage. Thus it is clear that A and B are stymied, even as between forcing C to cooperate in an equal division or freezing him out with alternating $2:1$ rewards for themselves.

The triadic version of the constant-sum game in which RCs and FCs are equal in magnitude but discordant is shown in Figure 9.20. In creating this type of pattern, it is necessary to set each person's RC equal in magnitude to the *sum* of the effects he has on his partners. Thus A's choice is between a_1 which benefits each of his partners by one unit and a_2 which benefits himself two units. His conflict, then, is between retaining all the benefit for himself or distributing it equally between his partners.

(Is it possible for the person to face a three-way conflict between benefiting himself or one particular partner or the other? The answer is no if we limit each person to two responses. Obviously, three responses are

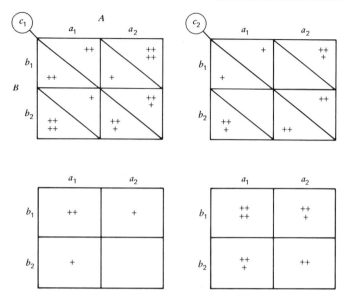

Figure 9.20   Constant-sum game based on FC-RC discordance.

needed in this case. This is one of several points at which moving from the dyad to the triad without a corresponding increase in number of responses creates peculiar constraints.)

Is it possible, in the constant-sum game in Figure 9.20, for A and B to freeze out C or to impose an equal distribution of the rewards? The answer to the first is no. They have no way of preventing C from having at least his share of the available rewards. The second problem is trivial for the same reason, that each person can be assured at least an equal share, simply by following his RC in the resultant matrix (which results in everyone keeping his two units at $a_2 b_2 c_2$).

A third kind of triadic constant-sum game is based strictly on FC components— $_A FC_B$, $_A FC_C$, $_B FC_A$, $_B FC_C$, $_C FC_A$, and $_C FC_B$. If each person's FCs are discordant, the result is the relationship shown in Figure 9.21. Each person has a choice of partner to benefit. Thus three units of benefit are available for distribution, except that a person may not receive the one for which he himself is responsible. It is obvious that this type of constant-sum game is unique to the triad in relation to the dyad. In the dyad, conflict of interest can occur only between the person and his partner. In the triad, as in this case, there is also a possible conflict between the two partners, reflected in the person's uncertainty about which one to help and in their competition for his assistance.

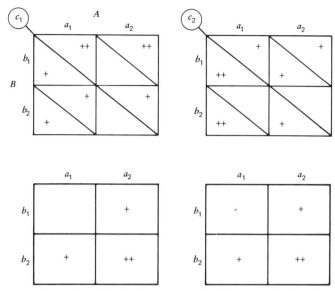

Figure 9.21   Constant-sum game based on discordant FC's.

It can be seen in Figure 9.21 that by benefiting each other (e.g., A and B exchange a_1 and b_1) any pair can freeze out the third. The excluded person's only leverage is to distribute his benefit unevenly between the two and thereby attempt to induce the disadvantaged person to reciprocate as the price for receiving help. Associated with a dyad's ability to freeze out the third person is their power to impose a $1:1:1$ division. Thus A and B can force C to accept such a division as the price for including him at all.

OUTCOME CORRESPONDENCE AND COGNITIVE BALANCE IN THE TRIAD

One meaning of certain kinds of interdependence is that a given person's rewards depend on the matching of behavior between two persons. Thus in $_ABC_B$ B's outcomes depend on the matches made between his and A's actions. If the sign of the BC term is positive, he will get a reward if the actions are matched (a_1b_1 or a_2b_2) or, if the sign is negative, he will get a reward if they are not matched (a_2b_1 or a_1b_2). Similarly, in $_{AC}FC_B$, if the term is positive, B will get a reward if A's and C's actions match, but if it is negative B will get a reward if they do not match.

One prime example to which the notion of matching or not matching applies is that of opinion expression. In certain contexts a person finds it rewarding to express the same opinion as another person—to match opinions with him, so to speak. In other contexts a person finds it rewarding to express disagreement with another. Viewing matching and not matching in this light, the question which sets of personal preferences regarding agreement and disagreement can be satisfied within the triad naturally arises. Is it possible for all three persons to satisfy such preferences at the same time? If so, for what sets of preferences is this possible? In other words, what preferences are compatible in the sense of generating an outcome matrix of high correspondence?

It will be clear that in the dyad only two sets of matching preferences generate correspondence: either both A and B must prefer agreement or both must prefer disagreement. A cannot satisfy his preference for matching at the same time that B satisfies his for not matching. Such preferences underlie noncorrespondent MBC.

It is readily shown that in the triad only two patterns of preferences can generate correspondence: either matching must be preferred in all three dyads or it must be preferred in one dyad but not in the other two. This is true, whether the matching refers (a) to BC terms (between the person and one of his partners), (b) to joint-FC terms (between the two partners of the person), or (c) to both. The proof of this statement is found in the possible patterns of actions in the $2 \times 2 \times 2$ matrix. Two patterns, $a_1b_1c_1$ and $a_2b_2c_2$, yield matching in each pair of persons. These patterns clearly make it possible for each person to satisfy preferences for agreement *with* each of his partners (the BC terms) and a preference for agreement *between* his partners (the joint-FC term). The remaining six possible patterns constitute three pairs of mirror-image patterns (e.g., $a_1b_1c_2$ and $a_2b_2c_1$), each of which yields matching in one pair of persons but not-matching in the other two pairs; for example, $a_1b_1c_2$ and $a_2b_2c_1$ yield matching between A and B but not-matching between A and C and between B and C. These patterns make it possible for one person (C in the example) to satisfy (1) his preferences for disagreement *with* each other person and (2) his preference for agreement *between* the two others, *and* for each of the other persons (A and B in the example) to satisfy (1) their respective preferences for agreement *with* one another and for disagreement *with* the first person and (2) their respective preferences for disagreement *between* the two others. In each case the first preferences correspond to the BC terms and the second preferences, to the joint-FC terms. The reverse side of the coin is that no response pattern permits two persons to satisfy their preferences for matching and, at the same time, the third person to satisfy his preference for not matching. Similarly, no response pattern permits three persons, each of whom prefers not matching, to be satisfied simultaneously.

We observe here a close equivalence between the conditions necessary for correspondence of outcomes and the requirements of cognitive balance (Heider, 1958). The sets of preferences that make possible correspondence of outcomes are also those that are in balance. At the dyadic level each person must want the same relation to exist between the two, either match or not-match. This corresponds to the balance rule for dyads that two positive or two negative relations are in balance. At the triadic level each person's preferences regarding his relations *with* each of the others must be consistent in a balance sense with his preference about the relation *between* them. If he wants to match each of them, he must also want them to match each other (the rule for the triad that three positive relations are in balance). On the other hand, if he wants not to match either of them, he must want them to match each other, or, if he wants to match one but not the other, he must want them not to match each other (the rule for the triad that one positive and two negative relations are in balance).

This equivalence between outcome correspondence and cognitive balance is provocative of speculation. At a descriptive level it means that the correspondent patterns are those that also permit each person to attain cognitive balance. Absence of interpersonal conflict is concurrent with lack of the intrapersonal tension associated with imbalance. Thus the three persons are not only not in conflict among themselves about which set of outcomes to attain, as they would be with noncorrespondent outcomes, but each of them is able to have a balanced view of the triad (and veridically so). Of course, the lack of conflict about outcomes need not mean a lack of opinion conflict. One of the correspondent (and balanced) patterns is that in which two persons agree with each other and disagree with the third. However, the correspondence means that even in this pattern the "need" of each for a consistent set of relations—his need for balance—is satisfied.

At a causal and more speculative level one wonders whether outcome correspondence may not constitute one of the antecedents of the preference for balanced interpersonal relations. If such relations are characterized by low conflict (at least in terms of outcomes), they may become intuitively recognized as such and subjectively valued. In the light of this analysis the individual's desire for triadic balance may reflect a sense of the interpersonal compatability of certain sets of preferences for matching and not-matching.

We must hasten to add an important caveat to these observations. The argument above applies only to the 2 × 2 and 2 × 2 × 2 interdependence patterns. With more alternative behaviors, there are many ways for persons not to match and it obviously becomes possible for all three persons to satisfy their respective desires simultaneously not to match each other. In other words, the equivalence between outcome correspondence and cognitive balance obtains only in a polarized, two-valued world; for example, when every action is either *pro* or *con* with respect to some central social issue. How frequently and extensively the real world has this property we leave for the reader to judge.

10

Negotiation and Coalition Formation

A Model of Independent and Joint Action in the Dyad, 282

ABSTRACT

This chapter first presents a model of independent and joint action in the dyad that identifies the framework within which negotiation between the members can occur. This framework consists of the various bargaining positions that may be available to the two persons and the settlement points that are viable in relation to the bargaining positions. A distinction is made between two types of bargaining position: (a) those created by each person simply pursuing his own interests and (b) those created explicitly, as threats, for the purpose of imposing on the other person a settlement favorable to the bargainer. The model is then extended to the triad where it forms the basis for an analysis of coalition formation—an analysis of which pair of the three persons, if any, will act in concert against the third. The basis for coalition formation exists in the mutual benefits to the coalition members of working together to create bargaining positions of the two types noted. The possibilities of coalition action are shown to increase the number of possible process and outcome patterns in the triad as compared with the dyad.

This chapter describes a model of action in the dyad and then generalizes the model to the triad. The latter enables us to examine the conditions underlying the formation of coalitions within the triad and the negotiations involved in the formation process. Here we do more systematically what we have done impressionistically throughout this book; that is, speculate about the *end state* of interaction in various interdependence relations (what the dyad or triad finally agrees, tacitly or explicitly, to do) and how they reach that end state (by threat, going their separate ways, negotiation, and so on).

We have considered interaction process at various other places in this book from a variety of perspectives. In the analysis of transformations we dealt with the evocation of outcome transformations, the transposition effects of preemption, and turn-taking sequential transformations. In Chapter 8 we dealt with the information processes by which interdependent persons make inferences about the *given* matrix and about how each other is transforming it. In this final chapter we adopt still another perspective on interaction process. We begin with the *transformed* or *effective* matrix and assume that the persons have good information about it. In other words, the problems of inferring the *given* matrix and the transformations have been solved. Each person knows what the *effective* values are for both persons in each possible outcome of their relationship. In the most interesting cases to be considered there still remains some degree of outcome noncorrespondence, and consequently there is room for further prosocial transformations of the matrix. In these cases the interaction includes appeals for further correspondence-heightening transformation. The values and rules that are sometimes elicited before interaction and that cause a person to treat the relationship as more correspondent than it is given are appealed to here as ways of settling the remaining conflict of interest. These prominently include proposals for sequential turn taking and pleas for justice (some variant of the *min diff* criterion). The conflictual aspects of the *effective* matrix also stimulate the use of egoistic criteria in devising means of settling the issues in favor of one's self. Chief among these is the *max rel* criterion as a means of identifying an effective threat action to use against one's partner. In addition to assuming that the participants have good information about the effective form of their interdependence, we assume that they have good control over the moment-to-moment temporal course of their interaction. Preemption is ruled out by assuming high alertness and equal motility of action. Neither person can plan on catching the other off guard in an undefended position. If one chooses to exercise his best threat action, the other one is assumed to be able to exercise his best defense or counteraction against it.

The above assumptions are, of course, unrealistic. Attribution about *given* values and transformations often occurs during negotiation and not before it. The transformation process is rarely complete before negotiation begins, and bargaining appeals and proposals are not simply routes to settlement but have an impact on the *effective* matrix itself. Alertness and motility are rarely equal between two persons; therefore one may act (or attempt to act) without the other being prepared. For a more realistic view of interaction process in all its complexity the reader will have to assemble the implications of our various analyses as they bear on a *given* pattern of interdependence, much as we have done, informally, in describing probable scenarios for various matrices.

A MODEL OF INDEPENDENT AND JOINT ACTION IN THE DYAD

Before considering coalitions in the triad it is necessary to specify the conditions for independent or joint action in the dyad. The essential elements of coalition formation are present in the dyad when the pair of persons agree to work together "against the game," so to speak.

In the pursuit of their best outcomes the members of a dyad may act in one of three ways:

1. *Independent action*, in which each person acts on his own, perhaps taking account of what his partner (acting in the same manner) is likely to do, to get the best outcomes he can.
2. *Cooperative joint action*, in which the two persons act in an agreed-on, coordinated manner, in the interest of providing each one with better outcomes than are available by individual action. (Value transformations serve the important purpose of facilitating such agreements, obviating the need for extensive analysis and negotiation. Thus the agreement may be tacit rather than explicit.)
3. *Imposed joint action*, in which the two persons act in an agreed-on, coordinated manner in the interest of preventing one of them from creating poorer outcomes for both, although particularly for the partner. The agreement here is imposed by the one person's wielding his threat power and consequently is usually explicit.

Which type of action occurs in the dyad (which is analogous to the question of which coalition, if any, will occur in the triad) depends upon the pairs of outcomes in the matrix and the way they are controlled by the two persons. For any given matrix, it is possible informally to anticipate how the interaction is likely to go and its probable conclusion. We now present a more systematic way of stating these expectations. This model is not presented as descriptive of behavior in the dyad. Nor is it a prescription of how the pair ought to behave. Rather, it is analytical of the possibilities, requirements, and constraints inherent to the interdependence matrix and suggestive of a scenario of the interaction that each person would find plausible. That is to say, the scenario takes account of the possible bases for action that the matrix provides for the pair and that they may present to each other. In short, this is a logical, coherent statement of the bases for action in interdependence relationships.

Our model entails a three-step analysis in which (a) two pivotal pairs of outcomes in the relationship are identified, (b) the remaining pairs of outcomes likely to come under consideration are classified in relation to the two crucial pairs, (c) each person's preferences for the pairs in (b) are examined to predict the probable outcome of the relationship; for example, whether it will result in independent action, cooperative joint action, or imposed joint action. By referring the predictions in (c) back to the matrix, it can be determined what specific form the action will take.

Identifying the IA and Th Pairs

Our model assumes that decisions are made in relation to two critical pairs of outcomes in the matrix, the independent action pair (IA) and the threat pair (Th). It is these two pairs that (in some instances) afford *bargaining positions* for the two persons and that (in all instances) give relationship-specific psychological meaning to their actions.

IA Pair. This is the pair of outcomes that A and B will get through their best "independent" actions as each one tries to maximize his own outcomes (follows a *max own* criterion). Each is assumed to follow his own RC or, lacking strong (dominant) RC, to take account of the other person's likely action (per the other person's RC) and to act accordingly (per own BC). In the absence of these conditions one or both are uncertain what the outcomes will be, so the pair of values is calculated on the basis of uncoordinated random action; for example, if there is uncertainty for both persons, as with pure MBC in a 2×2 matrix, the pair of values is simply GM_A and GM_B. In a larger matrix, if there is some section of the matrix through which the "If I . . ., then he . . ." reasoning cycles (i.e., there is no "saddlepoint"), then IA is calculated by averaging each person's outcomes over that section of the matrix.

In brief, the IA pair defines what each person can gain from the relationship if he goes his independent way, merely taking account of what the other is likely to do in his independent action.

Th Pair. The threat pair of values results from each person's best attempt unilaterally to establish a threat position from which to make demands for the good outcomes available in the relationship. As in the case of IA, the point is established by a person only in the face of his partner's similar efforts. Thus the Th pair represents both the best threat for A and his best defense against B's effort to establish a threat position.

The type of pair that can best serve A's purposes as a basis for threat depends on the particular distribution of the good outcomes or the "frontier" points. In general, however, it is a pair of points in which the difference $(A–B)$ is maximized. [The term $(A–B)$ refers to B's outcome subtracted from A's.] Generally, the Th pair of a matrix can be identified by examining the matrix of $(A–B)$ values (cf. Figure 5.6) and then assuming that A will do his best unilaterally to maximize this value while B will do his best to minimize it, that is, to maximize $(B–A)$. Each is assumed to take account of the other's efforts and to do the best he can in the light of what the other can be expected to do. (Our assumptions here amount to treating the pair as playing a constant-sum game. The Th pair is equivalent to the equilibrium pair of values, defined in one of the ways summarized in the discussion of Figure 6.14.)

We consider below the exceptions to the *max rel* rule as a basis for identifying the best Th pair, but meantime the reader will appreciate the general usefulness of the rule. To consider the matter from *A*'s point of view the ideal Th pair is one in which (*A–B*) is large and positive. This enables *A* to threaten unilaterally to move the pair to a point in the relationship at which, even though his own outcome will be low, *B*'s will be much lower. The value of such threat, of course, is to exert pressure on *B* to grant concessions to *A* in order to avoid the low outcomes.

The Th pair may be the same as the IA pair. If so, it is regarded as nonexistent. (It would be meaningless for a person to threaten his partner with outcomes they can get by independent action.) By its definition *the Th pair cannot yield either person higher outcomes than the IA pair*. If any pair selected by the threat criterion were to yield higher outcomes for either person than the (tentatively defined) IA pair, the Th pair would become the IA pair. The point is that as *A* and *B* attempt to maximize the difference to their own respective advantages neither can attain higher outcomes than he attains when each attempts merely to maximize his own outcomes. However, one or both (usually both) may attain lower outcomes in the pursuit of *max rel*.

Classification of Possible Outcomes

All possible pairs of outcomes in the matrix can be classified with respect to the bargaining positions defined by the IA and Th pairs. By "all possible pairs" we refer not only to those specified in the matrix but also to others produced by trade offs between the cells of the matrix; for example, a particular 2×2 matrix may have only the following four pairs of outcomes: (0,0), (10,0), (0,0), and (0,10). By coordinated trade offs between the second and fourth pairs other pairs of outcomes are possible; for example, (5,5), (6,4), and (2,8).

The classification of all possible pairs is shown in Figure 10.1. First, there may be *Reward* pairs in which both persons have higher outcomes than in the IA pair. These are the outcomes that the dyad can obtain by cooperative joint action. The action required is joint because some type of agreement is necessary to attain the outcomes. (Remember, IA is the best they can do without such agreement.) The action may be considered cooperative because *A* and *B* must work together with the common purpose of giving each person more than he can get if he acts independently. If there are no *Rew* pairs, *A* and *B* can do no better by agreement than by independent action.

Second, there may be *B-complies* (*B-comp*) pairs, in which B gets less than his outcome in IA but more than in Th, and A gets more than in IA. If there are such pairs, they include the outcomes to which A might hope to gain B's compliance by using his threat over B (hence the label *B-complies*); that is, by threatening B to take the dyad to the Th pair A can put pressure on B to accept something less good for him than IA but better than Th (and, of course, better for A than IA—the basis of A's interest in making the threat). The *B-complies* pairs can be attained only by agreement but it is an agreement imposed on B by A; hence these outcomes represent imposed joint action.

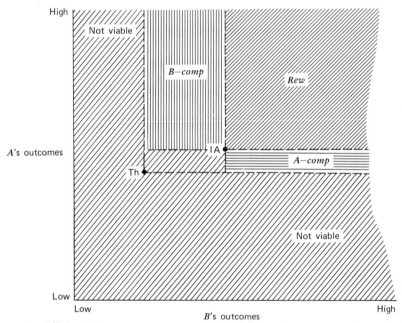

Figure 10.1   Classification of pairs of outcomes in relation to the IA and Th pairs.

Third, there may be *A-complies* (*A-comp*) pairs, defined for A in the same way as the *B-complies* pairs are defined for B, that is, better for A than Th but less good than IA and better for B than IA. B might hope to gain A's acquiescence to one of these pairs.

Finally, the remaining pairs may be dismissed from consideration as being not viable, that is, as having no basis for their bilateral acceptability. These pairs are either below the Th level for one person (why should he agree to accept less than the worst his partner can do to him?) or below

IA for both persons (why should they agree to a set of outcomes that both can exceed at IA?).

In fact, the notion of not viable pairs can be extended to include all pairs not on the frontier of the plot of pairs of outcomes. This is simply a way of precluding from consideration any pair of outcomes with respect to which another pair is better for *both* persons. In practice, this amounts to the assumption that the two persons have good information and use it carefully and skillfully. [With incomplete information, careless negotiation, and a complex bargaining task interdependent persons often fail to identify and agree on the frontier points (Kelley and Schenitzki, 1972; Pruitt and Lewis, 1975).] Thus in Figure 10.2 the nine large circles indicate the pairs of outcomes in a particular 3 × 3 relationship. As noted in Chapter 6, all possible trade offs among the cells in this relationship will yield pairs of outcomes that fall within the crosshatched convex polygon.

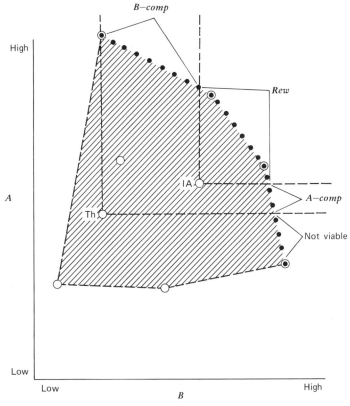

Figure 10.2   Classification of pairs of outcomes on the frontier.

Among them we consider only those denoted by solid circles; that is, those on the frontier of the polygon; and it is only the frontier pairs that we classify as *Rew*, *A-comp*, *B-comp*, not viable, or (see below) IA.

From the definition of the IA pair it will be noted that there may be no *Rew* pairs: the IA may be on the frontier itself, in which case it is given a special classification among the frontier points. Similarly, there may be no compliance pairs. The Th pair may equal IA, hence define no *Comp* pairs (and in that sense be nonexistent), or, even if Th is different from IA, there may be no outcomes on the frontier that satisfy the *Comp* criteria. If there are *Comp* pairs, the numbers of *A-comp* and *B-comp* pairs may differ greatly. If Th maximally favors *A* (his outcome there equals his outcome at IA), there will be no *A-comp* pairs and many *B-comp* pairs.

The relative locations of the several kinds of pairs will make it clear why we use the term compliance to describe some of them. Because a compliance set does not include any of the elements of the IA or *Rew* sets, the person forced to take a *Comp* pair is in a sense acting in a nonvoluntary way, unwillingly submitting to the partner's threat. He is required to accept lower outcomes than he might otherwise attain as through independent action or joint cooperative action. (In fact, the threatened person would be better off if no communication or agreement were possible! The IA is what two rational players might expect to get, on the average, with one-shot, no communication play.) The IA and the Th levels are somewhat similar in their psychological significance to the CL and CL_{alt}, respectively. Thus the IA defines a level of outcomes the person might minimally expect from the interaction, and the Th defines a level he will be forced to take if the partner acts to disrupt the relationship. Consequently the compliance set outcomes are analogous to those obtained in a nonvoluntary relationship, being below CL but above CL_{alt} (Thibaut and Kelley, 1959). (The IA and Th pairs are discussed in relation to the CL_{alt} on p. 296.)

Reconsideration of the Th pair

We have already noted that although identifying the Th pair by the *max rel* rule is generally appropriate there are exceptions. The *max rel* criterion always yields the pair that gives the bargainer the most favorable position from which to make an equity claim. Thus the larger the value $(B–A)$ for a particular pair of outcomes, the more favorable to *B* the frontier pair that comes closest to yielding him and *A* equal increments above that pair. The location of the Th pair, however, not only affects the location of an equitable outcome but also extends or curtails the two compliance sets. This effect of the threat pair is dependent not only on the value of $(B–A)$

but also on the value of $(B+A)$. Sometimes the effect is large enough that a point less favorable on the $(B-A)$ criterion will be preferred by B to one that is more favorable. The two cases are illustrated in Figure 10.3. In both cases diagonal lines indicating successive levels of $(B-A)$ have been drawn to permit easy comparison of different Th pairs. By the *max rel* criterion person B prefers points located farthest toward the lower right portion of the plot. Thus by this criterion he would prefer T to T' in both cases in Figure 10.3. In Case I, however, T' extends the *A-comp* set in a direction favorable to B and in Case II T' curtails the *B-comp* set in a direction favorable to him. In both cases the T' pairs seem to provide B with a better bargaining position. Thus, if the matrices were such that he could impose either T or T' on the dyad, the T' pair would be the better one.

The implication of these cases for our simulation of the interaction is that the Th point should be identified *after* the frontier points have been identified. The optimal threat point is the one that results when each person seeks a way in which unilaterally he can establish a favorable *max rel* position and either reduce the size of his own compliance set or increase the size of his partner's.

Predicting the Outcome of the Relationship

Once the viable points on the frontier have been identified and classified as IA or *Rew*, *A-comp*, and *B-comp* they are listed according to each person's preferences. The process of reaching agreement on some mode of action or trade off can then be thought of as one in which each person moves down his preference ordering until they come to the same outcome pair and this forms the basis for agreement. In A's preference ordering *B-comp* pairs, if any exist, will come first, followed by either the IA or *Rew* pairs. *A-comp* pairs will be at the bottom of the list. B's preference ordering will have a complementary structure, with *A-comp* pairs, if any exist, heading the list.

In the simplest cases the IA pair or the same *Rew* pair will be at the top of the two persons' preference orders and they can agree—either to leave each other alone and go their respective independent ways or to take joint action to attain the *Rew* pair. These two cases are illustrated in Figure 10.4 by correspondent MBC and MDG, respectively. In the more complex and common cases one or both will have *Comp* pairs as their first preferences and negotiation will ensue (see Chicken in Figure 10.4). Similarly, even when there are no *Comp* pairs, if there are multiple *Rew* pairs negotiation will be necessary to reach agreement on one of them (see PDG in Figure 10.4). When the negotiation includes *Comp* pairs, there is the possibility of imposed joint action; that is, of settlement on a pair that puts one person

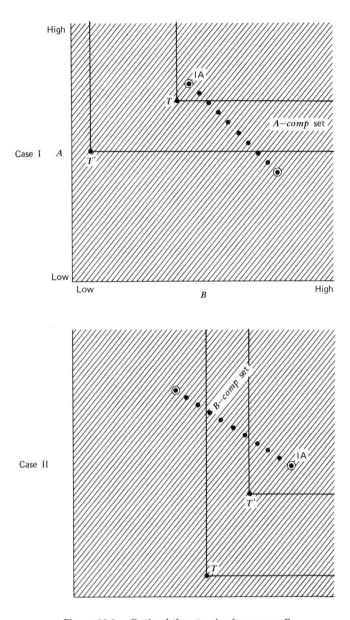

Figure 10.3 Optimal threat pairs for person B.

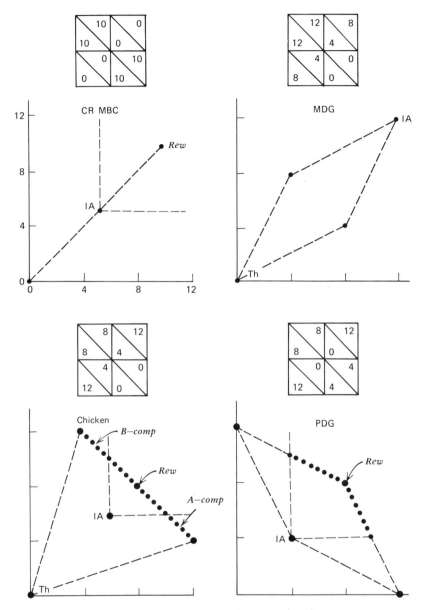

Figure 10.4   Analysis of four patterns in terms of settlement points.

below his IA level. This is particularly likely when the *Comp* sets are asymmetrical in relation to IA, as in Case I of Figure 10.3, in which A is likely to have to agree to a trade off that will put him below IA.

At this point we have made rough predictions about the course of the relationship. Depending on what each person finds at the top of his preference ordering of the frontier pairs of outcomes, each may act independently, jointly pursue a *Rew* point, or negotiate. Many relationships will require the last because the first preferences will not be compatible. Therefore, although we cannot make further clear predictions about the course of affairs, we must consider the process of negotiation. How is it that a person gives up his attempt to gain his preferred outcomes and looks further down in his preference order? What appeals does he make to and receive from his partner? What order is there to the process of finding a reasonable basis for agreement when the interests of the two persons, at least as among the frontier points, are in direct opposition? To these questions we now turn.

Negotiation

In general, negotiation involves two interdependent persons who are seeking an agreement that will make them both better off than at their respective bargaining positions. Figure 10.5 is a simple case. This is the situation we have described in which the two persons bargain over the values in the *Rew* set. In the absence of a Th pair, the IA pair of outcomes defines their respective bargaining positions. Three pairs of outcomes from the matrix are found in the *Rew* set, but inasmuch as there is the possibility of arranging a trade off between two or more of them only the most profitable (i.e., only the frontier pairs) are shown in the figure. Among the frontier pairs there is no *mutual* basis for selecting one rather than another. At this point our model of the process must become nonspecific, as we move from reasons for action that have a logical appeal for both persons to reasons that, although not without force, are more debatable and therefore less compelling. The former are epitomized by the argument that "We'll both be better off if . . ." and the latter by "We'll come out with equal gains if. . . ." The latter are the arguments of equality and equity. What force they have comes from the important fact that *some* agreement is to be preferred by both persons. Because in that basic sense both are in the same boat, the costs of nonagreement (it can be argued) should fall equally on both, and, conversely, the profits from agreement should be equally shared by both. Thus in Figure 10.5, although A prefers agreements close to x and B prefers those close to y, the equality argument can be made for one close to the 50:50 line.

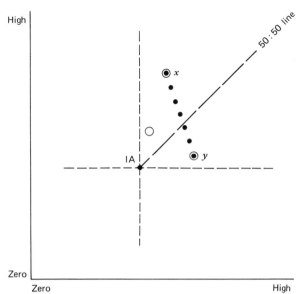

Figure 10.5   Negotiation diagram with bargaining among members of the *Rew* set.

Matters are rarely as simple as shown in Figure 10.5. Usually there are *multiple* baselines from which the bargaining occurs (Figure 10.6). In Case I the IA pair itself does not yield equal outcomes for *A* and *B* and two different equality arguments can be made, one with respect to the absolute values of any pair (to be referred to as an *equality* argument) and the other with respect to the two persons' gains in relation to the IA pair (to be referred to as an *equity* argument). The latter type of argument asserts that in a sense the IA pair represents the true zero point of the relationship, for it specifies what each person can generate "for himself," so to speak, in the absence of joint action. (In equity theory terms it represents his value, investments, and resources.) The argument continues that even though one person is better off than the other at IA he deserves to be so and accordingly deserves a similar advantage in the eventual agreement. It can be seen that in Case I in Figure 10.6 *A* will make this equity argument and *B* will make the equality argument. At this point our model has made its predictions about the process and must leave some uncertainty about the outcome. In general, of course, we might expect the final agreement to be some compromise between those indicated by the two arguments.

The most complex negotiation situation is shown in Case II in Figure 10.6. Here, in addition to the equity argument based on IA, *A* can introduce an equity argument based on the Th pair. His assertion is that

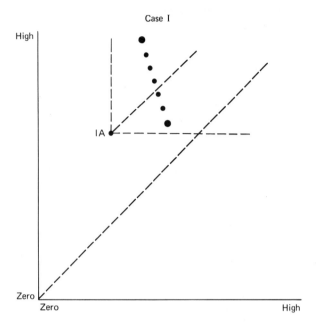

Case I

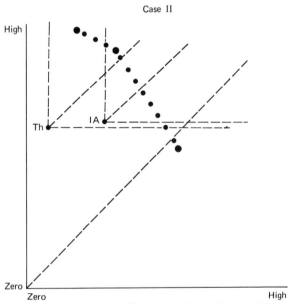

Case II

Figure 10.6   Negotiation diagrams with multiple baselines.

the Th pair defines the real baseline for each person in that he can ensure that they will get no more than their outcomes there. It will be clear from the figure that the force of this argument depends on how much A's outcomes in the Th pair surpass B's; that is, the amount A stands to gain from this equity consideration depends on how usable the Th pair is for A. Figure 10.7 shows the effect of the Th pair in a situation in which IA is on the frontier. From this example it is apparent that the threat-based equity argument may suffice to induce B to agree to an outcome below IA.

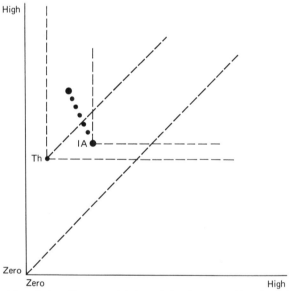

Figure 10.7   Negotiation diagram with bargaining between IA pair and *B-Comp* set.

Although the Th pair may afford a basis for one person's equity arguments, it would be wrong to conclude that these arguments have the same meaning and persuasiveness as those based on IA. In the one case (IA-based arguments) the assertion is "I deserve such and such because of what we would get if we go our individual ways." In the other case (Th-based arguments), the argument is "I deserve such and such because of what we would get if I impose the threat outcomes on us." There is clearly a difference in the implied locus of causation for the nonagreement outcomes, the former stemming from the structure of the relationship and the latter from the willful intervention of one person. The import of this difference is uncertain, but in general we might expect Th-based equity arguments to have less effect on the agreement because of the resistance they are likely to arouse by their implication that the relationship is subject to unilateral definition. Yet the difference is one of degree. It is, after all, the structure of the relationship that provides one person with the means for threatening the other. The difference is between (a) acting in a rather direct ends-oriented way (as in asserting one's intention to pursue the IA in the absence of agreement) and (b) acting in an indirect means-oriented way (as in asserting one's intention to impose the Th pair in the absence of a certain type of agreement).

Certainly one major exception to the generalization that a Th-based equity argument has less persuasiveness than one that is IA-based occurs when the Th-based argument coincides with (or is close to) the equality argument. This is illustrated by the version of the Threat game shown in Figure 10.8. The Th pair is useful for B, for the $(A–B)$ difference in outcomes is smaller than in the IA pair. It therefore becomes a basis for negotiating a trade off between the IA pair and the single member of the A-comp set. Because the Th pair is at $(0,0)$, its derivative equity argument coincides with an argument for equality of outcomes.

If the Th pair yields the same difference between A's and B's outcomes as the IA pair, it may provide no different basis for agreement than the IA pair. We may say that no usable threat exists for either person in such a case. Yet, if the Th point is different from the IA pair, it affords an additional argument for reaching *some* agreement; that is, it can be used by either person to press for agreement. We might expect the IA-based equity argument to carry more weight in this case.

The Comparison Level for Alternatives as a Bargaining Position

As noted in Chapter 3, the matrix may be used to represent the consequences of each person's being "in" or "out" of the dyadic relationship. Thibaut and Kelley (1959) defined the person's CL_{alt} as the lowest level of outcomes the person will accept in the light of his/her available alternative opportunities and relationships. The person's CL_{alt} thus constitutes a potential bargaining position from which to negotiate outcomes within the given relationship. We can now see that, depending on the circumstances, the CL_{alt} may correspond to an IA or a Th pair. The two possibilities are shown in Figure 10.9. Each person is shown to have two behavioral choices *within* the relationship (a_1 and a_2 for A and b_1 and b_2 for B). The consequences of one or both person's leaving the relationship are shown in terms of the values of their respective CL_{alt}s. (This glosses over a problem mentioned on p. 72.) In Case I, with independent action, B chooses b_2, and taking account of B's choice A chooses his CL_{alt}. Thus the

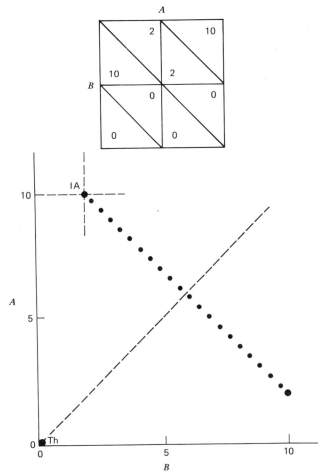

Figure 10.8 Matrix and negotiation diagram for the threat game.

CL_{alt} values (8 for A and 4 for B) constitute the IA pair. As shown in the bargaining space at the right, the IA affords a bargaining position from which it is reasonable for the two persons to negotiate some turn-taking arrangement between the a_2b_1 and a_2b_2 cells within the relationship.

By contrast, in Case II in Figure 10.9 the CL_{alt} values constitute a Th point. The IA pair (7,6) results from B's independent preference for b_2 and A's similar preference for a_2. In generating a threat point, A takes his CL_{alt} [this maximizes $(A–B)$ in the face of B's choice of b_2 as a way of minimizing $(A–B)$.] The Th point provided by the CL_{alt} values favors A and affords a

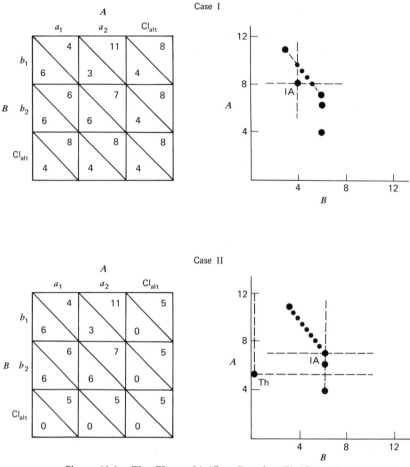

Figure 10.9   The CL$_{alt}$ as IA (Case I) and as Th (Case II).

basis for negotiating some trade off between the IA value and A's most preferred outcome (11,3 at a_2b_1).

The point of these examples is that the CL$_{alt}$ may have different meanings as a bargaining position, corresponding to the different meanings of the IA and Th pairs. The examples show that its meaning depends on how the two CL$_{alt}$s compare with the outcomes to be obtained within the relationship and with one another. When the CL$_{alt}$ values are known only to the persons to whom they apply, as is commonly the case in bargaining relationships, their potential significance as IA versus Th points creates a source of ambiguity and misunderstanding for the interaction. A person for whom the CL_{alt} provides an IA bargaining position may be viewed by the partner as using the alternatives as a threat and therefore as exerting undue pressure to gain a favorable agreement.

Some Qualifications

The preceding discussion has assumed that equity arguments are used to lay claim to outcomes that afford the two persons *equal increments* above the bargaining points, whether IA or Th. It must be noted that a different argument can be made, notably one that the *ratio* of outcomes at the bargaining point should be maintained at the settlement point. The implication of an *equal ratio* argument is shown in Figure 10.10 for the situation in Case I of Figure 10.6. Because the ratio of outcomes at IA favors A over B, the equal ratio argument favors him even more than the equal increment argument and the gap between the equity and the equality positions is widened. The equal ratio argument can be made only when there are meaningful zero points for the outcome scales, and is probably more likely to be invoked when ratio scales such as time, money, and weight are involved, and when they are commensurable between A and B.

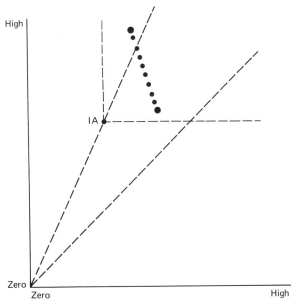

Figure 10.10   Equal-ratio equity argument for Case I in Figure 10.6.

Earlier we distinguished cooperative joint action from imposed joint action. It must now be admitted that there is no sharp dividing line between these categories. As the agreement within the *Rew* set moves closer to the IA level for one person, the agreement becomes to a degree imposed on that person. Similarly, as the agreement within the *B-comp* set approaches the IA level, it probably seems less a matter of compulsory agreement and takes on some of the qualities of a mutually cooperative action.

How do these equality arguments relate to value transformations? First, they are operative in relation to outcomes in the *effective* matrix, that is, in relation to outcomes that may already have been subjected to some transformation. Second, they are arguments directed toward producing a basis for agreement. As such they may introduce further prosocial transformation, but their primary function is that of facilitating agreement. The two phenomena are closely related because they derive their existence from the same facts of interdependence.

In concluding this description of a model of action for the dyad, it should be noted that involved here is a logical and analytical structure that is independent of the matrix analysis. The model begins with the definition of pivotal pairs of outcomes, the *bargaining positions*, and uses them to classify the frontier pairs in terms of possible *settlement points*. These pairs are then ranked according to each person's preferences and the two rank orders are examined for what they make probable in terms of negotiation, action, and so on. The latter implications can be translated readily back into matrix terms; for example, pairs of actions or co-ordinated trade offs between two pairs of actions. However, the intervening logic of the model, which consists of classification, rank orders, and implications, can be applied to sets of outcomes derived from any form of description of interdependence and does not require the matrix.

Although the matrix analysis of interdependence is not essential for the model of action, it illustrates the central role that some conceptualization of interdependence (outcome control) must play in linking the terms of the model to specific behaviors in the relationship. The model requires some way of specifying (a) the control over their individual and joint outcomes the two persons can exercise independently and by joint action, and (b) the bases for threat each can establish by unilateral control over, for example, the magnitude of the difference between their outcomes. The matrix provides a specification of both plausible bargaining positions and of reasonable settlement points. It also determines the nature of the joint action necessary to yield any agreed-on outcomes. It is not necessary to spell out here all the links between the matrix and the model because they have been implied in preceding sections of this book; for example, in

Chapter 5 on control over pair outcomes (the sum and difference scores) and in Chapters 4 and 6 on the turn-taking patterns and ratios necessary to yield certain allocations of outcomes between the two persons.

A MODEL OF ACTION IN THE TRIAD: COALITION FORMATION

In Chapter 9 we saw some reasons A and B might have for coordinating their actions in relation to C to induce him to act a certain way or to prevent him from taking some action. We have also seen, in their types of control over C, A's and B's means of exercising this influence. We now consider these matters more generally by attempting to answer such questions as the following: which pair of a triad, if any, will work in concert in relation to the third? What is their purpose and what is the nature of their concerted effort?

These questions concern the formation and actions of "coalitions," the term coalition meaning "an alliance for combined action of distinct . . . persons . . ." (Oxford English Dictionary). The essential observation is that two persons act in concert in relation to the third, usually *against* him. The combined action reflects an understanding between the two, either tacit or explicit, regarding some joint goal to be achieved and the means to do so. There may eventually be an agreement between the coalition and the third person, but there is always some difference between the within-coalition understanding and the understanding between it and the third person. A minimal difference is that the former precedes the latter.

Our model of action in the triad is simply an expansion of that for the dyad, except that we must take account of a new type of action, namely, *coalition action*. This action consists of two persons behaving in concert in relation to the third in regard for their special convergence of interest and their common conflict with him. By coalition action a pair is often able to establish special bargaining positions, analogous to the IA and Th pairs but differing from those defined by independent individual effort in the triad.

Figure 10.11 lists the possible types of viable outcome for the dyad and for the triad, respectively. For each kind of relationship the types of possible bargaining position are listed on the left and the settlement points associated with each bargaining position are listed on the right. (The reader will recall that for the dyad the IA point may also be a plausible settlement point, if it is on the frontier of the bargaining points. In the triad the same is true for IA and the various CoA points.) The greater number of possible bargaining positions and settlement points for the triad compared with the dyad reflects the greater number of different structural relations and dynamic processes possible in the triad. We shall now explain these various possibilities.

Identifying the IA, Th, CoA, and CoTh Triplets

Because each cell in the triadic relationship is specified by a triplet of outcomes, our first task is to define the various crucial triplets for the relationship. The IA and Th triplets are defined in the same way as the IA and Th pairs for the dyad except that they result from the pursuit by *all three* persons of their individual purposes. The IA triplet lists their respective outcomes when each one acts independently to maximize his outcomes, although taking account of what each of the others, similarly motivated, is likely to do. The Th triplet lists the outcomes resulting from the efforts of each to create an optimal bargaining position for himself. The same complications are here as for the dyad, but the Th triplet can be approximated by assuming that each person will try to maximize the difference between his own and the others' combined outcomes.

In addition to these triplets, there is the possibility that analogous but different triplets can be created by each pair of persons acting as a coalition against a third. These are referred to as *coalition action* (CoA) and *coalition threat* (CoTh) triplets. Each one that "exists" (that is different from the analogous IA or Th triplet) is given a prefix to indicate the particular pair of persons that create it. Thus the *AB*-CoA triplet listed in Figure 10.11 specifies the outcomes of the three persons when *A* and *B* work jointly to maximize their combined outcomes and when *C*, taking account of their actions, does his best to maximize his. Similarly, the *BC*-CoTh triplet describes what *B* and *C* can mobilize, by their joint effort, in the way of a threat to gain compliance from *A*.

The important property of these bilaterally defined triplets is that they *can be better* for both members of the particular coalition than the comparable unilaterally defined triplets *but never worse*. (If they are equivalent to the comparable IA or Th triplet, we disregard them.) That they will never be worse is easy to understand. Rather than generate positions that are less beneficial for themselves, *A* and *B* can agree to act in the same way they would act independently in generating the IA or Th triplets. That these coalition triplets may be better than the IA and Th triplets follows from the fact (illustrated in Chapter 9) that by joint action *A* and *B* can delimit the interaction in different ways than would be possible if they worked independently, and some of these ways may be to their mutual advantage.

DYAD		TRIAD	
Bargaining Positions	Settlement Points	Bargaining Positions	Settlement Points
IA	*Rew*	IA	*Rew*(IA)
Th	*A-comp*	Th	*A-comp* (Th)
	B-comp		*B-comp*(Th)
			C-comp(Th)
			AB-comp(Th)
			AC-comp(Th)
			BC-comp(Th)
		AB-CoA	*Rew*(AB-CoA)
		AC-CoA	*Rew*(AC-CoA)
		BC-CoA	*Rew*(BC-CoA)
		AB-CoTh	*C-comp*(AB-CoTh)
		AC-CoTh	*B-comp*(AC-CoTh)
		BC-CoTh	*A-comp*(BC-CoTh)

Figure 10.11 Possible types of bargaining positions and their associated settlement points in the dyad and triad.

Figure 10.12 shows two examples in which AB-CoA yields better outcomes than IA for both A and B. In the course of independent action among the three persons in Example I, C follows his RC to choose c_2 and, knowing this, A chooses a_2. Given the likelihood of those two actions, B follows his BC in the c_2 submatrix to choose b_2. These actions yield the triplet ($+4$, $+2$, $+5$). In contrast, by coalition action, A and B can ensure themselves the triplet ($+6$, $+6$, 0). In Example II the IA triplet ($+2$, $+2$, $+10$) results if, anticipating that C will choose c_2, A and B follow their respective RC's in the c_2 submatrix. By a coordinated trade off between a_1b_1 and a_2b_2 (assuming C stays at c_2) they can attain a number of triplets such as ($+3$, $+9$, $+2$) or ($+6$, $+6$, $+2$) which are better for both. This example shows the important fact that unlike IA the AB-CoA set can include a *number* of triplets rather than only one. More on this in a moment.

The example in Figure 10.13 shows how AB-CoTh can be more advantageous for A and B than the independently produced Th triplet. In their independent attempts to define self-advantageous threat points A maximizes the value $[A - (B + C)/2]$, B maximizes $[B - (A + C)/2]$, and C maximizes $[C - (A + B)/2]$. The last leads C to choose c_2 and in that half of the matrix A chooses a_1 and B chooses b_2. Acting as a coalition, A and B work together to maximize $[(A + B)/2 - C]$. With this criterion, given C's choice of c_2 (he continues to maximize $[C - (A + B)/2]$), they agree to the

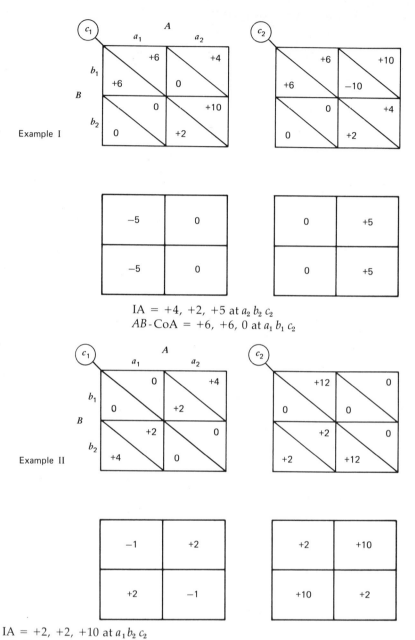

Example I

IA = +4, +2, +5 at $a_2 b_2 c_2$
AB-CoA = +6, +6, 0 at $a_1 b_1 c_2$

Example II

IA = +2, +2, +10 at $a_1 b_2 c_2$
AB-CoA = set of triplets resulting from alternation between $a_1 b_1 c_2$ and $a_2 b_2 c_2$.

Figure 10.12 Examples in which AB-CoA is better for both A and B than IA.

304

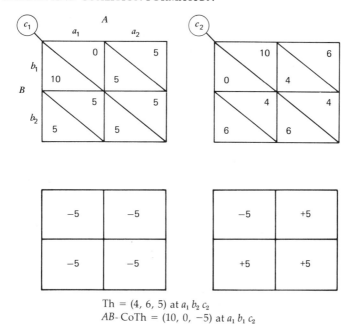

Th = (4, 6, 5) at $a_1 b_2 c_2$
AB- CoTh = (10, 0, −5) at $a_1 b_1 c_2$

Figure 10.13 Example in which AB-CoTh is more advantageous to both A and B than Th.

$a_1 b_1$ pair. The resulting AB-CoTh triplet is more useful for them as a threat than Th because their joint advantage over C is greater. By threatening to enact the $a_1 b_1$ pair they are in a better position to induce C's agreement to a contract favorable to their joint interest. It will be noted that the possible costs of the threat action are not borne equally by the members of the A–B coalition. If they find it necessary to carry out the threat action, B will suffer lower outcomes than A. This may be expected to affect differentially the two persons' willingness to establish a coaliton in order to threaten C.

Both CoA and CoTh sets may include more than one triplet of outcomes. This follows from the simple fact that any outcome or position *defined by agreement* among two or more persons may, for certain matrices, include a number of possible outcome triplets. This means that the coalition members may have to negotiate between themselves the division of rewards available in the CoA set. Also, in their use of the CoTh set as a bargaining baseline they may have to negotiate how the costs of the threat action, if taken, are to be borne. This means that the coalition is often working from a set of points in the negotiation space rather than a single one and this has implications for possible conflict within the coalition and for its vulnerability to counter offers and threats from the third person.

It will be clear from their definitions what the functions of the CoA and CoTh triplets are. Like IA, in some cases the CoA set may be part of what the persons negotiate *about* and in other cases, part of what they negotiate *from*. If functional at all, the CoTh triplet, like its Th counterpart, always plays the role of a position *from* which bargaining is conducted. Finally, it should be noted that just as a Th triplet may not differ from the IA triplet, so the *AB*-CoTh triplet may not differ from the *AB*-CoA triplet. From this it will be realized that although every triad will have an IA triplet it may or may not have a Th triplet and it may or may not have CoA triplets (i.e., different from the IA triplet). Given the existence of a Th triplet (different from the IA triplet), any coalition may or may not have a CoTh triplet (different both from the Th triplet and the appropriate CoA triplet).

Classification of Triplets on the Frontier

First, all the triplets of outcomes on the frontier can be classified with respect to the IA and Th triplets. The reader can visualize the possibilities here by imagining a three-dimensional version of Figure 10.1. The possible types of triplet that can be distinguished in relation to the IA and Th triplets are shown in the upper portion of the right-most column of Figure 10.11. Depending on the relative locations of the triplets in the three-dimensional space describing the outcomes of *A*, *B*, and *C* and depending on the location and extent of the frontier, there may be *Rew*(IA) triplets (better than IA for all three persons), *A-comp* triplets (better than IA for *B* and *C* but between IA and Th for *A*), *B-comp* and *C-comp* triplets, *AB–comp* triplets (better than IA for *C* but between IA and Th for *A* and *B*), and *BC-comp* and *AC-comp* triplets. The implication of the last type of compliance triplet is, of course, that the Th triplet may provide a basis for one member of the triad to bring threat pressure to bear on *both* of the others. It would be among the *BC-comp* triplets that *A* might attempt to gain *B*'s and *C*'s compliance to his threat. There may be six different types of compliance triplet because any one or pair of the triad can be below their IA outcomes but above Th. All remaining points on the frontier, at which one or more of the triad is below Th, are not viable. The person(s) below Th would have no reason to enter into an agreement that would make any of these points possible.

Second, as shown in Figure 10.11, the triplets on the frontier can also be classified with respect to each pair of CoA and CoTh triplets. Triplets better than *AB*-CoA for all three persons are labeled *Rew*(*AB*-CoA), those better than *AC*-CoA for all three, *Rew*(*AC*-CoA), and those better than

BC-CoA for all three, *Rew*(*BC*-CoA). Similarly, triplets better than *AB*-CoA for *A* and *B* but between *AB*-CoA and *AB*-CoTh for *C* will be labeled *C-comp* (*AB*-CoTh) triplets. Logically, the same types of triplet may be distinguished in relation to each pair of CoA and CoTh triplets as are defined by the IA and Th triplets. Certain of the *comp* types, however, do not make sense psychologically. Thus the *B-comp* (*AB*-CoTh) triplets (in which *A* and *C* are above *AB*-CoA, but *B* is below *AB*-CoA, though above *AB*-CoTh) are not viable because *B* cannot be expected to participate in creating the *AB*-CoTh point in order to induce his own compliance to sub-*AB*-CoA outcomes. Thus, as listed in Figure 10.11, the only meaningful compliance triplets relative to actions of the *A*-*B* coalition are the *C-comp* (*AB*-CoTh) triplets, the only ones relevant to the *A*-*C* coalition are the *B-comp* (*AC*-CoTh) triplets, and the only ones relevant to the *B*-*C* coalition are the *A-comp* (*BC*-CoTh) triplets. (Our notation is admittedly cumbersome for the reason that we have tried to preserve a high level of mnemonic value in the abbreviations. The reader will observe in Figure 10.11 that the notation for each settlement point includes a parenthetical suffix that describes the bargaining position with respect to which the settlement point is viable.)

The purpose of this second classification is, of course, to specify the ways in which coalition action in the triad may affect the meaning and control of the frontier points. A clear example of change in meaning would be a triplet that is labeled both *rew* and *AB*-CoA. Without the formation of a coalition, this triplet is accessible only by three-way cooperative action. The second label, however, means that by their concerted effort *A* and *B* can provide the triplet themselves (assuming only that *C* will not interfere with a threat).

In brief, each point on the frontier is potentially given four tags, one to indicate its position in relation to each of the four sets of reference points. If a given CoA or threat (Th or CoTh) triplet is missing, it, of course, does not affect the classification and is reflected in none of the labels. A triplet that is not viable with respect to a given set of reference points will simply receive no label referring to that set, and triplets that have no labels (i.e., that are not viable from any perspective) are simply eliminated from further consideration.

Predicting the Outcome of the Relationship

Again, once the frontier points have been tagged as described, they are listed for each person from most to least preferred. In general, each person's list will have the same general structure; for example, person *A*'s list will generally have *C-comp* (*AB*-CoTh), *B-comp* (*AC*-CoTh), *BC-comp*,

B-comp, and *C-comp* triplets as most preferred. Next in order will be *Rew*(AB-CoA) and *Rew*(AC-CoA) or *AB*-CoA and *AC*-CoA triplets, followed closely by IA or *Rew* triplets. Least preferred will be triplets requiring his compliance such as *A-comp* (*BC*-CoTh) or *AB-comp* triplets.

The decision process by which the triad agrees on a pattern of action can be thought of in terms of a series of concessions, with each person moving down his preference order until an appropriate set of labels is reached. This does not require agreement on the same triplet. One of the "emergent" phenomena of the triad is that under certain conditions a pair of persons can absolutely require the third to accept a nonpreferred triplet, namely, a CoA triplet. As mentioned earlier, the greater variety of possible events in the triad compared with the dyad is indicated by the greater variety of types of triplet that may occur in each person's preference list. The greater variety of means by which actions are decided on is indicated by the greater array of triplets that may be used to define minimal bargaining positions.

Triad Action Without Coalition

We consider first some of the possible situations in the triad that are similar to those in the dyad. In all these cases there is no CoA triplet not equal to the IA triplet and no CoTh triplet not equal to the Th triplet. Consequently, joint action by the members of any potential coalition is not relevant to the outcome. No pair can do any better for itself in the context of two-versus-one action than any individual can in the three-way context, and no pair can create a more useful threat position by concerted action than any individual can by independent action.

The simplest case is that in which there are also no Comp triplets, Th being equal to IA. Under these conditions the three persons may act independently and take the IA triplet (if it is on the frontier) or they may act jointly to attain one of the *Rew* triplets. If there are several *Rew* triplets, they will negotiate among them from the position of the IA triplet.

A somewhat more complex situation develops when there are *comp* triplets. The negotiation then proceeds over the union of the sets of *comp* triplets and either the IA or *Rew* triplets, each person making his claims from the Th position and, if it is not on the frontier, the IA point. The novel aspect of this situation in the triad is that the Th triplet may be usable in several quite different ways, namely, (a) by one person against the other two, (b) by two persons against the third, or (c) by one person against the other two and by the second person against the third. A simple example illustrates these possibilities. (It assumes *no* outcome transformation, it must be noted. The values given are the *effective* ones.)

Three youngsters will be given $15 if they can agree on how to divide it among themselves. If they cannot agree, each will be given $4 (IA = 4, 4, 4). An additional rule specifies that any one of them can by unilateral action (as by saying "I quit") cause them to receive a still different set of outcomes. In Case I this Th triplet yields 0, 0, 0 for A, B, and C, respectively; in Case II it yields 3, 0, 0; in Case III it yields 3, 3, 0; and in Case IV it yields 4, 2, 0.

In Case I Th is no more usable by one boy than by another. Its presence merely increases the importance of *some* agreement and of not aggravating any boy by pressing him to take a small share of the $15.

In Case II boy A stands to gain some advantage from using the threat because he has the least to lose by quitting. He might make the Th-based equity argument (an equal increment argument) that out of the $15 he should receive his $3 first and then the remaining $12 can be divided equally, yielding a 7, 4, 4 outcome (a triplet on the margin between the reward set and the BC-*comp* set).

Similarly, Case III favors both boy A and boy B. Either one of them can generate the Th triplet. If A suggests that it implies he should get a larger share than one-third, B will very likely assert that the same principle applies to his situation, and C becomes the one under pressure to move away from an equality-based agreement. Simple equity would give 3 each to A and B and divide the remaining 9 among the three, for a 6, 6, 3 outcome, a member of the C-*comp* set. Case III must not be confused with AB-CoTh, where A and B must work in concert to create the threat triplet. Case III is simply an example in which the rules of the game favor both A and B as individuals and work to the disadvantage of C. A and B are in the same respective situations in relation to their partners and therefore can be expected to act *similarly*, but there is no basis for their *joint* action.

Case IV is rather complex. Person A is no worse off if the threat is used than if they merely fail to agree. (Remember that he cannot be better off in the Th triplet than at IA or the Th triplet would simply become the IA point.) He clearly can be more casual about taking the threat action than either B or C. Boy B, though concerned to avoid anyone's quitting, is less so than C. An equity outcome would yield 7, 5, 3, again a member of the C-*comp* set.

One point of this example and its variations is simply that even in the absence of coalition action the phenomenon of threat takes a greater variety of forms in the triad than in the dyad.

Triad Action with Coalition

The simplest case of coalition involves no threat points (no Th or CoTh triplets) but only CoA triplets. Thus A's preference order, for example, may have $Rew(AB\text{-CoA})$, $Rew(AC\text{-CoA})$, $AB\text{-CoA}$, or $AC\text{-CoA}$ triplets at the top of the list and IA and Rew triplets at the bottom. If two persons come to their common CoA point as they work down their lists, they can require the third person to accept their set of outcomes; for example, if the AB-CoA point is on the frontier and A and B move to it in their respective preference orders (perhaps after each has passed up a few Rew triplets that were not acceptable to each other or to C), they can instate it as a settlement point. They can do so despite the fact that C may prefer one or more Rew triplets to the AB-CoA point. It is not a matter of imposing it by threat but simply a matter of A and B acting together and limiting C merely to doing his best for himself. Similarly, the AB-CoA point, although not on the frontier, may define some $Rew(AB\text{-CoA})$ triplets that A and B prefer to the Rew triplets but that C regards in a less favorable light. By their ability to force the trio to the AB-CoA triplet (in the absence of an effective threat for C), A and B can require C either to negotiate an agreement among the $Rew(AB\text{-CoA})$ triplets or to take the less good AB-CoA value.

Consider the following game as an example: by unanimous agreement on its allocation the three persons will be given \$15. Alternatively, if both agree to do so, A and B can receive \$6 each. In the absence of either type of agreement, each person gets nothing. Thus IA $= 0, 0, 0$; AB-CoA $= 6, 6, 0$; Rew = all triplets summing to 15 in which each person's outcome is greater than 0; and $Rew(AB\text{-CoA}) = 7, 7, 1$ (the single allocation of 15 that puts each person above AB-CoA). Persons A and B can limit C's choice to the Rew $(AB\text{-CoA})$ or the AB-CoA triplet. Note that there are Rew triplets that A might prefer to the $Rew(AB\text{-CoA})$ triplet (e.g., 9, 3, 3), but he has no better means of inducing the others to accept such triplets than each of them has for inducing him to accept other triplets disadvantageous to him. When A and B both recognize the futility of trying to attain such individually advantageous contracts, they will both move down their preference orders to the $Rew(AC\text{-CoA})$ triplet for which, as a coalition, they can make a compelling case.

Agreement *within* a coalition may not come so easily as the above example suggests. It will be recalled that AB-CoA may be a set of triplets rather than a single one and this may force A and B to negotiate among them or among a number of $Rew(AB\text{-CoA})$ triplets. Let us modify the above example merely by assuming that the alternative to a three-way agreement on a division of \$15 is A and B's agreement on a division of \$12 (rather than a fixed \$6 each). Now AB-CoA can yield any triplet in which both A and B have more than 0 (their outcomes in the IA triplet). Thus (11, 1, 0), (10, 2, 0), (9, 3, 0), . . ., (2, 10, 0), and (1, 11, 0) are members of the

AB-CoA set, and (12, 2, 1), (11, 3, 1), (10, 4, 1), and so on, are members of the *Rew*(*AB*-CoA) set. Clearly the *AB*-CoA set delimits the set of divisions of $15 that *A* and *B* will consider; for example, precluding an equal division (5, 5, 5). Although *A* and *B* can agree, however, that *C* should receive no more than 1 (his minimal price for agreeing to any three-way split of the $15 and all they can afford to give him while still giving themselves some motivation for a three-way rather than a two-way agreement), they have no structural basis for choosing among the *Rew*(*AB*-CoA) triplets. Therefore at the same time that they are jointly convincing *C* of the necessity of accepting a minimal share of the $15, they must negotiate between themselves a division of the rest. Of course, a (7, 7, 1) agreement has the appeal of equality between *A* and *B*, and in the absence of any basis for either of them to claim more we might expect it to be their ultimate allocation. The situation may change radically if, as we consider below, the Th or IA triplets favor either of them.

It may happen that any one of two or three coalitions is viable within the triad. Consider the simpler case first in which as the three move down their preference orders *A* comes to *AB*-CoA, *B* comes to both *AB*-CoA and *BC*-CoA, and *C* comes to *BC*-CoA. Person *A* now calls for the formation of the *A–B* coalition, *C* calls for the *B–C* coalition, and *B* has an interest in the formation of both coalitions. A simple example would be a game in which either *A* and *B* or *B* and *C* can divide $10, whichever pair can agree on an allocation. Person *B* is clearly in an enviable position, sought after by both *A* and *C* as a coalition partner. Because *A*'s and *C*'s alternatives to being in the coalition are both zero, each of them should be willing to offer *B* a lion's share of the $10. *B* bargains with each of them from the position of the CoA triplets he can generate with the other. Neither structurally nor in terms of equity arguments is there any basis for predicting which of the two coalitions will form—only that *B* will receive a large part of the $10.

A similar case is one in which each of the three possible coalitions is desired by both its members. The example game is one in which *any* pair can have $10 if it can agree on its allocation. This case, like the foregoing, permits of no prediction about which coalition will eventually form. Any tentative agreement by *A* and *B* can, in principle, always be upset by *C*'s offering one of them more if he will join the *A–C* or *B–C* coalition. The costs of negotiation and the risk of getting nothing by failure of some agreement exert influence toward stable agreement within some pair and the symmetry of dependence argues for an equal split within that pair.

These examples, lacking Th and CoTh triplets, involve bargaining merely from the IA and CoA triplets. With the addition of threat triplets the agreement process is likely to include pressures on one or more members of the triad to accept compliance triplets. For example, with a three-way agreement the trio can share $15; in the absence of agreement each one will receive $3. Alternatively, if A and B agree to it, they will divide $4 and C will receive nothing. The AB-CoTh triplets are as follows: (4, 0, 0), (3, 1, 0), (2, 2, 0), (1, 3, 0), and (0, 4, 0). By threatening to impose one of these A and B can agree that C should accept an asymmetrical split such as (7, 7, 1) which puts C below IA (3, 3, 3). A and B's position is not so clear-cut as it would be if there were only one AB-CoTh triplet (e.g., if their alternative pairwise agreement yielded each a fixed $2). Thus C would find some additional basis for resisting the threat (beyond the sizable inequality it implies) in the possibility that A and B might not readily agree on exactly how to back it up.

The reader will note the difference between the kinds of "game" rules in these allocation examples that underlie the CoA triplets versus the CoTh triplets. The AB-CoA triplet is based on a rule that permits A and B to assure themselves better outcomes than they would receive if a three-way agreement were not forthcoming. In contrast, the AB-CoTh triplet is based on a rule that gives them as well as C less than what the failure of three-way agreement yields.

From the preceding considerations it will be clear that once the possibilities exist for coalition formation within the triad (once there are CoA and CoTh triplets) the ideal position of a particular member of the triad is to be the favored member of a favored coalition. As we have seen, a number of different configurations can create this ideal position. One is that in which only one coalition has one highly favorable CoA triplet, and in that triplet the particular person is strongly favored; for example, a three-way agreement can divide $15, but a two-way agreement between A and B can yield them $9 and $6 respectively. A second case is one in which only two coalitions have highly favorable CoA triplets and the particular person is the common member of both. In a third case the AB-CoA or Rew(AB-CoA) triplets, whichever are on the frontier, are negotiable between A and B, and the other coalition triplets are missing, but the IA and/or Th triplets favor A. This puts A in a strong position to induce B to enter a coalition with him but on terms that yield A a large share of the coalition's benefits. It is instances of this last kind that form the basis for the generalization that each person will seek the coalition in which the coalition's power vis-à-vis the third person and his own power vis-à-vis his coalition mate are maximized. The importance of *both* factors in a person's choice is shown by the fact that he will sometimes prefer a less beneficial coalition in which he is the favored person to a more beneficial coalition in which he is disfavored.

11
Epilogue

313

ABSTRACT

This chapter provides a brief interpretive commentary on the theoretical ideas presented in this book. An outline of the kind of theory developed here lists its essential points. Some historical notes relate our central assumptions and orienting ideas to those of Kurt Lewin. A final section highlights several further lines of development of the present theoretical approach.

A KIND OF THEORY

Our purpose in this section is to make explicit what was implicit in the preceding chapters by describing in general terms the *kind* of theory presented in this book. It must be admitted that this represents a set of *post hoc* insights on our part. In advance of our work on this book we did not have clearly in mind the kind of theory outlined here. Rather we developed, in a rather exploratory and piecemeal way, the concepts we found to be needed to deal with certain basic observations and data from the social psychological study of interpersonal relations. After the fact we found it natural to organize the various ideas in the manner of the preceding chapters. Now, still further after the fact, we are able to step back and examine in more general terms the kind of theory we have evolved and perhaps suggest reasons why that kind of theory is needed.

To speak of and endorse the *kind* of theory that is represented is to imply that other versions of this kind of theory can be developed. It is precisely our purpose to emphasize that possibility and to urge its realization. We believe that as other means are developed for the systematic characterization and analysis of social interdependence a different theory of this sort can be developed. We also mean to suggest that any such theory should deal with the same problems that we have and will probably have the same general terms; in that sense, it will be the same *kind*. That is to indicate our confidence that our analysis has revealed many essential aspects of interpersonal relations—aspects that no theory can overlook—as well as our conviction that our general approach to conceptualizing these aspects is, in the long run, a viable one.

Limitations of the Matrix Concepts

It is our hope that the reader who has followed the successive developments in this book faithfully will agree with our high regard for the outcome matrix as a conceptual tool for the analysis of social interdependence. Even the minimal matrix, the 2 ×2, describes a diverse array of interpersonal structures and is richly suggestive of the processes associated with them. This matrix, however, has certain limitations that lead us to suspect that it will eventually be replaced as the central analytic device (with the result, as suggested, that the kind of theory presented here will have to be rewritten in terms of somewhat different interdependence concepts).

In its application to specific cases there are certain ambiguities in the delineation of the outcome matrix. One problem has to do with specifying the behavioral options for each person. This is misleadingly easy in experimental application of the matrix but often an uncertain matter for natural relationships. It seems clear that the options identified by an outsider may be quite different from those distinguished by the persons themselves. Our distinction (in Thibaut and Kelley, 1959, and in Chapter 1 of this book) between the "objective" and "subjective" matrix recognizes this fact. The notion of the objective matrix is based on the assumption that a well-informed and thorough analysis can identify more accurately than can the participants the structure of their relationship. (The attributional assumptions here are obvious: a number of independent, objective, and expert analysts, if given sufficient information—about this and similar relationships—can make more veridical discriminations and judgments than can the involved participants with their limited perspectives.) According to this view, the objective matrix represents a causal structure which, whether recognized or not, plays a shaping role in the relationship and is therefore a reality of which it would be well for the participants to become cognizant. An important line of analysis and research for the future will have the purpose of determining the course of development in persons' understandings of their interdependence. Because there can be two different subjective views of the same dyadic matrix (cf. Ingmar Bergman's *Scenes from a Marriage*), this analysis must identify the conditions that promote convergence in their understandings. In addition, as the concept of objective matrix highlights, we must identify processes that promote greater insight into and pursuit of the full range of possibilities immanent in their relationship. These processes will include the creative imagining and construction of new options that have not, perhaps, been available in the common examples of similar relationships.

Beyond the various ambiguities associated with the definition of the interdependence matrix its more serious limitations seem to lie in its static nature. The future elaboration of interdependence theory will profit most, in our estimation, from the development of concepts that lend themselves not only to characterizing the patterns at any given point in time but also to describing their temporal trends and changes. Fruitful initial steps would consist of specifying rules for generating scenarios of interaction from structural patterns of interdependence. Such rules would have to take account of the implications of the outcome matrix identified in Chapter 10. In addition, a temporal analysis will have to take account of various process constraints. It is well known, from numerous experimental studies, that the process that develops in a particular game depends not only on its pattern but also on such factors as the players' information, their opportunities for communication, and the conditions that determine the timing and visibility of their choices. [An important though often overlooked aspect of the original story of the Prisoner's Dilemma (see p. 42) is that the district attorney constrained the decision process in a particular way. By separating the prisoners and requiring them to make independent decisions without communication, he increased the likelihood of the particular outcome, mutual confession, that he preferred.]

We have long been aware of temporal changes in many of the rewards and costs associated with behavior (cf. e.g., Chapter 1 in Thibaut and Kelley, 1959). The short-term phenomena of satiation and fatigue require a model of interdependence that reflects the dependence of later outcomes on earlier ones. In addition, models intended to cover long-term trends in relationship dependencies must take account of changes, with maturation and aging, in motives and skills.

These brief comments simply point to some of the limitations of the outcome matrix as the central concept for the analysis of interdependence. The present theory was developed with the matrix as its major instrument. With drastic modifications in or replacements of that device, the theory will have to be rewritten. The general form of what we have done, however, is not dependent on the outcome matrix. We shall try to describe the general characteristics of the present formulation.

Essential Aspects of Present Theory

Taxonomy of Interdependent Relationships

Our analysis centers around an examination of types of interpersonal relationship in which they are described and differentiated in terms of interdependence. This is a uniquely social psychological focus, to be contrasted with a typology of persons (personality psychology) or of environments (environmental psychology).

Interdependence Patterns as Problems

The particular pattern of interdependence that characterizes a relationship determines the special set of problems confronting it. The taxonomy of relationships is, then, a taxonomy of problems, each type of interdependence pattern involving its unique problematic aspects and implying the necessary elements of solution. These problems exist for the individuals involved and for the collectivity (dyad, triad, etc.) they constitute. In the collectivity the problems are often shared in the sense that one person's solution depends on another's solution. Thus the possibility exists for dealing with the commonalities among the individual problems by way of coordinated or joint solutions.

Purposes Served by the Components Analysis.   The outcome matrix was our conceptual device for developing the taxonomy. It held out to us the attractive possibility of deriving qualitative differences among relationships from quantitative and configurational analysis. This analysis was conducted by identifying the components of the matrix, determining their relative magnitudes, and specifying their orientations (concordance, correspondence) in relation to one another. Specifically, the components analysis provided a useful bookkeeping system for exploring the domain of 2×2 interdependence matrices, identifying the salient patterns, and classifying them. It also pointed to a major kind of variation in type of joint problem; the central distinction between MFC and MBC served to highlight the difference between "exchange" and "coordination." The components analysis also provided an analytic framework for identifying the antecedents of various patterns; for example, the factors underlying correspondence versus noncorrespondence of outcomes. In Chapter 9 the components analysis provided guides for dealing with the third person and the complexities in pattern arising from the expansion of the dyad into a triad. In brief, the components constituted the elements of the structural aspects of our analysis. In analogy to the role of atoms and molecules in chemical theory, in their variations in magnitudes and relative orientations, the several types of component generated qualitatively different patterns and types of phenomena.

Functional Analysis

The taxonomy of problems provided a basis for a functional analysis. We assumed that in their experience with the various problems and from the necessity of coping with them, people develop solutions to them. Adaptation to situations of social interdependence is viewed as the source of both social norms and individual rules. Adaptation is seen to result from multiple processes. In his own direct experience in interdependent relationships each individual has opportunities to learn useful rules, including both the prosocial, moral concepts and the more egocentric, practical rules of thumb for "getting along with people." This experience is often preceded by and accompanied by social instruction in the moral and practical aspects of social relationships, which involve both explicit teaching and the provision of exemplars of social behavior. In the course of its history mankind has long encountered the basic types of interdependence and problems we have identified. In the collective wisdom about social life an understanding of the important variations of interpersonal relationships and of useful ways of dealing with them is implicit. Ordinarily, the instruction provided the individual by lecture and model will be consistent with his own experience; hence the two modes of acquisition will be mutually reinforcing. Inconsistency will occur at times of sharp social and technological change as when changing sex role conceptions render outmoded the earlier behavioral rules that assumed a high degree of asymmetry in dependence within the heterosexual dyad.

The preceding comments should not be taken to imply an assumption that the moral and practical rules that persons commonly follow are optimally adapted to the nature of their interdependent relationships. We have seen that the functionally optimal rules are highly contingent, that they depend both on the nature of the relationship and the transformations that partners make. This complexity suggests that the adaptation people make to the requirements of their relationships are often likely to be imperfect.

The Transformation Process

The solutions to the problems of interdependence often require that behavior be freed from control by the actor's immediate situation. It must become partially responsive to the situations of other persons and to possible future situations. This was demonstrable for various matrices in our taxonomy of relationships and must be true for interdependence problems, however described. We have found it useful to describe this process in terms of a shift from the *given* to the *effective* matrix—a transformation of the *given* matrix into one that controls behavior. The conceptual step taken here, of assuming that a person responds to a particular *given* situation as if it were a different one, has the important consequence of enabling both *given* and *effective* situations to be described in the same terms—in our case in matrix terms. The common terms of description in turn make it possible to examine the *given* situations from the point of view of what transformations are logically possible and which of them serve to yield better *given* outcomes than if the *given* situation were reacted to directly. The end result of this conceptual strategy is that it becomes plausible to describe what the person learns, as ways of dealing with problems of interdependence, in terms of matrix-transforming rules, values, and sequences. The specific psychological processes involved (control of attention and thought, binding of tension, and self-regulation of motivation) were not an explicit part of our analysis but it contains useful implications for the delineation of such processes (see pp. 202–206).

Attributional and Presentational Phenomena Created by the Transformation Process

The loosening of the linkage between behavior and the immediate situation involved in the transformation process introduces a set of causal factors into behavior that are intimately concerned with and, indeed, define the *person*. It is at the transformation junction in the chain of behavioral causation that the *person* appears as a causal agent. To other persons this means that the voluntary and conscious factors (e.g., ego strength, character, will power) underlying the person's behavior become apparent in contrast to external, situational factors (e.g., incentives, unconditioned stimuli) and internal, uncontrollable factors (biological drives, deeply rooted psychic needs). To the person himself the transformation process provides manifestations of the "self" as an agent in control of his own behavior and outcomes.

From the point of view of persons interdependent with an actor the transformation process creates the special set of attributional problems, outlined in Chapter 8, having to do with inferring the actor's orientation to and long-range goals for the relationship. For the actor the transformation process provides opportunities for self-presentation. The "self" as a causal agent is made apparent to others (as, also, to the self) by means of behavior that is independent of the structure of the immediate situation. Self-presentation and, indeed, the very properties it is possible for an individual to show to others and to know about himself are determined by the structure of the interdependent situations in which he finds himself. An understanding of this basic fact underlies his decisions about entering or arranging situations with particular patterns of interdependence.

The attributional problems of the actor's various partners, created by the transformational process, have their parallels in the assessment problems that face the social psychologist. Faced with a heterogeneity of reactions to a specific set of incentives, we find it difficult to distinguish variations in *given* matrices from variations in the transformations made of them. Our doubts about the proper generalizations to be drawn from observed behavior are heightened by our awareness of the special self-presentational tendencies that may be elicited by our subjects' consciousness of the assessment context for their behavior. Some of these contextual matters are discussed briefly in Chapter 7.

HISTORICAL NOTES

It may add to the understanding of the central ideas in this book to relate them to certain earlier conceptions in social psychology. It is particularly useful to link them to and compare them with the ideas of the man with whom we took our graduate studies—Kurt Lewin. Although it is not our principal intention here, to highlight these intellectual roots of our basic ideas may also help to discourage the notion that we have some "ultimate loyalties" to Hullian learning theory, as suggested by Chadwick-Jones (1976, p. 64). In this and our earlier book we have found that "behaviour theory" is useful at many points in our argument but the more fundamental notions are drawn from Lewin.

Lewin's influence is perhaps most strikingly present in the adoption of *interdependence* as the starting point of our analysis. This was the property to which Lewin gave a central position in his first papers in which he established the field of group dynamics. He wrote: "The essence of a group is not the similarity or dissimilarity of its members, but their interdependence. A group can be characterized as a 'dynamic whole'; this means that a change in the state of any subpart changes the state of any other subpart" (1948, p. 84). Interdependence, of course, can be given many different meanings depending on what changes in state are identified. Lewin's topological concepts have had great usefulness in the analysis of the flow of information or influence among the members of a group (as in French, 1956; and Harary, Norman, and Cartwright, 1965). The motivational concepts, however, involving valences and their related force fields, were not readily adaptable to problems of outcome interdependence. The interdependence between persons in their locomotion toward goals was only awkwardly represented in the life space and only gross distinctions in types of interdependence were suggested (e.g., Deutsch's promotive *versus* contrient interdependence, 1949). These limitations reflected the difficulties that Lewin encountered in formulating direction and the relative directions of different forces in the topologically defined life space (see Lewin, 1938, and Leeper's critique, 1943). It should be noted that Lewin's writings about social interdependence were limited to the last several years before his death. It seems clear that he was exploring a variety of ways to describe motivational interdependence and had not yet thoroughly developed any one way [cf. his pages on marital conflict (1948, pp. 84–102; 1951, pp. 188–237)]. As the reader of this book has seen, the analytic tool we have used, the outcome matrix, though not without its limitations, generates a rich set of suggestive distinctions among degrees and patterns of interdependence between persons in the attainment of their respective goals.

The life space, with its topological analysis of path and goal regions and its vector analysis of the forces acting on the person, deals essentially with the decisions and problems facing a single person. The outcome matrix, in contrast, deals with the interweaving of the decisions of several persons and often (when there is some correspondence of outcomes) with their joint problems. Despite the different purposes of the two kinds of analysis, certain aspects of our general strategy in developing the outcome matrix follow Lewin's precepts very closely.

The Principle of Contemporaneity.   Lewin emphasized that "any behavior or other change in a psychological field depends only upon the psychological field *at that time*" (1951, p. 45). This did not reflect a lack of interest in historical (developmental and learning) problems but was simply an insistence that the analysis of causal factors for a given event in the life space had to focus ultimately on processes contemporaneous with that event. We have followed this principle in our focus on the *effective* matrix. This summarizes the options and motives operative at the time of a given interaction and directly controlling the nature of that interaction. The antecedents of these causal factors are described in part by the *given* matrix and the transformations that are brought to bear on it. The more distal antecedents have been considered in our discussion of the psychological bases of rewards and costs and of behavioral facilitation and interference (Chapters 3 and 4 in Thibaut and Kelley, 1959). Changes in the *effective* matrix, from one point in time to another, are treated in terms of the effects of long- and short-run changes in factors underlying the *given* rewards and costs (e.g., changes in needs and skills, satiation and fatigue effects) and shifts in the prevailing transformations.

Taxonomy of Situations. Lewin was keenly aware of the importance of characterizing the behavioral field in ways that afford a basis for identifying different types of situation. Leeper (1943) made the following observation:

> The main point of departure for [Lewin's] work is the conviction that the influence of the situation (as personally organized or conceived) is . . . so important and so complex that specialized, technical concepts must be developed that will increase our capacity to identify and understand the factors and relationships that are involved here (p. 13).

Lewin's analytic concepts were types of goal and force field and their positions in relation to one another. Best known is his analysis of types of conflict (approach-approach, avoidance-avoidance, approach-avoidance) and variations in the locations of barriers (restraining forces) associated with each type of conflict (Lewin, 1935, pp. 87–94; 1946, pp. 809–815). This theoretical emphasis on a situational typology is directly reflected in Roger Barker's endeavor to identify the important "behavior settings" that an individual enters during his daily life (1968).

Our taxonomic efforts have focused on identifying types of interdependence in dyads and triads (see Chapter 11 in Thibaut and Kelley, 1959, and Chapters 4 and 9 of this book) and types of task that an interdependent pair may encounter (Chapter 9 in Thibaut and Kelley, 1959). Like Lewin, we analyze the types of situation for the patterns of behavior they are likely to generate. Additionally, we investigate (Chapter 7 of this book) the various interdependence patterns for what they encourage in the development of generalized adaptational tendencies—the transformational rules and evaluative criteria that they make it desirable for individuals to adopt in order to facilitate efficient management of the conflict-creating properties of the situations. This point relates to those that follow.

Cognitive Restructuring of the Field. Lewin (1946, pp. 802–804) observed that the behavioral field often posed problems for the person's locomotion that could be solved by a cognitive restructuring of the field. His favorite example was the detour or *Umweg* problem in which the child was unable to circumvent a barrier until he identified a path of connected regions that went around the barrier and included the goal region. This "distinguished path" often required the child to turn his back on the goal and to move away from it temporarily in order, ultimately, to reach it. The detour concept is clearly apparent in our notion of value transformations; for example, the person suppresses his interest in his own outcomes and concerns himself with those of the partner in order to improve his own outcomes *in the long run*. The notion of selective suppression of one's interests is similar to Lewin's concept of potency of the situation. A choice problem can be seen as involving overlapping situations, one coordinated to each of the several alternative goals. Lewin described a decision as raising the potency of one of the situations permanently, thus enabling it to dominate the other situations. This phenomenon can be described in transformational terms, the rule being to make up one's mind and then put the rejected alternatives out of mind. The functional value of this rule, in promoting conflict-free action, is apparent. The historical origin of Festinger's (1957) ideas about a process of postdecisional reduction of cognitive dissonance is suggested here.

The Motivational Properties of Conflict.   Lewin postulated that conflict situations (individual decision conflicts) give rise to emotional tension, the intensity of which is a function of the strength of the opposing forces (Lewin, 1951, p. 268). Similarly, tension develops in cognitively unstructured situations in which there is uncertainty about paths to goals, inasmuch as such situations result in psychological conflict (Deutsch and Krauss, 1965, p. 45). The tension motivates restless exploratory behavior and, if not too great, promotes the solution of detour and other cognitive problems.

We have relied on this property of situations of individual conflict and uncertainty in accounting for the existence of transformational tendencies. The motivation for the invention of transformations is seen to stem from the unpleasantness of situations that lack clear choice criteria and from the costs of interpersonal conflict and the thwarting of individual goals. In his experience with relief from conflict-based tension by following certain rules and criteria the individual's adherence to them is strengthened and gains a certain amount of autonomy. Also, the moral teachings that advocate the prosocial transformations gain support from tension reduction. [In using conflict-based tension as a motivational state, the reduction of which is reinforcing, our analysis essentially follows that of Brown and Farber (1951) who identify a frustration-produced drive.]

The Person as a Causal Agent.   In Chapter 7 we emphasized the fact that transformation processes reduce the control of the *given* outcomes over the behavior of the person. It is at this point in the causal sequence leading up to social behavior that the "person" appears, in fact and in an attributional sense, as a causal agent. The person who modifies his incentive conditions by producing a sharp transformation between the *given* and the *effective* matrix appears (to himself and others) as an active agent who, in part, governs his own behavior and limits its governance by the external environment and by his own drives and impulses. In short, he shows self-control of interests and self-regulation of action. In a special but real sense the transformation process is the juncture at which the person P becomes available for inclusion in Lewin's famous formula, $B = f(P, E)$: behavior is a function of the person and the environment.

FURTHER DEVELOPMENTS

Two of the implications of our analysis which have received little more than mention in the preceding chapters seem especially promising for further theoretical development.

Levels of Interdependence

The analysis of the transformation process reveals that people are interdependent not only at the level of the specific behaviors they enact but also at the level of the transformations they make of their *given* matrix; that is to say, a person's outcomes will depend not only on his own transformations but on those of his partners. In certain *given* patterns, such as the Prisoner's Dilemma, a person is ill-advised to adopt a joint-welfare orientation to the relationship unless he is assured that the partner will do likewise. This points to a more general phenomenon, that people are interdependent with respect to the general characteristics and attitudes they display in a relationship. From the internalization of social and personal values (as promoted by the functional utility of the transformational process) they gain rewards and incur costs not only from their own and their partner's behavior but also from the kind of person they are able to "be" in the interaction and the kind of person they find the partner to be. Persons are similarly interdependent in the norm and role preference and propensities they bring to their relationships.

The events at these higher levels of interdependence are constituted of real or perceived patterns of organization of events at the specific behavioral level. A person reveals that he has a particular attitude or personal characteristic by some consistency in his behavioral patterning. Thus "considerateness" is revealed by frequent acquiescence to the partner's conflicting interests. Similarly, his adoption of a particular norm for the relationship (e.g., his sex-derived right to precedence in instances of interest conflict) is revealed by a behavior pattern consistent with that norm (such as frequent preemption in Chicken-like patterns; persistence in overriding the partner's expressed preferences; advocacy of the same pattern for other males). Thus the higher levels of interdependence are linked to the behavioral level by the processes of attribution and self-presentation. This gives rise to what is probably a common kind of conflict having to do with whether a particular behavioral event is to be considered as having more general significance. A common form of this conflict, described as "attributional conflict" by Orvis, Kelley, and Butler (1976), appears to be that in which the enactor of a negative behavior believes it is to be taken only as a special instance and is not to be generalized from, whereas the partner is inclined to draw broad inferences from the event (the actor is a bad person or has negative attitudes toward the partner).

The conception of levels of interdependence deserves further thought. It seems reasonable to assume that interdependence can be described in the same terms at both the specific behavioral level and at the more abstract or general levels. (It will certainly be convenient, conceptually, if this proves to be the case.) Thus the basic interdependence components seem applicable to the level of personal characteristics, each person having RC-type preferences for how he himself appears, FC-type preferences for what the partner is like as a person, and BC-type preferences for combining the two (the latter corresponding to ideal models of person pairing). The central problems in developing the notion of levels of interdependence have to do with identifying the major levels and determining the dynamic relations among them. This will require a great expansion in our current understanding of the real and perceived organization of interpersonal behavior.

Functional Accounts of Motivation

The functional analysis underlying our conception of the transformational process points to some of the major components of social motivation (types of choice criterion and rules for social behavior) and their origin in the requirements of social interdependence. As briefly mentioned in Chapter 7, it seems likely to us that a more extensive analysis of this sort can be brought to bear on such phenomena as "unequivocal behavioral orientation," cognitive dissonance, reactance, competence, and social comparison. We have continued to be uneasy about the *ad hoc* invocation or postulation of such motives and tendencies as a means of defining areas of research or of solving social psychological problems (cf. Thibaut and Kelley, 1959, pp. 5, 116, 132). The major difficulties with this approach as we see it, are ambiguity about the ultimate "list" from which such tendencies are drawn and unclarity about the interrelations among the various tendencies (relative potency, domains of applicability, and so on). Thus it is difficult to see how motivational theory in social psychology can ever evolve from an *ad hoc* set of compartmentalized research topics into a coherent and inclusive set of interconnected principles.

It seems to us now to be possible to derive many of the qualitative variations in motivation from quantitative analysis of the structure of problems and especially from social interdependence problems. Our analysis in Chapter 7 merely scratches the surface of the rich possibilities. We focus on the rules and norms required by certain interpersonal relationships, but we take for granted many of the more basic motives and behavioral tendencies that these and other of life's problems require the individual to have. A primary requirement for all problems, impersonal as well as interpersonal, is that the individual be attentive to his environment and concerned about its causal structure. A realistic sense of own causal efficacy versus own dependence and helplessness is an essential aspect of one's causal knowledge. It is also usually essential to take account of the future and to plan ahead. Our analysis has taken for granted these basic necessities as they are reflected in the importance of paying attention to the partner's outcomes and future reactions to present events and in the necessity of expressing own needs and interests so that the partner's causal analysis of the relationship can also have some basic degree of veridicality. Few, or perhaps none, of these requirements are absolute. Most or all are contingent on circumstances, nature of the problem, and interdependence. We believe the same can be said of the kinds of motive and tendency mentioned at the outset—that they have a common functional utility but are always inappropriate for some of life's situations.

Our suggestion, then, is that attempts be made along the lines of functionalistic analysis to categorize both interpersonal and impersonal problems and to derive their implications for the dispositional and motivational repertory of the well-adapted person. An analysis of this sort will provide us with a sense of the total set of such tendencies, insights into their interrelations, and understanding of their contingent utility. This will, we believe, provide a framework within which order can be brought to the current plethora of arbitrary and disconnected motivational assumptions within social and personality psychology. It will also, as an incidental but important result, provide ways of dealing systematically with questions regarding the elements in a behavioral and motivational repertory that are spurious, maladaptive, and abnormal. Perhaps most important will be the ultimate relevance of this analysis to evaluating the quality of people's adaptation to their past, present, and future worlds. It seems clear that when there are massive changes in the distribution and locus of types of problematic situation and relationship the typical person's motives and tendencies are likely to become sharply inappropriate. For example, as social interdependence increases, as coordination problems assume greater importance than exchange problems, and as diminishing resources heighten the general level of noncorrespondence of outcomes, the once appropriate mixtures of cooperative and competitive tendencies and their associated rules for contingent application may become highly maladaptive. A description of the changing nature of interdependence and an analysis of its behavioral implications seem necessary if man's rate of adaptation is to keep pace with the rate of change in his world's requirements.

Bibliography

Alexander, C. N., Jr. and Weil, H. G. Players, persons, and purposes: Situational meaning and the Prisoner's Dilemma game. *Sociometry*, 1969, **32**, 121–144.

Aronfreed, J. *Conduct and conscience*. New York: Academic, 1968.

Aronson, E. and Linder, D. Gain and loss of esteem as determinants of interpersonal attractiveness. *Journal of Experimental Social Psychology*, 1965, **1**, 156–171.

Bandura, A. Social-learning theory of identificatory processes. In D. A. Goslin (Ed.), *Handbook of socialization theory and research*. Chicago: Rand McNally, 1969. Pp. 213-262.

Barker, R. G. *Ecological psychology*. Stanford: Stanford University Press, 1968.

Benton, A. A., Kelley, H. H., and Liebling, B. Effects of extremity of offers and concession rate on the outcomes of bargaining. *Journal of Personality and Social Psychology*, 1972, **24**, 73–83.

Bonacich, P. Norms and cohesion as adaptive responses to potential conflict: An experimental study. *Sociometry*, 1972, **35**, 357–375.

Braithwaite, R. B. *Theory of games as a tool for the moral philosopher*. Cambridge: Cambridge University Press, 1955.

Brehm, J. W. and Cole, A. H. Effect of a favor which reduces freedom. *Journal of Personality and Social Psychology*, 1966, **3**, 420–426.

Brown, B. The effects of need to maintain face on interpersonal bargaining. *Journal of Experimental Social Psychology*, 1968, **4**, 107–122.

Brown, J. S. and Farber, I. E. Emotions conceptualized as intervening variables with suggestions toward a theory of frustration. *Psychological Bulletin*, 1951, **48**, 465–495.

Chadwick-Jones, J. K. *Social exchange theory: Its structure and influence in social psychology*. New York: Academic, 1976.

Christie, R. and Geis, F. L. *Studies in Machiavellianism*. New York: Academic, 1970.

Daniels, F. V. Communication, incentive, and structural variables in interpersonal exchange and negotiation. *Journal of Experimental Social Psychology*, 1967, **3**, 47–74.

Deutsch, M. A theory of cooperation and competition. *Human Relations*, 1949, **2**, 129–152.

Deutsch, M. Trust and suspicion. *Journal of Conflict Resolution*, 1958, **2**, 265–279.

Deutsch, M. Bargaining, threat, and communication: Some experimental studies. In A. Archibald (Ed.), *Strategic interaction and conflict*. Berkeley, Calif.: Institute of International Studies, 1966. Pp. 19–41.

Deutsch, M. and Krauss, R. M. *Theories in social psychology*. New York: Basic Books, 1965.

329

Evans, G. Effect of unilateral promise and value of rewards upon cooperation and trust. *Journal of Abnormal and Social Psychology*, 1964, **69**, 587–590.

Festinger, L. *A theory of cognitive dissonance.* Evanston, Ill.: Row, Peterson, 1957.

Foa, U. G. and Foa, E. B. *Resource theory of social exchange.* Morristown, N. J.: General Learning Press, 1975.

French, J. R. P., Jr. A formal theory of social power. *Psychological Review*, 1956, **63**, 181–194.

Friedland, N., Arnold, S. E., and Thibaut, J. W. Motivational bases in mixed-motive interactions: The effects of comparison levels. *Journal of Experimental Social Psychology*, 1974, **10**, 188–199.

Gallo, P. J., Jr. Effects of increased incentives upon the use of threat in bargaining. *Journal of Personality and Social Psychology*, 1966, **4**, 14–20.

Gouldner, A. W. The norm of reciprocity. *American Sociological Review*, 1960, **25**, 165–167.

Gruder, C. L. Relationships with opponents and partner in mixed-motive bargaining. *Journal of Conflict Resolution*, 1971, **15**, 403–416.

Gumpert, P., Deutsch, M., and Epstein, Y. Effect of incentive magnitude on cooperation in the Prisoner's Dilemma game. *Journal of Personality and Social Psychology*, 1969, **11**, 66–69.

Guyer, M. and Rapoport, A. Threat in a two-person game. *Journal of Experimental Social Psychology*, 1970, **6**, 11–26.

Hamburger, H. Separable games. *Behavioral Science*, 1969, **14**, 121–132.

Hamburger, H. N-person Prisoner's Dilemma. *Journal of Mathematical Sociology*, 1973, **3**, 27–48.

Hamilton, E. and Cairns, H. (Eds.), *The collected dialogues of Plato (including the letters).* Princeton, N. J.: Princeton University Press, 1969.

Hamilton, W. D. The genetical evolution of social behavior. *Journal of Theoretical Biology*, 1964, **7**, 1–52.

Harary, F., Norman, R. Z., and Cartwright, D. *Structural models: An introduction to the theory of directed graphs.* New York: Wiley, 1958.

Heider, F. *The psychology of interpersonal relations.* New York: Wiley, 1958.

Homans, G. C. *Social behavior: Its elementary forms.* New York: Harcourt Brace Jovanovich, 1974.

Howard, N. *The paradoxes of rationality: Theory of metagames and political behavior.* Cambridge: MIT Press, 1971.

Jones, E. E. *Ingratiation.* New York: Appleton-Century, 1964.

Jones, E. E. and Davis, K. E. From acts to dispositions: The attribution process in person perception. In L. Berkowitz (Ed.), *Advances in experimental social psychology*, Vol. 2. New York: Academic, 1965. Pp. 219–266.

Jones, E. E. and Gerard, H. B. *Foundations of social psychology.* New York: Wiley, 1967.

Jones, E. E. and Goethals, G. R. *Order effects in impression formation: Attribution context and the nature of the entity.* Morristown, N. J.: General Learning Press, 1971.

Jones, E. E. and Nisbett, R. E. *The actor and the observer: Divergent perceptions of the causes of behavior.* Morristown, N. J.: General Learning Press, 1971.

Jones, E. E. and Wortman, C. *Ingratiation: An attributional approach.* Morristown, N. J.: General Learning Press, 1973.

Kelley, H. H. Attribution theory in social psychology. In D. Levine (Ed.), *Nebraska Symposium on Motivation, 1967.* Lincoln: University of Nebraska Press, 1967. Pp. 192–238.

Kelley, H. H. *Attribution in social interaction*. Morristown, N. J.: General Learning Press, 1971.

Kelley, H. H. *Causal schemata and the attribution process*. Morristown, N. J.: General Learning Press, 1972.

Kelley, H. H. and Schenitski, D. P. Bargaining. Chapter 10 in C. G. McClintock (Ed.), *Experimental social psychology*. New York: Holt, Rinehart, and Winston, 1972. Pp. 298–337.

Kelley, H. H., Shure, G. H., Deutsch, M., Faucheux, C., Lanzetta, J. T., Moscovici, S., Nuttin, J. M., Jr., Rabbie, J. M. and Thibaut, J. W. A comparative experimental study of negotiation behavior, *Journal of Personality and Social Psychology*, 1970, **16**, 411-438.

Kelley, H. H. and Stahelski, A. J. The inference of intentions from moves in the Prisoner's Dilemma game. *Journal of Experimental Social Psychology*, 1970a, **6**, 401–419.

Kelley, H. H. and Stahelski, A. J. The social interaction basis of cooperators' and competitors' beliefs about others. *Journal of Personality and Social Psychology*, 1970b, **16**, 66–91.

Kelley, H. H. and Thibaut, J. W. Group problem solving. Chapter 29 in G. Lindzey and E. Aronson (Eds.), *The handbook of social psychology*, second edition. Reading, Mass.: Addison-Wesley, 1969. Volume 4, pp. 1–101.

Kelley, H. H., Thibaut, J. W., Radloff, R., and Mundy, D. The development of cooperation in the "minimal social situation." *Psychological Monographs*, 1962, **76**, (19) (whole no. 538).

Kulhman, D. M. and Marshello, A. F. J. Individual differences in game motivation as moderators of preprogrammed strategy effects in Prisoner's Dilemma. *Journal of Personality and Social Psychology*, 1975, **32**, 922–931.

Leeper, R. W. *Lewin's topological and vector psychology: A digest and a critique*. Eugene, Oregon: University of Oregon, 1943.

Lewin, K. *A dynamic theory of personality*. New York: McGraw-Hill, 1935.

Lewin, K. The conceptual representation and the measurement of psychological forces. *Contributions to Psychological Theory*, 1938, **1** (4), Serial No. 4, 1–247.

Lewin, K. Behavior and development as a function of the total situation. In L. Carmichael (Ed.), *Manual of Child Psychology*. New York: Wiley, 1946. Pp. 791–844.

Lewin, K. *Resolving social conflicts*. New York: Harper, 1948.

Lewin, K. *Field theory in social science*. New York: Harper and Row, 1951.

Luce, R. D. and Raiffa, H. *Games and Decisions*. New York: Wiley, 1957.

McClintock, C. G. Game behavior and social motivation in interpersonal settings. In C. G. McClintock (Ed.), *Experimental social psychology*. New York: Holt, Rinehart, and Winston, 1972a. Pp. 271–297.

McClintock, C. G. Social motivation—a set of propositions. *Behavioral Science*, 1972b, **17**, 438–454.

McClintock, C. G. and McNeel, S. P. Reward level and game playing behavior. *Journal of Conflict Resolution*, 1966a, **10**, 98–102.

McClintock, C. G. and McNeel, S. P. Reward and score feedback as determinants of cooperative and competitive game behavior. *Journal of Personality and Social Psychology*, 1966b, **4**, 606–613.

McClintock, C. G. and McNeel, S. P. Prior dyadic experience and monetary reward as determinants of cooperative and competitive game behavior. *Journal of Personality and Social Psychology*, 1967, **5**, 282–294.

Madsen, M. C. and Shapira, A. Cooperative and competitive behavior of urban Afro-American, Anglo-American, Mexican-American, and Mexican village children. *Developmental Psychology*, 1970, **3**, 16–20.

Marlowe, D., Gergen, K. J., and Doob, A. N. Opponent's personality, expectation of social interaction, and interpersonal bargaining. *Journal of Personality and Social Psychology*, 1966, **3**, 206–213.

Marwell, G., Ratcliff, K., and Schmitt, D. R. Minimizing differences in a maximizing difference game. *Journal of Personality and Social Psychology*, 1969, **12**, 158–163.

Mehrabian, A. *Nonverbal communication*. Chicago: Aldine-Atherton, 1972.

Messick, D. M. and McClintock, C. G. Motivational bases of choice in experimental games. *Journal of Personality and Social Psychology*, 1968, **4**, 1–25.

Messick, D. M. and Thorngate, W. Relative gain maximization in experimental games. *Journal of Experimental Social Psychology*, 1967, **3**, 85–101.

Miller, D. T. and Holmes, J. G. The role of situational restrictiveness on self-fulfilling prophecies: A theoretical and empirical extension of Kelley and Stahelski's Triangle Hypothesis. *Journal of Personality and Social Psychology*, 1975, **31**, 661–673.

Mischel, W. Toward a cognitive learning reconceptualization of personality. *Psychological Review*, 1973, **80**, 252–283.

Mischel, W. Processes in delay of gratification. In L. Berkowitz (Ed.), *Advances in experimental social psychology, Volume 7*. New York: Academic, 1974. Pp. 249–272.

Montague, A. *On being human*. New York: Schuman, 1951.

Morgan, W. R. and Sawyer, J. Bargaining, expectations, and the preference for equality over equity. *Journal of Personality and Social Psychology*, 1967, **6**, 139–149.

Orvis, B. R., Kelley, H. H., and Butler, D. Attributional conflict in young couples. In J. H. Harvey, W. J. Ickes, and R. E. Kidd (Eds.), *New directions in attribution research, Vol. 1*. Hillsdale, N. J.: Erlbaum Associates, 1976. Pp. 353–386.

Osgood, C. E. *An alternative to war or surrender*. Urbana: University of Illinois Press, 1962.

Osgood, C. E., Suci, G. J., and Tannenbaum, P. H. *The measurement of meaning*. Urbana: University of Illinois Press, 1957.

Oskamp, S. Effects of programmed strategies on cooperation in the Prisoner's Dilemma and other mixed-motive games. *Journal of Conflict Resolution*, 1971, **15**, 225–259.

Pepitone, A., Maderna, A., Caporicci, E., Tiberi, E., Iacono, G., de Majo, G., Perfetto, M., Asprea, A., Villone, G., Fua, G., and Tonucci, F. Justice in choice behavior: A cross-cultural study. *International Journal of Psychology*. 1970, **5**, 1–10.

Pilisuk, M. and Skolnick, P. Inducing trust: A test of the Osgood proposal. *Journal of Personality and Social Psychology*, 1968, **8**, 121–133.

Pruitt, D. G. Reward structure and cooperation: The decomposed Prisoner's Dilemma game. *Journal of Personality and Social Psychology*, 1967, **7**, 21–27.

Pruitt, D. G. Reciprocity and credit building in the laboratory dyad. *Journal of Personality and Social Psychology*, 1968, **8**, 143–147.

Pruitt, D. G. Motivational processes in the decomposed Prisoner's Dilemma game. *Journal of Personality and Social Psychology*, 1970, **14**, 227–238.

Pruitt, D. G. and Drews, J. L. The effect of time pressure, time elapsed, and the opponent's concession rate on behavior in negotiation. *Journal of Experimental Social Psychology*, 1969, **5**, 43–60.

Pruitt, D. G. and Lewis, S. A. Development of integrative solutions in bilateral negotiation. *Journal of Personality and Social Psychology*, 1975, **31**, 621–633.

Radlow, R., Weidner, M. F., and Hurst, P. M. The effect of incentive magnitude and "motivational orientation" upon choice behavior in a two-person non-zero-sum game. *Journal of Social Psychology*, 1968, **74**, 199–208.

Rapoport, A. and Guyer, M. A taxonomy of 2 × 2 games. *General Systems*, 1966, **11**, 203–214.

Schelling, T. C. *The strategy of conflict*. Cambridge: Harvard University Press, 1960.

Schopler, J. and Thompson, V. Role of attribution processes in mediating amount of reciprocity for a favor. *Journal of Personality and Social Psychology*, 1968, **10**, 243–250.

Shapira, A. and Madsen, M. C. Cooperative and competitive behavior of kibbutz and urban children in Israel. *Child Development*, 1969, **40**, 609–617.

Shure, G H. and Meeker, R. J. Empirical demonstration of normative behavior in the Prisoner's Dilemma. *Proceedings of the 76th Annual Convention, American Psychological Association*, 1968, 61–62.

Shure, G. H. and Meeker, R. J. Bargaining processes in experimental territorial conflict situations. *Peace Research Society: Papers*, 1969, **11**, 109–122.

Siegel, S. Level of aspiration and decision making. *Psychological Review*, 1957, **64**, 253–262.

Steiner, I. D. *Group process and productivity*. New York: Academic, 1972.

Swinth, R. L. The establishment of the trust relationship. *Journal of Conflict Resolution*, 1967, **11**, 335–344.

Terhune, K. W. The effects of personality in cooperation and conflict. In P. Swingle (Ed.), *The structure of conflict*. New York: Academic, 1970. Pp. 193–234.

Thibaut, J. W. The development of contractual norms in bargaining: Replication and variation. *Journal of Conflict Resolution*, 1968, **12**, 102–112.

Thibaut, J. W. and Faucheux, C. The development of contractual norms in a bargaining situation under two types of stress. *Journal of Experimental Social Psychology*, 1965. **1**, 89–102.

Thibaut, J. W. and Kelley, H. H. *The social psychology of groups*. New York: Wiley, 1959.

Thibaut, J. W. and Ross, M. Commitment and experience as determinants of assimilation and contrast. *Journal of Personality and Social Psychology*, 1969, **13**, 322–329.

Thibaut, J. W. and Walker, L. *Procedural justice: A psychological analysis*. Hillsdale, N. J.: Erlbaum Associates, 1975.

Thorngate, W. Person perception and the prediction of behavior in decomposed games. Technical Report 73–2, Social Psychology Labs, University of Alberta, Edmonton, Canada. (Undated.)

Tolstoy, L. *The Kreutzer sonata and other tales*. Oxford: World's Classics, Oxford University Press, 1940.

Triandis, H. C., Vassiliou, V., and Nassiakou, M. Three cross-cultural studies of subjective culture. *Journal of Personality and Social Psychology Monograph Supplement*, 1968, **8**, No. 4, Part 2.

Trivers, R. L. Parent-offspring conflict. *American Zoologist*, 1974, **14**, 249–264.

Tversky, A. and Kahneman, D. Availability: A heuristic for judging frequency and probability. *Cognitive Psychology*, 1973, **5**, 207–232.

Vinacke, W. E. and Arkoff, A. An experimental study of coalitions in the triad. *American Sociological Review,* 1957, **22,** 406–414.

Waller, W. W. and Hill, R. *The family, a dynamic interpretation*. New York: Dryden, 1951.

Wilson, K. V. and Bixenstine, V. E. Forms of social control in two-person, two-choice games. *Behavioral Science,* 1962, **7,** 92–102.

Winch, R. F. *The modern family*. New York: Holt, 1952.

Wish, M., Deutsch, M., and Kaplan, S. J. Perceived dimensions of interpersonal relations. *Journal of Personality and Social Psychology*, 1976, **33,** 409–420.

Wolf, G. Evaluation within interpersonal systems. *General Systems,* 1972, **17,** 43–51.

Wrightsman, L. S. Personality and attitudinal correlates of trusting and trustworthy behaviors in a two-person game. *Journal of Personality and Social Psychology,* 1966, **4,** 328–332.

Wyer, R. S. Prediction of behavior in two-person games. *Journal of Personality and Social Psychology,* 1969, **13,** 222–238.

Author Index

Subject Index

ς